To:

Andrew

From:

_K.U.M.C._

Date:

May 6, 2015

THE
BIBLE
IN 366 DAYS
FOR MEN

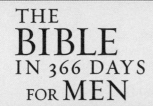

STEPHAN JOUBERT

CHRISTIAN ART
PUBLISHERS

Originally published by Christelike Uitgewersmaatskappy
under the title *Die Bybel in 366 dae vir mans*

© 2010

English edition
© 2011 Christian Art Publishers
PO Box 1599, Vereeniging, 1930, RSA

First edition 2011

Translated by Mairi-Ann Bonnet

Cover designed by Christian Art Publishers

Images used under license from Shutterstock.com

Scripture quotations are taken from the *Holy Bible*,
New Living Translation, second edition, copyright © 1996, 2004.
Used by permission of Tyndale House Publishers, Inc.,
Carol Stream, Illinois 60188. All rights reserved.

Set in 9 on 12 pt Arial
by Christian Art Publishers

Printed in China

ISBN 978-1-77036-442-4

11 12 13 14 15 16 17 18 19 20 – 11 10 9 8 7 6 5 4 3 2

All Scripture is inspired by God and is useful to teach us what is true and to make us realize what is wrong in our lives. It corrects us when we are wrong and teaches us to do what is right. God uses it to prepare and equip His people to do every good work.

~ 2 Timothy 3:16-17 ~

Foreword

The Bible is different from any other book in the world. It is the living Word of God which does not exist merely to increase our wisdom. It points to and tells of Jesus, the Word that became flesh and came to deliver us from sin and death, and to show us how God wants us to live. That is why it is the Word that gives life and changes lives.

The Bible in 366 Days for Men contains core passages of the Bible that have been compiled chronologically from the *New Living Translation*®, and each day's reading opens with a short devotional thought by Stephan Joubert.

You will be encouraged and inspired to receive your daily power and guidance from the One who's kingdom is different from the kingdoms of the world – the One who has a unique calling for you as a man in a world that needs Him now more than ever.

JANUARY

Not alone

God said that it was not good for man to be alone so He made a helper for Adam. A helper is someone who can do something better than you can. Wives are helpers. A wife is God's answer to a man's great loneliness.

[18]Then the LORD God said, "It is not good for the man to be alone. I will make a helper who is just right for him." [19]So the LORD God formed from the ground all the wild animals and all the birds of the sky. He brought them to the man to see what he would call them, and the man chose a name for each one. [20]He gave names to all the livestock, all the birds of the sky, and all the wild animals. But still there was no helper just right for him.

[21]So the LORD God caused the man to fall into a deep sleep. While the man slept, the LORD God took out one of the man's ribs and closed up the opening. [22]Then the LORD God made a woman from the rib, and he brought her to the man.

[23]"At last!" the man exclaimed. "This one is bone from my bone, and flesh from my flesh! She will be called 'woman,' because she was taken from 'man.'"

[24]This explains why a man leaves his father and mother and is joined to his wife, and the two are united into one.

~ Genesis 2:18-24

One in a million

The whole earth was filled with evil and everyone was wicked, except for one man – Noah. He found favor with God, and for this reason God showed mercy instead of inflicting punishment. Why? Well, because God is first and foremost a God of grace. And He still shows us mercy today!

¹Then the people began to multiply on the earth, and daughters were born to them. ²The sons of God saw the beautiful women and took any they wanted as their wives. ³Then the LORD said, "My Spirit will not put up with humans for such a long time, for they are only mortal flesh. In the future, their normal lifespan will be no more than 120 years."

⁴In those days, and for some time after, giant Nephilites lived on the earth, for whenever the sons of God had intercourse with women, they gave birth to children who became the heroes and famous warriors of ancient times.

⁵The LORD observed the extent of human wickedness on the earth, and he saw that everything they thought or imagined was consistently and totally evil. ⁶So the LORD was sorry he had ever made them and put them on the earth. It broke his heart. ⁷And the LORD said, "I will wipe this human race I have created from the face of the earth. Yes, and I will destroy every living thing— all the people, the large animals, the small animals that scurry along the ground, and even the birds of the sky. I am sorry I ever made them." ⁸But Noah found favor with the LORD.

~ Genesis 6:1-8

God has time

Abram was seventy-five years old when God called him. But only after twenty-five years did God fulfill His promises. You see, God has time and we don't. We are in a hurry and God isn't. The challenge for us is to fall into step with His rhythms and will, and not the other way around.

¹When Abram was ninety-nine years old, the Lord appeared to him and said, "I am El-Shaddai—'God Almighty.' Serve me faithfully and live a blameless life. ²I will make a covenant with you, by which I will guarantee to give you countless descendants."

³At this, Abram fell face down on the ground. Then God said to him, ⁴"This is my covenant with you: I will make you the father of a multitude of nations! ⁵What's more, I am changing your name. It will no longer be Abram. Instead, you will be called Abraham, for you will be the father of many nations. ⁶I will make you extremely fruitful. Your descendants will become many nations, and kings will be among them!

⁷"I will confirm my covenant with you and your descendants after you, from generation to generation. This is the everlasting covenant: I will always be your God and the God of your descendants after you. ⁸And I will give the entire land of Canaan, where you now live as a foreigner, to you and your descendants. It will be their possession forever, and I will be their God."

⁹Then God said to Abraham, "Your responsibility is to obey the terms of the covenant. You and all your descendants have this continual responsibility. ¹⁰This is the covenant that you and your descendants must keep: Each male among you must be circumcised.

~ Genesis 17:1-10

Don't laugh

You should never laugh at God's promises – just ask Sarah. She underestimated God and overemphasized her and Abraham's old age. Yet God proved that He can do the impossible. After Isaac's birth, Sarah could laugh with joy over the miracle that took place in their old age.

[6]So Abraham ran back to the tent and said to Sarah, "Hurry! Get three large measures of your best flour, knead it into dough, and bake some bread." [7]Then Abraham ran out to the herd and chose a tender calf and gave it to his servant, who quickly prepared it. [8]When the food was ready, Abraham took some yogurt and milk and the roasted meat, and he served it to the men. As they ate, Abraham waited on them in the shade of the trees.

[9]"Where is Sarah, your wife?" the visitors asked.

"She's inside the tent," Abraham replied.

[10]Then one of them said, "I will return to you about this time next year, and your wife, Sarah, will have a son!"

Sarah was listening to this conversation from the tent. [11]Abraham and Sarah were both very old by this time, and Sarah was long past the age of having children. [12]So she laughed silently to herself and said, "How could a worn-out woman like me enjoy such pleasure, especially when my master—my husband—is also so old?"

[13]Then the LORD said to Abraham, "Why did Sarah laugh? Why did she say, 'Can an old woman like me have a baby?' [14]Is anything too hard for the LORD? I will return about this time next year, and Sarah will have a son."

[15]Sarah was afraid, so she denied it, saying, "I didn't laugh."

But the LORD said, "No, you did laugh."

~ Genesis 18:6-15

Dare to pray

Abraham prayed daringly and asked the Lord to spare the city of Sodom if, in the end, only ten righteous people could be found there. Sometimes it is necessary to pray boldly and courageously. Boldness in prayer can change difficult circumstances.

26And the LORD replied, "If I find fifty righteous people in Sodom, I will spare the entire city for their sake."

27Then Abraham spoke again. "Since I have begun, let me speak further to my Lord, even though I am but dust and ashes. 28Suppose there are only forty-five righteous people rather than fifty? Will you destroy the whole city for lack of five?"

And the LORD said, "I will not destroy it if I find forty-five righteous people there."

29Then Abraham pressed his request further. "Suppose there are only forty?"

And the LORD replied, "I will not destroy it for the sake of the forty."

30"Please don't be angry, my Lord," Abraham pleaded. "Let me speak—suppose only thirty righteous people are found?"

And the LORD replied, "I will not destroy it if I find thirty."

31Then Abraham said, "Since I have dared to speak to the Lord, let me continue—suppose there are only twenty?"

And the LORD replied, "Then I will not destroy it for the sake of the twenty."

32Finally, Abraham said, "Lord, please don't be angry with me if I speak one more time. Suppose only ten are found there?"

And the LORD replied, "Then I will not destroy it for the sake of the ten."

33When the LORD had finished his conversation with Abraham, he went on his way, and Abraham returned to his tent.

~ Genesis 18:26-33

God's stairway to heaven

To meet God in your dreams is an unexpected and unforgettable encounter. No wonder it changed a liar like Jacob into a man of God. God is everywhere, just open your eyes and notice Him. Wake up from your sleep and live for Him.

[10]Meanwhile, Jacob left Beersheba and traveled toward Haran. [11]At sundown he arrived at a good place to set up camp and stopped there for the night. Jacob found a stone to rest his head against and lay down to sleep. [12]As he slept, he dreamed of a stairway that reached from the earth up to heaven. And he saw the angels of God going up and down the stairway.

[13]At the top of the stairway stood the LORD, and he said, "I am the LORD, the God of your grandfather Abraham, and the God of your father, Isaac. The ground you are lying on belongs to you. I am giving it to you and your descendants. [14]Your descendants will be as numerous as the dust of the earth! They will spread out in all directions—to the west and the east, to the north and the south. And all the families of the earth will be blessed through you and your descendants. [15]What's more, I am with you, and I will protect you wherever you go. One day I will bring you back to this land. I will not leave you until I have finished giving you everything I have promised you."

[16]Then Jacob awoke from his sleep and said, "Surely the LORD is in this place, and I wasn't even aware of it!" [17]But he was also afraid and said, "What an awesome place this is! It is none other than the house of God, the very gateway to heaven!"

[18]The next morning Jacob got up very early. He took the stone he had rested his head against, and he set it upright as a memorial pillar. Then he poured olive oil over it. [19]He named that place Bethel (which means "house of God"), although it was previously called Luz.

~ Genesis 28:10-19

Wrestling with God

Jacob wrestled with God's heavenly messenger – and this was no easy task. God blessed him for his bravery. Jacob's name changed to Israel because he had wrestled with God. Later, a whole nation was named after him because of his courage to take on heaven and earth.

²²During the night Jacob got up and took his two wives, his two servant wives, and his eleven sons and crossed the Jabbok River with them. ²³After taking them to the other side, he sent over all his possessions.

²⁴This left Jacob all alone in the camp, and a man came and wrestled with him until the dawn began to break. ²⁵When the man saw that he would not win the match, he touched Jacob's hip and wrenched it out of its socket. ²⁶Then the man said, "Let me go, for the dawn is breaking!"

But Jacob said, "I will not let you go unless you bless me."

²⁷"What is your name?" the man asked.

He replied, "Jacob."

²⁸"Your name will no longer be Jacob," the man told him. "From now on you will be called Israel, because you have fought with God and with men and have won."

²⁹"Please tell me your name," Jacob said.

"Why do you want to know my name?" the man replied. Then he blessed Jacob there.

³⁰Jacob named the place Peniel (which means "face of God"), for he said, "I have seen God face to face, yet my life has been spared." ³¹The sun was rising as Jacob left Peniel, and he was limping because of the injury to his hip. ³²(Even today the people of Israel don't eat the tendon near the hip socket because of what happened that night when the man strained the tendon of Jacob's hip.)

~ Genesis 32:22-32

Blessed

It is wonderful to be in the presence of those who are blessed by the Lord. Their presence changes their surroundings. Joseph was such a man. God blessed him everywhere he went and in everything he did. God's people are always a living blessing to those around them.

¹When Joseph was taken to Egypt by the Ishmaelite traders, he was purchased by Potiphar, an Egyptian officer.

²The LORD was with Joseph, so he succeeded in everything he did as he served in the home of his Egyptian master. ³Potiphar noticed this and realized that the LORD was with Joseph, giving him success in everything he did. ⁴This pleased Potiphar, so he soon made Joseph his personal attendant. He put him in charge of his entire household and everything he owned. ⁵From the day Joseph was put in charge of his master's household and property, the LORD began to bless Potiphar's household for Joseph's sake. All his household affairs ran smoothly, and his crops and livestock flourished. ⁶So Potiphar gave Joseph complete administrative responsibility over everything he owned. With Joseph there, he didn't worry about a thing.

Joseph was a very handsome and well-built young man.

¹⁹Potiphar was furious when he heard his wife's story about how Joseph had treated her. ²⁰So he took Joseph and threw him into the prison where the king's prisoners were held, and there he remained. ²¹But the LORD was with Joseph in the prison and showed him his faithful love. And the LORD made Joseph a favorite with the prison warden. ²²Before long, the warden put Joseph in charge of all the other prisoners and over everything that happened in the prison. ²³The warden had no more worries, because Joseph took care of everything. The LORD was with him and caused everything he did to succeed.

~ Genesis 39:1-6, 19-23

Forget the past

Joseph never used his power to take revenge on his brothers. Instead, he firmly closed the book on what they did to him in the past. He started over with his brothers. Joseph had tasted God's mercy and he was therefore able to show mercy to others.

[14]After burying Jacob, Joseph returned to Egypt with his brothers and all who had accompanied him to his father's burial. [15]But now that their father was dead, Joseph's brothers became fearful. "Now Joseph will show his anger and pay us back for all the wrong we did to him," they said.

[16]So they sent this message to Joseph: "Before your father died, he instructed us [17]to say to you: 'Please forgive your brothers for the great wrong they did to you—for their sin in treating you so cruelly.' So we, the servants of the God of your father, beg you to forgive our sin." When Joseph received the message, he broke down and wept. [18]Then his brothers came and threw themselves down before Joseph. "Look, we are your slaves!" they said.

[19]But Joseph replied, "Don't be afraid of me. Am I God, that I can punish you? [20]You intended to harm me, but God intended it all for good. He brought me to this position so I could save the lives of many people. [21]No, don't be afraid. I will continue to take care of you and your children." So he reassured them by speaking kindly to them.

[22]So Joseph and his brothers and their families continued to live in Egypt. Joseph lived to the age of 110. [23]He lived to see three generations of descendants of his son Ephraim, and he lived to see the birth of the children of Manasseh's son Makir, whom he claimed as his own.

~ Genesis 50:14-23

Faith is no guarantee

Life is not necessarily easier because you believe in God. Ask Moses. He stood up for what he believed in and had to flee for his life as a result. Even so, he placed his principles above his own comfort although it cost him greatly.

9"Take this baby and nurse him for me," the princess told the baby's mother. "I will pay you for your help." So the woman took her baby home and nursed him.

10Later, when the boy was older, his mother brought him back to Pharaoh's daughter, who adopted him as her own son. The princess named him Moses, for she explained, "I lifted him out of the water."

11Many years later, when Moses had grown up, he went out to visit his own people, the Hebrews, and he saw how hard they were forced to work. During his visit, he saw an Egyptian beating one of his fellow Hebrews. 12After looking in all directions to make sure no one was watching, Moses killed the Egyptian and hid the body in the sand.

13The next day, when Moses went out to visit his people again, he saw two Hebrew men fighting. "Why are you beating up your friend?" Moses said to the one who had started the fight.

14The man replied, "Who appointed you to be our prince and judge? Are you going to kill me as you killed that Egyptian yesterday?"

Then Moses was afraid, thinking, "Everyone knows what I did." 15And sure enough, Pharaoh heard what had happened, and he tried to kill Moses. But Moses fled from Pharaoh and went to live in the land of Midian.

~ Exodus 2:9-15

God is greater than His name

When Moses asked God who he must say sent him to the Israelites, he learnt that God can't be confined to a name. He is greater than even the most holy name we can use to address Him. God is the Lord, the great I AM! It is before Him alone that we bow today.

⁸"So I have come down to rescue them from the power of the Egyptians and lead them out of Egypt into their own fertile and spacious land. It is a land flowing with milk and honey—the land where the Canaanites, Hittites, Amorites, Perizzites, Hivites, and Jebusites now live. ⁹Look! The cry of the people of Israel has reached me, and I have seen how harshly the Egyptians abuse them. ¹⁰Now go, for I am sending you to Pharaoh. You must lead my people Israel out of Egypt."

¹¹But Moses protested to God, "Who am I to appear before Pharaoh? Who am I to lead the people of Israel out of Egypt?"

¹²God answered, "I will be with you. And this is your sign that I am the one who has sent you: When you have brought the people out of Egypt, you will worship God at this very mountain."

¹³But Moses protested, "If I go to the people of Israel and tell them, 'The God of your ancestors has sent me to you,' they will ask me, 'What is his name?' Then what should I tell them?"

¹⁴God replied to Moses, "I AM WHO I AM. Say this to the people of Israel: I AM has sent me to you." ¹⁵God also said to Moses, "Say this to the people of Israel: Yahweh, the God of your ancestors—the God of Abraham, the God of Isaac, and the God of Jacob—has sent me to you. This is my eternal name, my name to remember for all generations."

~ Exodus 3:8-15

God uses me, in spite of me

God did not accept Moses' stuttering as a reason not to send him to Pharaoh. God uses people, not because of their wonderful talents, but often despite the absence thereof. Learn from Moses and take heart!

¹⁰But Moses pleaded with the LORD, "O Lord, I'm not very good with words. I never have been, and I'm not now, even though you have spoken to me. I get tongue-tied, and my words get tangled."

¹¹Then the LORD asked Moses, "Who makes a person's mouth? Who decides whether people speak or do not speak, hear or do not hear, see or do not see? Is it not I, the LORD? ¹²Now go! I will be with you as you speak, and I will instruct you in what to say."

¹³But Moses again pleaded, "Lord, please! Send anyone else."

¹⁴Then the LORD became angry with Moses. "All right," he said. "What about your brother, Aaron the Levite? I know he speaks well. And look! He is on his way to meet you now. He will be delighted to see you. ¹⁵Talk to him, and put the words in his mouth. I will be with both of you as you speak, and I will instruct you both in what to do. ¹⁶Aaron will be your spokesman to the people. He will be your mouthpiece, and you will stand in the place of God for him, telling him what to say. ¹⁷And take your shepherd's staff with you, and use it to perform the miraculous signs I have shown you."

~ Exodus 4:10-17

The older, the better

There is no retirement age when you serve the Lord. Moses only started warming up when he was eighty. Only then did he start his true service when he and Aaron confronted Pharaoh. It's never too late to start serving the Lord.

¹Then the LORD said to Moses, "Pay close attention to this. I will make you seem like God to Pharaoh, and your brother, Aaron, will be your prophet. ²Tell Aaron everything I command you, and Aaron must command Pharaoh to let the people of Israel leave his country. ³But I will make Pharaoh's heart stubborn so I can multiply my miraculous signs and wonders in the land of Egypt. ⁴Even then Pharaoh will refuse to listen to you. So I will bring down my fist on Egypt. Then I will rescue my forces—my people, the Israelites—from the land of Egypt with great acts of judgment. ⁵When I raise my powerful hand and bring out the Israelites, the Egyptians will know that I am the LORD."

⁶So Moses and Aaron did just as the LORD had commanded them. ⁷Moses was eighty years old, and Aaron was eighty-three when they made their demands to Pharaoh.

⁸Then the LORD said to Moses and Aaron, ⁹"Pharaoh will demand, 'Show me a miracle.' When he does this, say to Aaron, 'Take your staff and throw it down in front of Pharaoh, and it will become a serpent.'"

~ Exodus 7:1-9

Celebrate God's victories

The feasts in the Bible, in this case Passover, served as a celebration of God's great victories in the past. But the first Passover was in anticipation of a victory that was still to take place. God soon made this victory a reality. God is faithful – yesterday, today, and tomorrow. Therefore we can celebrate today.

¹While the Israelites were still in the land of Egypt, the LORD gave the following instructions to Moses and Aaron: ²"From now on, this month will be the first month of the year for you. ³Announce to the whole community of Israel that on the tenth day of this month each family must choose a lamb or a young goat for a sacrifice, one animal for each household. ⁴If a family is too small to eat a whole animal, let them share with another family in the neighborhood. Divide the animal according to the size of each family and how much they can eat. ⁵The animal you select must be a one-year-old male, either a sheep or a goat, with no defects.

⁶"Take special care of this chosen animal until the evening of the fourteenth day of this first month. Then the whole assembly of the community of Israel must slaughter their lamb or young goat at twilight. ⁷They are to take some of the blood and smear it on the sides and top of the doorframes of the houses where they eat the animal. ⁸That same night they must roast the meat over a fire and eat it along with bitter salad greens and bread made without yeast. ⁹Do not eat any of the meat raw or boiled in water. The whole animal—including the head, legs, and internal organs—must be roasted over a fire. ¹⁰Do not leave any of it until the next morning. Burn whatever is not eaten before morning."

~ Exodus 12:1-10

The Lord fights in your place

You are always on the winning side if you are on God's side. Even the charging Egyptian army was defeated before the battle began. Heavenly wisdom tells us that one plus One is still the only winning combination. Make sure God is that One!

⁵When word reached the king of Egypt that the Israelites had fled, Pharaoh and his officials changed their minds. "What have we done, letting all those Israelite slaves get away?" they asked. ⁶So Pharaoh harnessed his chariot and called up his troops. ⁷He took with him 600 of Egypt's best chariots, along with the rest of the chariots of Egypt, each with its commander. ⁸The LORD hardened the heart of Pharaoh, the king of Egypt, so he chased after the people of Israel, who had left with fists raised in defiance. ⁹The Egyptians chased after them with all the forces in Pharaoh's army—all his horses and chariots, his charioteers, and his troops. The Egyptians caught up with the people of Israel as they were camped beside the shore near Pi-hahiroth, across from Baal-zephon.

¹⁰As Pharaoh approached, the people of Israel looked up and panicked when they saw the Egyptians overtaking them. They cried out to the LORD, ¹¹and they said to Moses, "Why did you bring us out here to die in the wilderness? Weren't there enough graves for us in Egypt? What have you done to us? Why did you make us leave Egypt? ¹²Didn't we tell you this would happen while we were still in Egypt? We said, 'Leave us alone! Let us be slaves to the Egyptians. It's better to be a slave in Egypt than a corpse in the wilderness!'"

¹³But Moses told the people, "Don't be afraid. Just stand still and watch the LORD rescue you today. The Egyptians you see today will never be seen again. ¹⁴The LORD himself will fight for you. Just stay calm."

~ Exodus 14:5-14

God takes care of today

One day at a time – that is God's way of caring for us. Every day He made sure that there was precisely enough manna for all the Israelites. He is still the same today – providing us with our daily bread right on time.

17So the people of Israel did as they were told. Some gathered a lot, some only a little. 18But when they measured it out, everyone had just enough. Those who gathered a lot had nothing left over, and those who gathered only a little had enough. Each family had just what it needed.

19Then Moses told them, "Do not keep any of it until morning." 20But some of them didn't listen and kept some of it until morning. But by then it was full of maggots and had a terrible smell. Moses was very angry with them.

21After this the people gathered the food morning by morning, each family according to its need. And as the sun became hot, the flakes they had not picked up melted and disappeared. 22On the sixth day, they gathered twice as much as usual—four quarts for each person instead of two. Then all the leaders of the community came and asked Moses for an explanation. 23He told them, "This is what the LORD commanded: Tomorrow will be a day of complete rest, a holy Sabbath day set apart for the LORD. So bake or boil as much as you want today, and set aside what is left for tomorrow."

24So they put some aside until morning, just as Moses had commanded. And in the morning the leftover food was wholesome and good, without maggots or odor. 25Moses said, "Eat this food today, for today is a Sabbath day dedicated to the LORD. There will be no food on the ground today. 26You may gather the food for six days, but the seventh day is the Sabbath. There will be no food on the ground that day."

~ Exodus 16:17-26

The Jethro principle

Moses had bitten of more than he could chew. He tried to be everything to everybody. By taking Jethro's advice he empowered others to serve God.

[13]The next day, Moses took his seat to hear the people's disputes against each other. They waited before him from morning till evening. [14]When Moses' father-in-law saw all that Moses was doing for the people, he asked, "What are you really accomplishing here? Why are you trying to do all this alone while everyone stands around you from morning till evening?"

[15]Moses replied, "Because the people come to me to get a ruling from God. [16]When a dispute arises, they come to me, and I am the one who settles the case between the quarreling parties. I inform the people of God's decrees and give them his instructions."

[17]"This is not good!" Moses' father-in-law exclaimed. [18]"You're going to wear yourself out—and the people, too. This job is too heavy a burden for you to handle all by yourself. [19]Now listen to me, and let me give you a word of advice, and may God be with you. You should continue to be the people's representative before God, bringing their disputes to him. [20]Teach them God's decrees, and give them his instructions. Show them how to conduct their lives. [21]But select from all the people some capable, honest men who fear God and hate bribes. Appoint them as leaders over groups of one thousand, one hundred, fifty, and ten. [22]They should always be available to solve the people's common disputes, but have them bring the major cases to you. Let the leaders decide the smaller matters themselves. They will help you carry the load, making the task easier for you. [23]If you follow this advice, and if God commands you to do so, then you will be able to endure the pressures, and all these people will go home in peace."

~ Exodus 18:13-23

Help those in need

Speak out for those who don't have a voice – strangers, widows and orphans. Stand up for those who have been knocked down by life. Bring relief to the suffering. Prevent the authorities from exploiting the poor. Then God's will is lived out.

21"You must not mistreat or oppress foreigners in any way. Remember, you yourselves were once foreigners in the land of Egypt.

22"You must not exploit a widow or an orphan. 23If you exploit them in any way and they cry out to me, then I will certainly hear their cry. 24My anger will blaze against you, and I will kill you with the sword. Then your wives will be widows and your children fatherless.

25"If you lend money to any of my people who are in need, do not charge interest as a money lender would. 26If you take your neighbor's cloak as security for a loan, you must return it before sunset. 27This coat may be the only blanket your neighbor has. How can a person sleep without it? If you do not return it and your neighbor cries out to me for help, then I will hear, for I am merciful.

28"You must not dishonor God or curse any of your rulers.

29"You must not hold anything back when you give me offerings from your crops and your wine.

"You must give me your firstborn sons."

~ Exodus 22:21-29

Negotiating with God

Only Moses, and later Paul, was prepared to sacrifice his place in heaven in order to save God's people. Talk about dedication and love for a bunch of stubborn people! Moses even tried to negotiate with God and change the decision He made about the sinful nation.

[29]Then Moses told the Levites, "Today you have ordained yourselves for the service of the LORD, for you obeyed him even though it meant killing your own sons and brothers. Today you have earned a blessing."

[30]The next day Moses said to the people, "You have committed a terrible sin, but I will go back up to the LORD on the mountain. Perhaps I will be able to obtain forgiveness for your sin."

[31]So Moses returned to the LORD and said, "Oh, what a terrible sin these people have committed. They have made gods of gold for themselves. [32]But now, if you will only forgive their sin—but if not, erase my name from the record you have written!"

[33]But the LORD replied to Moses, "No, I will erase the name of everyone who has sinned against me. [34]Now go, lead the people to the place I told you about. Look! My angel will lead the way before you. And when I come to call the people to account, I will certainly hold them responsible for their sins."

[35]Then the LORD sent a great plague upon the people because they had worshiped the calf Aaron had made.

~ Exodus 32:29-35

An ever-present God

God is present among His people. Sometimes His glory is tangible, while at other times it is something that must be embraced by faith. But the fact remains: God is always present. For this reason every coming together in His name is special.

¹⁵Next Aaron presented the offerings of the people. He slaughtered the people's goat and presented it as an offering for their sin, just as he had first done with the offering for his own sin. ¹⁶Then he presented the burnt offering and sacrificed it in the prescribed way. ¹⁷He also presented the grain offering, burning a handful of the flour mixture on the altar, in addition to the regular burnt offering for the morning.

¹⁸Then Aaron slaughtered the bull and the ram for the people's peace offering. His sons brought him the blood, and he splattered it against all sides of the altar. ¹⁹Then he took the fat of the bull and the ram—the fat of the broad tail and from around the internal organs—along with the kidneys and the long lobes of the livers. ²⁰He placed these fat portions on top of the breasts of these animals and burned them on the altar. ²¹Aaron then lifted up the breasts and right thighs as a special offering to the LORD, just as Moses had commanded.

²²After that, Aaron raised his hands toward the people and blessed them. Then, after presenting the sin offering, the burnt offering, and the peace offering, he stepped down from the altar. ²³Then Moses and Aaron went into the Tabernacle, and when they came back out, they blessed the people again, and the glory of the LORD appeared to the whole community. ²⁴Fire blazed forth from the LORD's presence and consumed the burnt offering and the fat on the altar. When the people saw this, they shouted with joy and fell face down on the ground.

~ Leviticus 9:15-24

Avoid forbidden fruit

Sexuality is one of God's many good gifts. It is beautiful and holy when it takes place within His will. But the moment it steps outside the borders of His will it becomes a soul-destroying fire. Therefore God warns His people not to play with fire which they can't control or extinguish.

¹Then the LORD said to Moses, ²"Give the following instructions to the people of Israel. I am the LORD your God. ³So do not act like the people in Egypt, where you used to live, or like the people of Canaan, where I am taking you. You must not imitate their way of life. ⁴You must obey all my regulations and be careful to obey my decrees, for I am the LORD your God. ⁵If you obey my decrees and my regulations, you will find life through them. I am the LORD.

⁶"You must never have sexual relations with a close relative, for I am the LORD. ⁷"Do not violate your father by having sexual relations with your mother. She is your mother; you must not have sexual relations with her. ⁸"Do not have sexual relations with any of your father's wives, for this would violate your father.

⁹"Do not have sexual relations with your sister or half sister, whether she is your father's daughter or your mother's daughter, whether she was born into your household or someone else's.

¹⁰"Do not have sexual relations with your granddaughter, whether she is your son's daughter or your daughter's daughter, for this would violate yourself. ¹¹"Do not have sexual relations with your stepsister, the daughter of any of your father's wives, for she is your sister. ¹²"Do not have sexual relations with your father's sister, for she is your father's close relative. ¹³"Do not have sexual relations with your mother's sister, for she is your mother's close relative."

~ Leviticus 18:1-13

For the first time:
Love each other

Leviticus 19 is very important and in verse 18 we read for the first time in the Bible that we must love our neighbors as ourselves. How can we do this? By judging fairly; not stealing from others; not gossiping and by not nursing hatred in our hearts.

¹The LORD also said to Moses, ⁹"When you harvest the crops of your land, do not harvest the grain along the edges of your fields, and do not pick up what the harvesters drop. ¹⁰It is the same with your grape crop—do not strip every last bunch of grapes from the vines, and do not pick up the grapes that fall to the ground. Leave them for the poor and the foreigners living among you. I am the LORD your God.

¹¹"Do not steal. Do not deceive or cheat one another.

¹²"Do not bring shame on the name of your God by using it to swear falsely. I am the LORD.

¹³"Do not defraud or rob your neighbor. Do not make your hired workers wait until the next day to receive their pay.

¹⁴"Do not insult the deaf or cause the blind to stumble. You must fear your God; I am the LORD.

¹⁵"Do not twist justice in legal matters by favoring the poor or being partial to the rich and powerful. Always judge people fairly.

¹⁶"Do not spread slanderous gossip among your people. Do not stand idly by when your neighbor's life is threatened. I am the LORD.

¹⁷"Do not nurse hatred in your heart for any of your relatives. Confront people directly so you will not be held guilty for their sin.

¹⁸"Do not seek revenge or bear a grudge against a fellow Israelite, but love your neighbor as yourself. I am the LORD."

~ Leviticus 19:1, 9-18

Give God what He deserves

To give is evidence of your love for God. The Israelites gave a tenth of all their income to the Lord. But tithing is not only rigid and fixed things, it is also to give of yourself and your possessions to God and to others.

[1]The LORD said to Moses, [26]"You may not dedicate a firstborn animal to the LORD, for the firstborn of your cattle, sheep, and goats already belong to him. [27]However, you may buy back the firstborn of a ceremonially unclean animal by paying the priest's assessment of its worth, plus 20 percent. If you do not buy it back, the priest will sell it at its assessed value.

[28]"However, anything specially set apart for the LORD—whether a person, an animal, or family property—must never be sold or bought back. Anything devoted in this way has been set apart as holy, and it belongs to the LORD. [29]No person specially set apart for destruction may be bought back. Such a person must be put to death.

[30]"One tenth of the produce of the land, whether grain from the fields or fruit from the trees, belongs to the LORD and must be set apart to him as holy. [31]If you want to buy back the LORD's tenth of the grain or fruit, you must pay its value, plus 20 percent. [32]Count off every tenth animal from your herds and flocks and set them apart for the LORD as holy. [33]You may not pick and choose between good and bad animals, and you may not substitute one for another. But if you do exchange one animal for another, then both the original animal and its substitute will be considered holy and cannot be bought back."

[34]These are the commands that the LORD gave through Moses on Mount Sinai for the Israelites.

~ Leviticus 27:1, 26-34

Follow the cloud

God is not static. No, He is dynamic. He is on the move. When His cloud moves, His people move with! The trick is to know when to set up camp and when to get going again. This requires obedience and great discernment.

[15]On the day the Tabernacle was set up, the cloud covered it. But from evening until morning the cloud over the Tabernacle looked like a pillar of fire. [16]This was the regular pattern—at night the cloud that covered the Tabernacle had the appearance of fire. [17]Whenever the cloud lifted from over the sacred tent, the people of Israel would break camp and follow it. And wherever the cloud settled, the people of Israel would set up camp. [18]In this way, they traveled and camped at the LORD's command wherever he told them to go. Then they remained in their camp as long as the cloud stayed over the Tabernacle. [19]If the cloud remained over the Tabernacle for a long time, the Israelites stayed and performed their duty to the LORD. [20]Sometimes the cloud would stay over the Tabernacle for only a few days, so the people would stay for only a few days, as the LORD commanded. Then at the LORD's command they would break camp and move on. [21]Sometimes the cloud stayed only overnight and lifted the next morning. But day or night, when the cloud lifted, the people broke camp and moved on. [22]Whether the cloud stayed above the Tabernacle for two days, a month, or a year, the people of Israel stayed in camp and did not move on. But as soon as it lifted, they broke camp and moved on. [23]So they camped or traveled at the LORD's command, and they did whatever the LORD told them through Moses.

~ Numbers 9:15-23

Are you following the majority?

The twelve spies delivered a minority and majority report to Moses. The majority were against moving to the Promised Land, but Joshua and Caleb were for it. In contrast to the ten, they and Moses chose the most difficult route as God's route. Even today, the right path is often the most difficult.

^{25}After exploring the land for forty days, the men returned ^{26}to Moses, Aaron, and the whole community of Israel at Kadesh in the wilderness of Paran. They reported to the whole community what they had seen and showed them the fruit they had taken from the land. ^{27}This was their report to Moses: "We entered the land you sent us to explore, and it is indeed a bountiful country—a land flowing with milk and honey. Here is the kind of fruit it produces. ^{28}But the people living there are powerful, and their towns are large and fortified. We even saw giants there, the descendants of Anak! ^{29}The Amalekites live in the Negev, and the Hittites, Jebusites, and Amorites live in the hill country. The Canaanites live along the coast of the Mediterranean Sea and along the Jordan Valley."

^{30}But Caleb tried to quiet the people as they stood before Moses. "Let's go at once to take the land," he said. "We can certainly conquer it!"

^{31}But the other men who had explored the land with him disagreed. "We can't go up against them! They are stronger than we are!" ^{32}So they spread this bad report about the land among the Israelites: "The land we traveled through and explored will devour anyone who goes to live there. All the people we saw were huge. ^{33}We even saw giants there, the descendants of Anak. Next to them we felt like grasshoppers, and that's what they thought, too!"

~ Numbers 13:25-33

To care for your people

It is sometimes difficult to love your own people, especially when they moan and complain the whole time. But Moses never lost his love for the people. For this reason he hastily made atonement for them when God wanted to punish them for their rebellion.

⁴¹But the very next morning the whole community of Israel began muttering again against Moses and Aaron, saying, "You have killed the Lord's people!" ⁴²As the community gathered to protest against Moses and Aaron, they turned toward the Tabernacle and saw that the cloud had covered it, and the glorious presence of the Lord appeared.

⁴³Moses and Aaron came and stood in front of the Tabernacle, ⁴⁴and the Lord said to Moses, ⁴⁵"Get away from all these people so that I can instantly destroy them!" But Moses and Aaron fell face down on the ground.

⁴⁶And Moses said to Aaron, "Quick, take an incense burner and place burning coals on it from the altar. Lay incense on it, and carry it out among the people to purify them and make them right with the Lord. The Lord's anger is blazing against them—the plague has already begun."

⁴⁷Aaron did as Moses told him and ran out among the people. The plague had already begun to strike down the people, but Aaron burned the incense and purified the people. ⁴⁸He stood between the dead and the living, and the plague stopped. ⁴⁹But 14,700 people died in that plague, in addition to those who had died in the affair involving Korah. ⁵⁰Then because the plague had stopped, Aaron returned to Moses at the entrance of the Tabernacle.

~ Numbers 16:41-50

Only One

In the midst of all the new gods that Israel encountered in the new land, they heard that the Lord is the only God. All the other gods are stone dead. God's visible deeds throughout history show who He is. His actions tell of His greatness.

⁵While the Israelites were in the land of Moab east of the Jordan River, Moses carefully explained the LORD's instructions as follows.

4³²"Now search all of history, from the time God created people on the earth until now, and search from one end of the heavens to the other. Has anything as great as this ever been seen or heard before? ³³Has any nation ever heard the voice of God speaking from fire—as you did—and survived? ³⁴Has any other god dared to take a nation for himself out of another nation by means of trials, miraculous signs, wonders, war, a strong hand, a powerful arm, and terrifying acts? Yet that is what the LORD your God did for you in Egypt, right before your eyes.

³⁵"He showed you these things so you would know that the LORD is God and there is no other. ³⁶He let you hear his voice from heaven so he could instruct you. He let you see his great fire here on earth so he could speak to you from it. ³⁷Because he loved your ancestors, he chose to bless their descendants, and he personally brought you out of Egypt with a great display of power. ³⁸He drove out nations far greater than you, so he could bring you in and give you their land as your special possession, as it is today. ³⁹"So remember this and keep it firmly in mind: The LORD is God both in heaven and on earth, and there is no other. ⁴⁰If you obey all the decrees and commands I am giving you today, all will be well with you and your children. I am giving you these instructions so you will enjoy a long life in the land the LORD your God is giving you for all time."

~ Deuteronomy 1:5, 4:32-40

"Listen, O Israel!"

Deuteronomy 6:4 is still one of the most well-known verses to every Israelite. It confirms that the Lord is the only God. We must love and serve this one Lord with everything within us. Our love for Him must become visible in our daily lives – where we and our children live, work and play.

⁴"Listen, O Israel! The LORD is our God, the LORD alone. ⁵And you must love the LORD your God with all your heart, all your soul, and all your strength. ⁶And you must commit yourselves wholeheartedly to these commands that I am giving you today. ⁷Repeat them again and again to your children. Talk about them when you are at home and when you are on the road, when you are going to bed and when you are getting up. ⁸Tie them to your hands and wear them on your forehead as reminders. ⁹Write them on the doorposts of your house and on your gates.

¹⁰"The LORD your God will soon bring you into the land he swore to give you when he made a vow to your ancestors Abraham, Isaac, and Jacob. It is a land with large, prosperous cities that you did not build. ¹¹The houses will be richly stocked with goods you did not produce. You will draw water from cisterns you did not dig, and you will eat from vineyards and olive trees you did not plant. When you have eaten your fill in this land, ¹²be careful not to forget the LORD, who rescued you from slavery in the land of Egypt. ¹³You must fear the LORD your God and serve him. When you take an oath, you must use only his name."

¹⁴"You must not worship any of the gods of neighboring nations, ¹⁵for the LORD your God, who lives among you, is a jealous God. His anger will flare up against you, and he will wipe you from the face of the earth.

~ Deuteronomy 6:4-15

Don't forget to remember

Forgetfulness is something many of us seem to suffer from. For this reason God calls us to sidestep forgetfulness by keeping His commandments. To forget God's will is to miss life itself. Personal comfort and convenience can be great memory-thieves. Don't forget God's goodness to you.

⁶"So obey the commands of the LORD your God by walking in his ways and fearing him. ⁷For the LORD your God is bringing you into a good land of flowing streams and pools of water, with fountains and springs that gush out in the valleys and hills. ⁸It is a land of wheat and barley; of grapevines, fig trees, and pomegranates; of olive oil and honey. ⁹It is a land where food is plentiful and nothing is lacking. It is a land where iron is as common as stone, and copper is abundant in the hills. ¹⁰When you have eaten your fill, be sure to praise the LORD your God for the good land he has given you.

¹¹"But that is the time to be careful! Beware that in your plenty you do not forget the LORD your God and disobey his commands, regulations, and decrees that I am giving you today. ¹²For when you have become full and prosperous and have built fine homes to live in, ¹³and when your flocks and herds have become very large and your silver and gold have multiplied along with everything else, be careful! ¹⁴Do not become proud at that time and forget the LORD your God, who rescued you from slavery in the land of Egypt. ¹⁵Do not forget that he led you through the great and terrifying wilderness with its poisonous snakes and scorpions, where it was so hot and dry. He gave you water from the rock! ¹⁶He fed you with manna in the wilderness, a food unknown to your ancestors. He did this to humble you and test you for your own good."

~ Deuteronomy 8:6-16

What does God ask?

God's expectation of His people is simple – we must love Him with everything in us. He doesn't ask obedience to dead laws and difficult regulations. Rather, it is about having a living relationship with the Lord of heaven and earth. And about having an all-encompassing love for Him.

[12]"And now, Israel, what does the LORD your God require of you? He requires only that you fear the LORD your God, and live in a way that pleases him, and love him and serve him with all your heart and soul. [13]And you must always obey the LORD's commands and decrees that I am giving you today for your own good.

[14]"Look, the highest heavens and the earth and everything in it all belong to the LORD your God. [15]Yet the LORD chose your ancestors as the objects of his love. And he chose you, their descendants, above all other nations, as is evident today. [16]Therefore, change your hearts and stop being stubborn.

[17]"For the LORD your God is the God of gods and Lord of lords. He is the great God, the mighty and awesome God, who shows no partiality and cannot be bribed. [18]He ensures that orphans and widows receive justice. He shows love to the foreigners living among you and gives them food and clothing. [19]So you, too, must show love to foreigners, for you yourselves were once foreigners in the land of Egypt. [20]You must fear the LORD your God and worship him and cling to him. Your oaths must be in his name alone. [21]He alone is your God, the only one who is worthy of your praise, the one who has done these mighty miracles that you have seen with your own eyes. [22]When your ancestors went down into Egypt, there were only seventy of them. But now the LORD your God has made you as numerous as the stars in the sky!"

~ Deuteronomy 10:12-22

True prophecy

Prophecy is not religious fortune telling in a disguised form. It is concerned with making God's will known, not with predicting the future. Therefore, true prophecy sometimes goes against the grain. The test of prophecy is the practical realization of God's will. If this doesn't happen, the prophecy is false.

¹⁵Moses continued, "The LORD your God will raise up for you a prophet like me from among your fellow Israelites. You must listen to him. ¹⁶For this is what you yourselves requested of the LORD your God when you were assembled at Mount Sinai. You said, 'Don't let us hear the voice of the LORD our God anymore or see this blazing fire, for we will die.'

¹⁷"Then the LORD said to me, 'What they have said is right. ¹⁸I will raise up a prophet like you from among their fellow Israelites. I will put my words in his mouth, and he will tell the people everything I command him. ¹⁹I will personally deal with anyone who will not listen to the messages the prophet proclaims on my behalf. ²⁰But any prophet who falsely claims to speak in my name or who speaks in the name of another god must die.'

²¹"But you may wonder, 'How will we know whether or not a prophecy is from the LORD?' ²²If the prophet speaks in the LORD's name but his prediction does not happen or come true, you will know that the LORD did not give that message. That prophet has spoken without my authority and need not be feared."

~ Deuteronomy 18:15-22

FEBRUARY

Teach the children too

Faith is not only meant for grown-ups, but especially for children. Therefore, adults must educate children in the ways of the Lord. It is not only the church and the school's responsibility – parents must raise their children for the Lord. Faith shows first in the home!

[7]Then Moses called for Joshua, and as all Israel watched, he said to him, "Be strong and courageous! For you will lead these people into the land that the LORD swore to their ancestors he would give them. You are the one who will divide it among them as their grants of land. [8]Do not be afraid or discouraged, for the LORD will personally go ahead of you. He will be with you; he will neither fail you nor abandon you."

[9]So Moses wrote this entire body of instruction in a book and gave it to the priests, who carried the Ark of the LORD's Covenant, and to the elders of Israel. [10]Then Moses gave them this command: "At the end of every seventh year, the Year of Release, during the Festival of Shelters, [11]you must read this Book of Instruction to all the people of Israel when they assemble before the LORD your God at the place he chooses. [12]Call them all together—men, women, children, and the foreigners living in your towns—so they may hear this Book of Instruction and learn to fear the LORD your God and carefully obey all the terms of these instructions. [13]Do this so that your children who have not known these instructions will hear them and will learn to fear the LORD your God. Do this as long as you live in the land you are crossing the Jordan to occupy."

~ Deuteronomy 31:7-13

Think about it …

How do you take over from Moses if your name is Joshua? Well, the Lord tells you to think about Moses' words day and night. That is how you abide in God's will and live a blessed life in His presence.

[1]After the death of Moses the LORD's servant, the LORD spoke to Joshua son of Nun, Moses' assistant. He said, [2]"Moses my servant is dead. Therefore, the time has come for you to lead these people, the Israelites, across the Jordan River into the land I am giving them. [3]I promise you what I promised Moses: 'Wherever you set foot, you will be on land I have given you—[4]from the Negev wilderness in the south to the Lebanon mountains in the north, from the Euphrates River in the east to the Mediterranean Sea in the west, including all the land of the Hittites.' [5]No one will be able to stand against you as long as you live. For I will be with you as I was with Moses. I will not fail you or abandon you.

[6]"Be strong and courageous, for you are the one who will lead these people to possess all the land I swore to their ancestors I would give them. [7]Be strong and very courageous. Be careful to obey all the instructions Moses gave you. Do not deviate from them, turning either to the right or to the left. Then you will be successful in everything you do. [8]Study this Book of Instruction continually. Meditate on it day and night so you will be sure to obey everything written in it. Only then will you prosper and succeed in all you do. [9]This is my command—be strong and courageous! Do not be afraid or discouraged. For the LORD your God is with you wherever you go."

~ Joshua 1:1-9

A memorial stone

God speaks in many ways – even through stones! He reminds His people everywhere of His care and salvation. Throughout Israel's history visible monuments of the Lord's mighty intervention and care were erected. There should be similar memorials in our lives too.

¹When all the people had crossed the Jordan, the LORD said to Joshua, ²"Now choose twelve men, one from each tribe. ³Tell them, 'Take twelve stones from the very place where the priests are standing in the middle of the Jordan. Carry them out and pile them up at the place where you will camp tonight.'"

⁴So Joshua called together the twelve men he had chosen—one from each of the tribes of Israel. ⁵He told them, "Go into the middle of the Jordan, in front of the Ark of the LORD your God. Each of you must pick up one stone and carry it out on your shoulder—twelve stones in all, one for each of the twelve tribes of Israel. ⁶We will use these stones to build a memorial. In the future your children will ask you, 'What do these stones mean?' ⁷Then you can tell them, 'They remind us that the Jordan River stopped flowing when the Ark of the LORD's Covenant went across.' These stones will stand as a memorial among the people of Israel forever."

⁸So the men did as Joshua had commanded them. They took twelve stones from the middle of the Jordan River, one for each tribe, just as the LORD had told Joshua. They carried them to the place where they camped for the night and constructed the memorial there.

⁹Joshua also set up another pile of twelve stones in the middle of the Jordan, at the place where the priests who carried the Ark of the Covenant were standing. And they are there to this day.

~ Joshua 4:1-9

God brings the universe to a halt

Anything is possible for God. He could even halt the universe when His servant Joshua asked Him to make the sun stand still. The earth stopped right there in its orbit around the sun. We serve a mighty God! Great is His name.

⁹Joshua traveled all night from Gilgal and took the Amorite armies by surprise. ¹⁰The LORD threw them into a panic, and the Israelites slaughtered great numbers of them at Gibeon. Then the Israelites chased the enemy along the road to Beth-horon, killing them all along the way to Azekah and Makkedah. ¹¹As the Amorites retreated down the road from Beth-horon, the LORD destroyed them with a terrible hailstorm from heaven that continued until they reached Azekah. The hail killed more of the enemy than the Israelites killed with the sword.

¹²On the day the LORD gave the Israelites victory over the Amorites, Joshua prayed to the LORD in front of all the people of Israel. He said,

"Let the sun stand still over Gibeon, and the moon over the valley of Aijalon."

¹³So the sun stood still and the moon stayed in place until the nation of Israel had defeated its enemies.

Is this event not recorded in *The Book of Jashar*? The sun stayed in the middle of the sky, and it did not set as on a normal day. ¹⁴There has never been a day like this one before or since, when the LORD answered such a prayer. Surely the LORD fought for Israel that day!

~ Joshua 10:9-14

At your post to the end

Caleb, one of the original two scouts, followed the Lord wholeheartedly. He was never overwhelmed by pride, laziness or fear. His zeal never faltered. Caleb was a living example of how to walk on God's path.

⁶A delegation from the tribe of Judah, led by Caleb son of Jephunneh the Kenizzite, came to Joshua at Gilgal. Caleb said to Joshua, "Remember what the LORD said to Moses, the man of God, about you and me when we were at Kadesh-barnea. ⁷I was forty years old when Moses, the servant of the LORD, sent me from Kadesh-barnea to explore the land of Canaan. I returned and gave an honest report, ⁸but my brothers who went with me frightened the people from entering the Promised Land. For my part, I wholeheartedly followed the LORD my God. ⁹So that day Moses solemnly promised me, 'The land of Canaan on which you were just walking will be your grant of land and that of your descendants forever, because you wholeheartedly followed the LORD my God.'

¹⁰"Now, as you can see, the LORD has kept me alive and well as he promised for all these forty-five years since Moses made this promise—even while Israel wandered in the wilderness. Today I am eighty-five years old. ¹¹I am as strong now as I was when Moses sent me on that journey, and I can still travel and fight as well as I could then. ¹²So give me the hill country that the LORD promised me. You will remember that as scouts we found the descendants of Anak living there in great, walled towns. But if the LORD is with me, I will drive them out of the land, just as the LORD said."

¹³So Joshua blessed Caleb son of Jephunneh and gave Hebron to him as his portion of land. ¹⁴Hebron still belongs to the descendants of Caleb son of Jephunneh the Kenizzite because he wholeheartedly followed the LORD, the God of Israel.

~ Joshua 14:6-14

True obedience

Joshua's farewell words tell the story of a man who knew only one type of loyalty throughout his life – namely loyalty toward God. He shares the secret of this life: carefully obey God's will. There is no other route that leads to Life.

[1]The years passed, and the LORD had given the people of Israel rest from all their enemies. Joshua, who was now very old, [2]called together all the elders, leaders, judges, and officers of Israel. He said to them, "I am now a very old man. [3]You have seen everything the LORD your God has done for you during my lifetime. The LORD your God has fought for you against your enemies. [4]I have allotted to you as your homeland all the land of the nations yet unconquered, as well as the land of those we have already conquered—from the Jordan River to the Mediterranean Sea in the west. [5]This land will be yours, for the LORD your God will himself drive out all the people living there now. You will take possession of their land, just as the LORD your God promised you.

[6]"So be very careful to follow everything Moses wrote in the Book of Instruction. Do not deviate from it, turning either to the right or to the left. [7]Make sure you do not associate with the other people still remaining in the land. Do not even mention the names of their gods, much less swear by them or serve them or worship them. [8]Rather, cling tightly to the LORD your God as you have done until now."

~ Joshua 23:1-8

The tragedy of a godless generation

After Joshua's death a godless generation of Israelites appeared on the scene. Parents did not raise God-fearing children, and therefore God was constantly pushed to the background. The only solution is for parents to love God with and in front of their children.

7And the Israelites served the LORD throughout the lifetime of Joshua and the leaders who outlived him—those who had seen all the great things the LORD had done for Israel.

8Joshua son of Nun, the servant of the LORD, died at the age of 110. 9They buried him in the land he had been allocated, at Timnath-serah in the hill country of Ephraim, north of Mount Gaash.

10After that generation died, another generation grew up who did not acknowledge the LORD or remember the mighty things he had done for Israel.

11The Israelites did evil in the LORD's sight and served the images of Baal. 12They abandoned the LORD, the God of their ancestors, who had brought them out of Egypt. They went after other gods, worshiping the gods of the people around them. And they angered the LORD. 13They abandoned the LORD to serve Baal and the images of Ashtoreth. 14This made the LORD burn with anger against Israel, so he handed them over to raiders who stole their possessions. He turned them over to their enemies all around, and they were no longer able to resist them. 15Every time Israel went out to battle, the LORD fought against them, causing them to be defeated, just as he had warned. And the people were in great distress.

~ Judges 2:7-15

Hope for the fearful

Gideon was not the bravest person called to service by God – he was also not the godliest. But he was still called to be a mighty hero for the Lord. Luckily God doesn't fall for people's excuses and little faith when He calls them.

[11]Then the angel of the Lord came and sat beneath the great tree at Ophrah, which belonged to Joash of the clan of Abiezer. Gideon son of Joash was threshing wheat at the bottom of a winepress to hide the grain from the Midianites. [12]The angel of the Lord appeared to him and said, "Mighty hero, the Lord is with you!"

[13]"Sir," Gideon replied, "if the Lord is with us, why has all this happened to us? And where are all the miracles our ancestors told us about? Didn't they say, 'The Lord brought us up out of Egypt'? But now the Lord has abandoned us and handed us over to the Midianites."

[14]Then the Lord turned to him and said, "Go with the strength you have, and rescue Israel from the Midianites. I am sending you!"

[15]"But Lord," Gideon replied, "how can I rescue Israel? My clan is the weakest in the whole tribe of Manasseh, and I am the least in my entire family!"

[16]The Lord said to him, "I will be with you. And you will destroy the Midianites as if you were fighting against one man."

~ Judges 6:11-16

Talent and character are not the same

Samson was one of the most talented judges ever. His strength knew no end, but he had little character. Talent usually only regulates your world on the outside, while character controls our inner world before God. Character carries you through this life and the next.

¹One day Samson went to the Philistine town of Gaza and spent the night with a prostitute. ²Word soon spread that Samson was there, so the men of Gaza gathered together and waited all night at the town gates. They kept quiet during the night, saying to themselves, "When the light of morning comes, we will kill him."

³But Samson stayed in bed only until midnight. Then he got up, took hold of the doors of the town gate, including the two posts, and lifted them up, bar and all. He put them on his shoulders and carried them all the way to the top of the hill across from Hebron.

⁴Some time later Samson fell in love with a woman named Delilah, who lived in the valley of Sorek. ⁵The rulers of the Philistines went to her and said, "Entice Samson to tell you what makes him so strong and how he can be overpowered and tied up securely. Then each of us will give you 1,100 pieces of silver."

⁶So Delilah said to Samson, "Please tell me what makes you so strong and what it would take to tie you up securely."

⁷Samson replied, "If I were tied up with seven new bowstrings that have not yet been dried, I would become as weak as anyone else."

⁸So the Philistine rulers brought Delilah seven new bowstrings, and she tied Samson up with them.

~ Judges 16:1-8

Do only God's will

What a shocking solution to the men of Benjamin who still needed wives. No wonder Judges 21:25 concludes with the words, "All the people did whatever seemed right in their own eyes." We must only do what is right in God's eyes, not as we see fit. His will is all that matters.

²⁰They told the men of Benjamin who still needed wives, "Go and hide in the vineyards. ²¹When you see the young women of Shiloh come out for their dances, rush out from the vineyards, and each of you can take one of them home to the land of Benjamin to be your wife! ²²And when their fathers and brothers come to us in protest, we will tell them, 'Please be sympathetic. Let them have your daughters, for we didn't find wives for all of them when we destroyed Jabesh-gilead. And you are not guilty of breaking the vow since you did not actually give your daughters to them in marriage.'"

²³So the men of Benjamin did as they were told. Each man caught one of the women as she danced in the celebration and carried her off to be his wife. They returned to their own land, and they rebuilt their towns and lived in them.

²⁴Then the people of Israel departed by tribes and families, and they returned to their own homes.

²⁵In those days Israel had no king; all the people did whatever seemed right in their own eyes.

~ Judges 21:20-25

Women on God's path

Who doesn't know Ruth's famous words in verses 16-17? How moving! In a strange country she discovered the living God's fingerprints and footprints in her mother-in-law, Naomi's life. Therefore, she could and would not live without this God and one of His people.

8But on the way, Naomi said to her two daughters-in-law, "Go back to your mothers' homes. And may the Lord reward you for your kindness to your husbands and to me. 9May the Lord bless you with the security of another marriage." Then she kissed them good-bye, and they all broke down and wept.

10"No," they said. "We want to go with you to your people."

11But Naomi replied, "Why should you go on with me? Can I still give birth to other sons who could grow up to be your husbands? 12No, my daughters, return to your parents' homes, for I am too old to marry again. And even if it were possible, and I were to get married tonight and bear sons, then what? 13Would you wait for them to grow up and refuse to marry someone else? No, of course not, my daughters! Things are far more bitter for me than for you, because the Lord himself has raised his fist against me."

14And again they wept together, and Orpah kissed her mother-in-law good-bye. But Ruth clung tightly to Naomi. 15"Look," Naomi said to her, "your sister-in-law has gone back to her people and to her gods. You should do the same."

16But Ruth replied, "Don't ask me to leave you and turn back. Wherever you go, I will go; wherever you live, I will live. Your people will be my people, and your God will be my God. 17Wherever you die, I will die, and there I will be buried. May the Lord punish me severely if I allow anything but death to separate us!"

~ Ruth 1:8-17

Use your head

Faith is not only about matters of the heart, but also about matters of the mind. Naomi used her head and taught Ruth how to attract the right man's attention. Learn from her how to go through life with godly wisdom.

¹Now there was a wealthy and influential man in Bethlehem named Boaz, who was a relative of Naomi's husband, Elimelech. ²One day Ruth the Moabite said to Naomi, "Let me go out into the harvest fields to pick up the stalks of grain left behind by anyone who is kind enough to let me do it." Naomi replied, "All right, my daughter, go ahead." ³So Ruth went out to gather grain behind the harvesters. And as it happened, she found herself working in a field that belonged to Boaz, the relative of her father-in-law, Elimelech.

⁴While she was there, Boaz arrived from Bethlehem and greeted the harvesters. "The LORD be with you!" he said.

"The LORD bless you!" the harvesters replied.

⁵Then Boaz asked his foreman, "Who is that young woman over there? Who does she belong to?"

⁶And the foreman replied, "She is the young woman from Moab who came back with Naomi. ⁷She asked me this morning if she could gather grain behind the harvesters. She has been hard at work ever since, except for a few minutes' rest in the shelter."

⁸Boaz went over and said to Ruth, "Listen, my daughter. Stay right here with us when you gather grain; don't go to any other fields. Stay right behind the young women working in my field. ⁹See which part of the field they are harvesting, and then follow them. I have warned the young men not to treat you roughly. And when you are thirsty, help yourself to the water they have drawn from the well."

~ Ruth 2:1-9

All's well that ends well

Ruth and Boaz's story ends well, for them and for Naomi too. In His own ways, God intervened in Naomi's life and realized His will in and through her pain and hardship. Eventually she could have descendants and experience God's goodness. God stays faithful to the end!

¹³So Boaz took Ruth into his home, and she became his wife. When he slept with her, the LORD enabled her to become pregnant, and she gave birth to a son. ¹⁴Then the women of the town said to Naomi, "Praise the LORD, who has now provided a redeemer for your family! May this child be famous in Israel. ¹⁵May he restore your youth and care for you in your old age. For he is the son of your daughter-in-law who loves you and has been better to you than seven sons!"

¹⁶Naomi took the baby and cuddled him to her breast. And she cared for him as if he were her own. ¹⁷The neighbor women said, "Now at last Naomi has a son again!" And they named him Obed. He became the father of Jesse and the grandfather of David.

¹⁸This is the genealogical record of their ancestor Perez:

Perez was the father of Hezron. ¹⁹Hezron was the father of Ram. Ram was the father of Amminadab. ²⁰Amminadab was the father of Nahshon. Nahshon was the father of Salmon. ²¹Salmon was the father of Boaz. Boaz was the father of Obed. ²²Obed was the father of Jesse. Jesse was the father of David.

~ Ruth 4:13-22

Petition does not fall on deaf ears

Samuel's name explains everything, "I asked the Lord for him." A childless mother's endless plea opened the way for a great prophet. See what praying to a loving God can accomplish? It can bring about individuals who can change a country's history!

¹⁹The entire family got up early the next morning and went to worship the LORD once more. Then they returned home to Ramah. When Elkanah slept with Hannah, the LORD remembered her plea, ²⁰and in due time she gave birth to a son. She named him Samuel, for she said, "I asked the LORD for him."

²¹The next year Elkanah and his family went on their annual trip to offer a sacrifice to the LORD. ²²But Hannah did not go. She told her husband, "Wait until the boy is weaned. Then I will take him to the Tabernacle and leave him there with the LORD permanently."

²³"Whatever you think is best," Elkanah agreed. "Stay here for now, and may the LORD help you keep your promise." So she stayed home and nursed the boy until he was weaned.

²⁴When the child was weaned, Hannah took him to the Tabernacle in Shiloh. They brought along a three-year-old bull for the sacrifice and a basket of flour and some wine. ²⁵After sacrificing the bull, they brought the boy to Eli. ²⁶"Sir, do you remember me?" Hannah asked. "I am the woman who stood here several years ago praying to the LORD. ²⁷I asked the LORD to give me this boy, and he has granted my request. ²⁸Now I am giving him to the LORD, and he will belong to the LORD his whole life." And they worshiped the LORD there.

~ 1 Samuel 1:19-28

Rein them in

It is tragic that Eli's sons had no respect for God. Therefore the urgent warning to discipline them. He was more afraid of his children than of God! Loving God requires a home where respect and strong principles still count.

[27]One day a man of God came to Eli and gave him this message from the LORD: "I revealed myself to your ancestors when the people of Israel were slaves in Egypt. [28]I chose your ancestor Aaron from among all the tribes of Israel to be my priest, to offer sacrifices on my altar, to burn incense, and to wear the priestly vest as he served me. And I assigned the sacrificial offerings to you priests. [29]So why do you scorn my sacrifices and offerings? Why do you give your sons more honor than you give me—for you and they have become fat from the best offerings of my people Israel!

[30]"Therefore, the LORD, the God of Israel, says: I promised that your branch of the tribe of Levi would always be my priests. But I will honor those who honor me, and I will despise those who think lightly of me. [31]The time is coming when I will put an end to your family, so it will no longer serve as my priests. All the members of your family will die before their time. None will reach old age. [32]You will watch with envy as I pour out prosperity on the people of Israel. But no members of your family will ever live out their days. [33]Those who survive will live in sadness and grief, and their children will die a violent death. [34]And to prove that what I have said will come true, I will cause your two sons, Hophni and Phinehas, to die on the same day!"

~ 1 Samuel 2:27-34

Mercy

When Samuel spoke to the nation, the sky thundered. They asked him to pray for them. Samuel's answer confirmed God's mercy – for sinners too. But it also emphasized that mercy is not a license for sinning continually. Mercy calls for righteous living.

¹Then Samuel addressed all Israel: "I have done as you asked and given you a king.

¹⁶"Now stand here and see the great thing the LORD is about to do. ¹⁷You know that it does not rain at this time of the year during the wheat harvest. I will ask the LORD to send thunder and rain today. Then you will realize how wicked you have been in asking the LORD for a king!"

¹⁸So Samuel called to the LORD, and the LORD sent thunder and rain that day. And all the people were terrified of the LORD and of Samuel. ¹⁹"Pray to the LORD your God for us, or we will die!" they all said to Samuel. "For now we have added to our sins by asking for a king."

²⁰"Don't be afraid," Samuel reassured them. "You have certainly done wrong, but make sure now that you worship the LORD with all your heart, and don't turn your back on him. ²¹Don't go back to worshiping worthless idols that cannot help or rescue you—they are totally useless! ²²The LORD will not abandon his people, because that would dishonor his great name. For it has pleased the LORD to make you his very own people.

²³"As for me, I will certainly not sin against the LORD by ending my prayers for you. And I will continue to teach you what is good and right. ²⁴But be sure to fear the LORD and faithfully serve him. Think of all the wonderful things he has done for you. ²⁵But if you continue to sin, you and your king will be swept away."

~ 1 Samuel 12:1, 16-25

When God abandons you

Saul's reign ended in chaos. God's Spirit abandoned Saul. What can be worse than that? But God is never caught off guard by our sin. He raises up new people to do His will, people like David.

¹³So as David stood there among his brothers, Samuel took the flask of olive oil he had brought and anointed David with the oil. And the Spirit of the Lord came powerfully upon David from that day on. Then Samuel returned to Ramah.

¹⁴Now the Spirit of the Lord had left Saul, and the Lord sent a tormenting spirit that filled him with depression and fear. ¹⁵Some of Saul's servants said to him, "A tormenting spirit from God is troubling you. ¹⁶Let us find a good musician to play the harp whenever the tormenting spirit troubles you. He will play soothing music, and you will soon be well again."

¹⁷"All right," Saul said. "Find me someone who plays well, and bring him here."

¹⁸One of the servants said to Saul, "One of Jesse's sons from Bethlehem is a talented harp player. Not only that—he is a brave warrior, a man of war, and has good judgment. He is also a fine-looking young man, and the Lord is with him."

¹⁹So Saul sent messengers to Jesse to say, "Send me your son David, the shepherd." ²⁰Jesse responded by sending David to Saul, along with a young goat, a donkey loaded with bread, and a wineskin full of wine. ²¹So David went to Saul and began serving him. Saul loved David very much, and David became his armor bearer.

²²Then Saul sent word to Jesse asking, "Please let David remain in my service, for I am very pleased with him." ²³And whenever the tormenting spirit from God troubled Saul, David would play the harp. Then Saul would feel better, and the tormenting spirit would go away.

~ 1 Samuel 16:13-23

David picked up five stones

Five small stones versus an armored giant – but David was ready for the fight with Goliath. His stones were missiles in the hands of God that day. The impossible happens when ordinary people place their lives in God's hands. Then giants fall in battle and the weak conquer great establishments.

⁴¹Goliath walked out toward David with his shield bearer ahead of him, ⁴²sneering in contempt at this ruddy-faced boy. ⁴³"Am I a dog," he roared at David, "that you come at me with a stick?" And he cursed David by the names of his gods. ⁴⁴"Come over here, and I'll give your flesh to the birds and wild animals!" Goliath yelled.

⁴⁵David replied to the Philistine, "You come to me with sword, spear, and javelin, but I come to you in the name of the LORD of Heaven's Armies—the God of the armies of Israel, whom you have defied. ⁴⁶Today the LORD will conquer you, and I will kill you and cut off your head. And then I will give the dead bodies of your men to the birds and wild animals, and the whole world will know that there is a God in Israel! ⁴⁷And everyone assembled here will know that the LORD rescues his people, but not with sword and spear. This is the LORD's battle, and he will give you to us!"

⁴⁸As Goliath moved closer to attack, David quickly ran out to meet him. ⁴⁹Reaching into his shepherd's bag and taking out a stone, he hurled it with his sling and hit the Philistine in the forehead. The stone sank in, and Goliath stumbled and fell face down on the ground.

⁵⁰So David triumphed over the Philistine with only a sling and a stone, for he had no sword. ⁵¹Then David ran over and pulled Goliath's sword from its sheath. David used it to kill him and cut off his head.

~ 1 Samuel 17:41-51

Friendship expects everything

David and Jonathan's friendship is legendary. In 1 Samuel 20 it is portrayed grippingly. Their bond was so strong that Jonathan faced the anger of his father, Saul, to save David's life. True friendship is rare and precious. It sacrifices everything for each other.

⁸"Show me this loyalty as my sworn friend—for we made a solemn pact before the LORD—or kill me yourself if I have sinned against your father. But please don't betray me to him!"

⁹"Never!" Jonathan exclaimed. "You know that if I had the slightest notion my father was planning to kill you, I would tell you at once."

¹⁰Then David asked, "How will I know whether or not your father is angry?"

¹¹"Come out to the field with me," Jonathan replied. And they went out there together. ¹²Then Jonathan told David, "I promise by the LORD, the God of Israel, that by this time tomorrow, or the next day at the latest, I will talk to my father and let you know at once how he feels about you. If he speaks favorably about you, I will let you know. ¹³But if he is angry and wants you killed, may the LORD strike me and even kill me if I don't warn you so you can escape and live. May the LORD be with you as he used to be with my father. ¹⁴And may you treat me with the faithful love of the LORD as long as I live. But if I die, ¹⁵treat my family with this faithful love, even when the LORD destroys all your enemies from the face of the earth."

¹⁶So Jonathan made a solemn pact with David, saying, "May the LORD destroy all your enemies!" ¹⁷And Jonathan made David reaffirm his vow of friendship again, for Jonathan loved David as he loved himself.

~ 1 Samuel 20:8-17

We have no right to revenge

When David heard about Saul and Jonathan's deaths, he mourned. He did not rejoice even though Saul had caused him so much grief. The same is true for us. Our calling is to live and forgive – not to hate.

¹⁷Then David composed a funeral song for Saul and Jonathan, ¹⁸and he commanded that it be taught to the people of Judah. It is known as the Song of the Bow, and it is recorded in *The Book of Jashar.*

¹⁹Your pride and joy, O Israel, lies dead on the hills! Oh, how the mighty heroes have fallen! ²⁰Don't announce the news in Gath, don't proclaim it in the streets of Ashkelon, or the daughters of the Philistines will rejoice and the pagans will laugh in triumph. ²¹O mountains of Gilboa, let there be no dew or rain upon you, nor fruitful fields producing offerings of grain. For there the shield of the mighty heroes was defiled; the shield of Saul will no longer be anointed with oil. ²²The bow of Jonathan was powerful, and the sword of Saul did its mighty work. They shed the blood of their enemies and pierced the bodies of mighty heroes. ²³How beloved and gracious were Saul and Jonathan! They were together in life and in death. They were swifter than eagles, stronger than lions. ²⁴O women of Israel, weep for Saul, for he dressed you in luxurious scarlet clothing, in garments decorated with gold.

²⁵Oh, how the mighty heroes have fallen in battle! Jonathan lies dead on the hills.

²⁶How I weep for you, my brother Jonathan!

Oh, how much I loved you! And your love for me was deep, deeper than the love of women! ²⁷Oh, how the mighty heroes have fallen!

Stripped of their weapons, they lie dead.

~ 2 Samuel 1:17-27

Dance before God

I'm glad I don't have to do what David had done once – dance naked in front of God's ark. He did not have a hidden agenda. His dancing was a demonstration of his humility and love for God.

[14]And David danced before the LORD with all his might, wearing a priestly garment. [15]So David and all the people of Israel brought up the Ark of the LORD with shouts of joy and the blowing of rams' horns. [16]But as the Ark of the LORD entered the City of David, Michal, the daughter of Saul, looked down from her window. When she saw King David leaping and dancing before the LORD, she was filled with contempt for him.

[17]They brought the Ark of the LORD and set it in its place inside the special tent David had prepared for it. And David sacrificed burnt offerings and peace offerings to the LORD. [18]When he had finished his sacrifices, David blessed the people in the name of the LORD of Heaven's Armies. [19]Then he gave to every Israelite man and woman in the crowd a loaf of bread, a cake of dates, and a cake of raisins. Then all the people returned to their homes.

[20]When David returned home to bless his own family, Michal, the daughter of Saul, came out to meet him. She said in disgust, "How distinguished the king of Israel looked today, shamelessly exposing himself to the servant girls like any vulgar person might do!" [21]David retorted to Michal, "I was dancing before the LORD, who chose me above your father and all his family! He appointed me as the leader of Israel, the people of the LORD, so I celebrate before the LORD. [22]Yes, and I am willing to look even more foolish than this, even to be humiliated in my own eyes! But those servant girls you mentioned will indeed think I am distinguished!"

~ 2 Samuel 6:14-22

Sin is costly

Sin can cost you. Ask David. His spying on Bathsheba lead to an evil cycle of adultery, murder and cover-ups. But you can't hide anything from God. Therefore, rather bring your sins to the Light. For Christ's sake God will erase your sins.

²Late one afternoon, after his midday rest, David got out of bed and was walking on the roof of the palace. As he looked out over the city, he noticed a woman of unusual beauty taking a bath. ³He sent someone to find out who she was, and he was told, "She is Bathsheba, the daughter of Eliam and the wife of Uriah the Hittite." ⁴Then David sent messengers to get her; and when she came to the palace, he slept with her. She had just completed the purification rites after having her menstrual period. Then she returned home. ⁵Later, when Bathsheba discovered that she was pregnant, she sent David a message, saying, "I'm pregnant."

⁶Then David sent word to Joab: "Send me Uriah the Hittite." So Joab sent him to David. ⁷When Uriah arrived, David asked him how Joab and the army were getting along and how the war was progressing. ⁸Then he told Uriah, "Go on home and relax." David even sent a gift to Uriah after he had left the palace. ⁹But Uriah didn't go home. He slept that night at the palace entrance with the king's palace guard.

¹⁰When David heard that Uriah had not gone home, he summoned him and asked, "What's the matter? Why didn't you go home last night after being away for so long?"

¹¹Uriah replied, "The Ark and the armies of Israel and Judah are living in tents, and Joab and my master's men are camping in the open fields. How could I go home to wine and dine and sleep with my wife? I swear that I would never do such a thing."

~ 2 Samuel 11:2-11

Don't cover up sin

The mistake David made after his trespasses with Bathsheba was to try and cover it up. It pulled him down deeper and deeper. Therefore, Nathan brought it out into the open and tore down David's mask. The best place to openly repent of sin is at God's feet. Only He can take it away.

¹So the Lord sent Nathan the prophet to tell David this story: "There were two men in a certain town. One was rich, and one was poor. ²The rich man owned a great many sheep and cattle. ³The poor man owned nothing but one little lamb he had bought. He raised that little lamb, and it grew up with his children. It ate from the man's own plate and drank from his cup. He cuddled it in his arms like a baby daughter. ⁴One day a guest arrived at the home of the rich man. But instead of killing an animal from his own flock or herd, he took the poor man's lamb and killed it and prepared it for his guest."

⁵David was furious. "As surely as the Lord lives," he vowed, "any man who would do such a thing deserves to die! ⁶He must repay four lambs to the poor man for the one he stole and for having no pity."

⁷Then Nathan said to David, "You are that man! The Lord, the God of Israel, says: I anointed you king of Israel and saved you from the power of Saul. ⁸I gave you your master's house and his wives and the kingdoms of Israel and Judah. And if that had not been enough, I would have given you much, much more. ⁹Why, then, have you despised the word of the Lord and done this horrible deed? For you have murdered Uriah the Hittite with the sword of the Ammonites and stolen his wife."

~ 2 Samuel 12:1-9

A valiant warrior in a lion's den

Benaiah was one of David's heroes. He was such a brave man! He once killed a lion in a pit. David's heroes were fighters who always charged into battle. The Lord's heroes are those who hold on to Him against the current and are always at their post.

¹⁶So the Three broke through the Philistine lines, drew some water from the well by the gate in Bethlehem, and brought it back to David. But he refused to drink it. Instead, he poured it out as an offering to the LORD. ¹⁷"The LORD forbid that I should drink this!" he exclaimed. "This water is as precious as the blood of these men who risked their lives to bring it to me." So David did not drink it. These are examples of the exploits of the Three.

¹⁸Abishai son of Zeruiah, the brother of Joab, was the leader of the Thirty. He once used his spear to kill 300 enemy warriors in a single battle. It was by such feats that he became as famous as the Three. ¹⁹Abishai was the most famous of the Thirty and was their commander, though he was not one of the Three.

²⁰There was also Benaiah son of Jehoiada, a valiant warrior from Kabzeel. He did many heroic deeds, which included killing two champions of Moab. Another time, on a snowy day, he chased a lion down into a pit and killed it. ²¹Once, armed only with a club, he killed a great Egyptian warrior who was armed with a spear. Benaiah wrenched the spear from the Egyptian's hand and killed him with it. ²²Deeds like these made Benaiah as famous as the Three mightiest warriors. ²³He was more honored than the other members of the Thirty, though he was not one of the Three. And David made him captain of his bodyguard.

~ 2 Samuel 23:16-23

Firmly grip that baton

There comes a time to pass the baton. It must be done correctly, like David did when he passed down kingship to his son Solomon. The most important lesson that he passed on was that Solomon must serve the Lord faithfully and obey His Word. In this way successors can continue successfully.

¹As the time of King David's death approached, he gave this charge to his son Solomon:

²"I am going where everyone on earth must someday go. Take courage and be a man. ³Observe the requirements of the Lord your God, and follow all his ways. Keep the decrees, commands, regulations, and laws written in the Law of Moses so that you will be successful in all you do and wherever you go. ⁴If you do this, then the Lord will keep the promise he made to me. He told me, 'If your descendants live as they should and follow me faithfully with all their heart and soul, one of them will always sit on the throne of Israel.'

⁵"And there is something else. You know what Joab son of Zeruiah did to me when he murdered my two army commanders, Abner son of Ner and Amasa son of Jether. He pretended that it was an act of war, but it was done in a time of peace, staining his belt and sandals with innocent blood. ⁶Do with him what you think best, but don't let him grow old and go to his grave in peace.

⁷"Be kind to the sons of Barzillai of Gilead. Make them permanent guests at your table, for they took care of me when I fled from your brother Absalom."

~ 1 Kings 2:1-7

God is with His people

God wants to be with His people. In Solomon's time He did it by using the temple as a symbol of His presence. God does not physically stay in man-made buildings, but He binds Himself to us through His Spirit.

¹¹Then the LORD gave this message to Solomon: ¹²"Concerning this Temple you are building, if you keep all my decrees and regulations and obey all my commands, I will fulfill through you the promise I made to your father, David. ¹³I will live among the Israelites and will never abandon my people Israel."

¹⁴So Solomon finished building the Temple. ¹⁵The entire inside, from floor to ceiling, was paneled with wood. He paneled the walls and ceilings with cedar, and he used planks of cypress for the floors. ¹⁶He partitioned off an inner sanctuary—the Most Holy Place—at the far end of the Temple. It was 30 feet deep and was paneled with cedar from floor to ceiling. ¹⁷The main room of the Temple, outside the Most Holy Place, was 60 feet long. ¹⁸Cedar paneling completely covered the stone walls throughout the Temple, and the paneling was decorated with carvings of gourds and open flowers.

¹⁹He prepared the inner sanctuary at the far end of the Temple, where the Ark of the LORD's Covenant would be placed. ²⁰This inner sanctuary was 30 feet long, 30 feet wide, and 30 feet high. He overlaid the inside with solid gold. He also overlaid the altar made of cedar. ²¹Then Solomon overlaid the rest of the Temple's interior with solid gold, and he made gold chains to protect the entrance to the Most Holy Place. ²²So he finished overlaying the entire Temple with gold, including the altar that belonged to the Most Holy Place.

~ 1 Kings 6:11-22

Welcome the Lord

Not even the highest heavens are good enough for the living God, but still He reveals Himself to us here on earth. He makes His home with us. For this reason Solomon joyfully welcomed God with the inauguration of the temple. When God appears, there is always rejoicing among His people.

²²Then Solomon stood before the altar of the Lord in front of the entire community of Israel. He lifted his hands toward heaven, ²³and he prayed,

"O Lord, God of Israel, there is no God like you in all of heaven above or on the earth below. You keep your covenant and show unfailing love to all who walk before you in whole-hearted devotion. ²⁴You have kept your promise to your servant David, my father. You made that promise with your own mouth, and with your own hands you have fulfilled it today.

²⁵"And now, O Lord, God of Israel, carry out the additional promise you made to your servant David, my father. For you said to him, 'If your descendants guard their behavior and faithfully follow me as you have done, one of them will always sit on the throne of Israel.' ²⁶Now, O God of Israel, fulfill this promise to your servant David, my father.

²⁷"But will God really live on earth? Why, even the highest heavens cannot contain you. How much less this Temple I have built! ²⁸Nevertheless, listen to my prayer and my plea, O Lord my God. Hear the cry and the prayer that your servant is making to you today. ²⁹May you watch over this Temple night and day, this place where you have said, 'My name will be there.' May you always hear the prayers I make toward this place. ³⁰May you hear the humble and earnest requests from me and your people Israel when we pray toward this place. Yes, hear us from heaven where you live, and when you hear, forgive."

~ 1 Kings 8:22-30

Wisdom

The queen of Sheba was overwhelmed by Solomon's reign. It was especially his wisdom that gripped her. Right there she honored God for showering His servants with His favor and insight. God's heavenly wisdom continually transforms earthly people into living gifts to each other.

¹When the queen of Sheba heard of Solomon's fame, which brought honor to the name of the LORD, she came to test him with hard questions. ²She arrived in Jerusalem with a large group of attendants and a great caravan of camels loaded with spices, large quantities of gold, and precious jewels. When she met with Solomon, she talked with him about everything she had on her mind. ³Solomon had answers for all her questions; nothing was too hard for the king to explain to her. ⁴When the queen of Sheba realized how very wise Solomon was, and when she saw the palace he had built, ⁵she was overwhelmed. She was also amazed at the food on his tables, the organization of his officials and their splendid clothing, the cup-bearers, and the burnt offerings Solomon made at the Temple of the LORD.

⁶She exclaimed to the king, "Everything I heard in my country about your achievements and wisdom is true! ⁷I didn't believe what was said until I arrived here and saw it with my own eyes. In fact, I had not heard the half of it! Your wisdom and prosperity are far beyond what I was told. ⁸How happy your people must be! What a privilege for your officials to stand here day after day, listening to your wisdom! ⁹Praise the LORD your God, who delights in you and has placed you on the throne of Israel. Because of the LORD's eternal love for Israel, he has made you king so you can rule with justice and righteousness."

~ 1 Kings 10:1-9

Survival food for a refugee

One day Elijah was still the great hero of faith on Carmel, and the next day he was fleeing. Eventually he came to a broom tree and prayed that he might die. But an angel appeared with enough food for Elijah to survive the forty days he would need to reach God's mountain.

¹When Ahab got home, he told Jezebel everything Elijah had done, including the way he had killed all the prophets of Baal. ²So Jezebel sent this message to Elijah: "May the gods strike me and even kill me if by this time tomorrow I have not killed you just as you killed them."

³Elijah was afraid and fled for his life. He went to Beersheba, a town in Judah, and he left his servant there. ⁴Then he went on alone into the wilderness, traveling all day. He sat down under a solitary broom tree and prayed that he might die. "I have had enough, LORD," he said. "Take my life, for I am no better than my ancestors who have already died."

⁵Then he lay down and slept under the broom tree. But as he was sleeping, an angel touched him and told him, "Get up and eat!" ⁶He looked around and there beside his head was some bread baked on hot stones and a jar of water! So he ate and drank and lay down again.

⁷Then the angel of the LORD came again and touched him and said, "Get up and eat some more, or the journey ahead will be too much for you."

⁸So he got up and ate and drank, and the food gave him enough strength to travel forty days and forty nights to Mount Sinai, the mountain of God.

~ 1 Kings 19:1-8

March

God provides pure drinking water

Jericho's water was undrinkable until the prophet Elisha ordered the people to put salt in the pit. The water became pure. God's compassion makes the most basic resources for survival available to humans and animals. He doesn't only supply drinking water, but also living water for all who are thirsty.

¹⁹One day the leaders of the town of Jericho visited Elisha. "We have a problem, my lord," they told him. "This town is located in pleasant surroundings, as you can see. But the water is bad, and the land is unproductive."

²⁰Elisha said, "Bring me a new bowl with salt in it." So they brought it to him. ²¹Then he went out to the spring that supplied the town with water and threw the salt into it. And he said, "This is what the LORD says: I have purified this water. It will no longer cause death or infertility." ²²And the water has remained pure ever since, just as Elisha said.

²³Elisha left Jericho and went up to Bethel. As he was walking along the road, a group of boys from the town began mocking and making fun of him. "Go away, baldy!" they chanted. "Go away, baldy!" ²⁴Elisha turned around and looked at them, and he cursed them in the name of the LORD. Then two bears came out of the woods and mauled forty-two of them. ²⁵From there Elisha went to Mount Carmel and finally returned to Samaria.

~ 2 Kings 2:19-25

Food for the hungry

Elisha's miracle-working power was only used in God's service. He never displayed his special gifts in honor of himself. When people were hungry, Elisha provided food abundantly in God's name. In this way God's name was honored in everyday life and His presence made visible.

³⁸Elisha now returned to Gilgal, and there was a famine in the land. One day as the group of prophets was seated before him, he said to his servant, "Put a large pot on the fire, and make some stew for the rest of the group."

³⁹One of the young men went out into the field to gather herbs and came back with a pocketful of wild gourds. He shredded them and put them into the pot without realizing they were poisonous. ⁴⁰Some of the stew was served to the men. But after they had eaten a bite or two they cried out, "Man of God, there's poison in this stew!" So they would not eat it.

⁴¹Elisha said, "Bring me some flour." Then he threw it into the pot and said, "Now it's all right; go ahead and eat." And then it did not harm them.

⁴²One day a man from Baal-shalishah brought the man of God a sack of fresh grain and twenty loaves of barley bread made from the first grain of his harvest. Elisha said, "Give it to the people so they can eat."

⁴³"What?" his servant exclaimed. "Feed a hundred people with only this?"

But Elisha repeated, "Give it to the people so they can eat, for this is what the Lord says: Everyone will eat, and there will even be some left over!" ⁴⁴And when they gave it to the people, there was plenty for all and some left over, just as the Lord had promised.

~ 2 Kings 4:38-44

God opens the floodgates of heaven

When famine was prevalent in Samaria, most of the people's faith was long gone. Even the king and his officer mocked God. But Elisha knew that God would open the floodgates of heaven at the same time the next day. Nothing is ever too hopeless for God. He will intervene.

[32] Elisha was sitting in his house with the elders of Israel when the king sent a messenger to summon him. But before the messenger arrived, Elisha said to the elders, "A murderer has sent a man to cut off my head. When he arrives, shut the door and keep him out. We will soon hear his master's steps following him."

[33] While Elisha was still saying this, the messenger arrived. And the king said, "All this misery is from the Lord! Why should I wait for the Lord any longer?"

7 [1] Elisha replied, "Listen to this message from the Lord! This is what the Lord says: By this time tomorrow in the markets of Samaria, five quarts of choice flour will cost only one piece of silver, and ten quarts of barley grain will cost only one piece of silver."

[2] The officer assisting the king said to the man of God, "That couldn't happen even if the Lord opened the windows of heaven!"

But Elisha replied, "You will see it happen with your own eyes, but you won't be able to eat any of it!"

~ 2 Kings 6:32-7:2

Enough is enough!

God had enough of the ten tribes of Israel's sins. The Assyrians destroyed them all in 722 BC and took over their country. God does not allow His name to be mocked. Yet, He is also merciful – as we can see from His journey with Benjamin and Judah.

18Because the LORD was very angry with Israel, he swept them away from his presence. Only the tribe of Judah remained in the land. 19But even the people of Judah refused to obey the commands of the LORD their God, for they followed the evil practices that Israel had introduced. 20The LORD rejected all the descendants of Israel. He punished them by handing them over to their attackers until he had banished Israel from his presence.

21For when the LORD tore Israel away from the kingdom of David, they chose Jeroboam son of Nebat as their king. But Jeroboam drew Israel away from following the LORD and made them commit a great sin. 22And the people of Israel persisted in all the evil ways of Jeroboam. They did not turn from these sins 23until the LORD finally swept them away from his presence, just as all his prophets had warned. So Israel was exiled from their land to Assyria, where they remain to this day.

24The king of Assyria transported groups of people from Babylon, Cuthah, Avva, Hamath, and Sepharvaim and resettled them in the towns of Samaria, replacing the people of Israel. They took possession of Samaria and lived in its towns. 25But since these foreign settlers did not worship the LORD when they first arrived, the LORD sent lions among them, which killed some of them.

~ 2 Kings 17:18-25

Death delayed

When King Hezekiah heard that he was going to die soon, he refused to accept it. Immediately he pleaded with God for mercy. And fifteen years were suddenly added to his life. Now that's mercy!

¹Hezekiah became deathly ill, and the prophet Isaiah son of Amoz went to visit him. He gave the king this message: "This is what the LORD says: Set your affairs in order, for you are going to die. You will not recover from this illness." ²When Hezekiah heard this, he turned his face to the wall and prayed to the LORD, ³"Remember, O LORD, how I have always been faithful to you and have served you single-mindedly, always doing what pleases you." Then he broke down and wept bitterly.

⁴But before Isaiah had left the middle courtyard, this message came to him from the LORD: ⁵"Go back to Hezekiah, the leader of my people. Tell him, 'This is what the LORD, the God of your ancestor David, says: I have heard your prayer and seen your tears. I will heal you, and three days from now you will get out of bed and go to the Temple of the LORD. ⁶I will add fifteen years to your life, and I will rescue you and this city from the king of Assyria. I will defend this city for my own honor and for the sake of my servant David.'" ⁷Then Isaiah said, "Make an ointment from figs." So Hezekiah's servants spread the ointment over the boil, and Hezekiah recovered! ⁸Meanwhile, Hezekiah had said to Isaiah, "What sign will the LORD give to prove that he will heal me and that I will go to the Temple of the LORD three days from now?" ⁹Isaiah replied, "This is the sign from the LORD to prove that he will do as he promised. Would you like the shadow on the sundial to go forward ten steps or backward ten steps?" ¹⁰"The shadow always moves forward," Hezekiah replied, "so that would be easy. Make it go ten steps backward instead." ¹¹So Isaiah the prophet asked the LORD to do this.

~ 2 Kings 20:1-11

Celebrate!

Josiah was no doubt one of the greatest religious reformers in the history of Judah. He ended idolatry and instituted Passover again when the Book of the Covenant was rediscovered. Reformers always bring people back to a living relationship with God.

²¹King Josiah then issued this order to all the people: "You must celebrate the Passover to the Lord your God, as required in this Book of the Covenant." ²²There had not been a Passover celebration like that since the time when the judges ruled in Israel, nor throughout all the years of the kings of Israel and Judah. ²³This Passover was celebrated to the Lord in Jerusalem in the eighteenth year of King Josiah's reign.

²⁴Josiah also got rid of the mediums and psychics, the household gods, the idols, and every other kind of detestable practice, both in Jerusalem and throughout the land of Judah. He did this in obedience to the laws written in the scroll that Hilkiah the priest had found in the Lord's Temple. ²⁵Never before had there been a king like Josiah, who turned to the Lord with all his heart and soul and strength, obeying all the laws of Moses. And there has never been a king like him since.

²⁶Even so, the Lord was very angry with Judah because of all the wicked things Manasseh had done to provoke him. ²⁷For the Lord said, "I will also banish Judah from my presence just as I have banished Israel. And I will reject my chosen city of Jerusalem and the Temple where my name was to be honored."

~ 2 Kings 23:21-27

The shepherd of the flock

The writer(s) of Chronicles tells how the Israelites appointed David as their earthly shepherd. His shepherding days flowed over into taking care of God's people as their king. What a responsibility to lead others in God's name! But in the end, God is the true Shepherd.

¹Then all Israel gathered before David at Hebron and told him, "We are your own flesh and blood. ²In the past, even when Saul was king, you were the one who really led the forces of Israel. And the LORD your God told you, 'You will be the shepherd of my people Israel. You will be the leader of my people Israel.'"

³So there at Hebron, David made a covenant before the LORD with all the elders of Israel. And they anointed him king of Israel, just as the LORD had promised through Samuel.

⁴Then David and all Israel went to Jerusalem (or Jebus, as it used to be called), where the Jebusites, the original inhabitants of the land, were living. ⁵The people of Jebus taunted David, saying, "You'll never get in here!" But David captured the fortress of Zion, which is now called the City of David.

⁶David had said to his troops, "Whoever is first to attack the Jebusites will become the commander of my armies!" And Joab, the son of David's sister Zeruiah, was first to attack, so he became the commander of David's armies.

⁷David made the fortress his home, and that is why it is called the City of David. ⁸He extended the city from the supporting terraces to the surrounding area, while Joab rebuilt the rest of Jerusalem. ⁹And David became more and more powerful, because the LORD of Heaven's Armies was with him.

~ 1 Chronicles 11:1-9

A king praises God

It is wonderful when mighty earthly leaders are humble before God. It is even more wonderful when they write songs of praise to Him, like David did. In the end we are only dust; but despite that we are people who must sing and cheer before God while we are still alive.

[23]Let the whole earth sing to the LORD! Each day proclaim the good news that he saves. [24]Publish his glorious deeds among the nations. Tell everyone about the amazing things he does.

[25]Great is the LORD! He is most worthy of praise! He is to be feared above all gods. [26]The gods of other nations are mere idols, but the LORD made the heavens! [27]Honor and majesty surround him; strength and joy fill his dwelling.

[28]O nations of the world, recognize the LORD, recognize that the LORD is glorious and strong. [29]Give to the LORD the glory he deserves! Bring your offering and come into his presence. Worship the LORD in all his holy splendor. [30]Let all the earth tremble before him. The world stands firm and cannot be shaken.

[31]Let the heavens be glad, and the earth rejoice! Tell all the nations, "The LORD reigns!" [32]Let the sea and everything in it shout his praise! Let the fields and their crops burst out with joy! [33]Let the trees of the forest rustle with praise, for the LORD is coming to judge the earth.

[34]Give thanks to the LORD, for he is good! His faithful love endures forever.

[35]Cry out, "Save us, O God of our salvation! Gather and rescue us from among the nations, so we can thank your holy name and rejoice and praise you."

[36]Praise the LORD, the God of Israel, who lives from everlasting to everlasting!

~ 1 Chronicles 16:23-36

In God's hands

When David arrogantly counted his people to emphasize his own power, God's judgment hit him hard. When he had to choose his punishment, he chose to rather end up in God's hands than in people's. With God there is always mercy.

⁷God was very displeased with the census, and he punished Israel for it. ⁸Then David said to God, "I have sinned greatly by taking this census. Please forgive my guilt for doing this foolish thing."

⁹Then the LORD spoke to Gad, David's seer. This was the message: ¹⁰"Go and say to David, 'This is what the LORD says: I will give you three choices. Choose one of these punishments, and I will inflict it on you.'"

¹¹So Gad came to David and said, "These are the choices the LORD has given you. ¹²You may choose three years of famine, three months of destruction by the sword of your enemies, or three days of severe plague as the angel of the LORD brings devastation throughout the land of Israel. Decide what answer I should give the LORD who sent me."

¹³"I'm in a desperate situation!" David replied to Gad. "But let me fall into the hands of the LORD, for his mercy is very great. Do not let me fall into human hands."

¹⁴So the LORD sent a plague upon Israel, and 70,000 people died as a result. ¹⁵And God sent an angel to destroy Jerusalem. But just as the angel was preparing to destroy it, the LORD relented and said to the death angel, "Stop! That is enough!" At that moment the angel of the LORD was standing by the threshing floor of Araunah the Jebusite.

~ 1 Chronicles 21:7-15

What would you choose?

Solomon had the opportunity of a lifetime when God told him in a dream that he could ask anything he wanted. Solomon asked for wisdom – not for wealth, honor, a long life, or the death of his enemies. God was so impressed that He gave His servant all these other things as well.

⁵But the bronze altar made by Bezalel son of Uri and grandson of Hur was there at Gibeon in front of the Tabernacle of the Lord. So Solomon and the people gathered in front of it to consult the Lord. ⁶There in front of the Tabernacle, Solomon went up to the bronze altar in the Lord's presence and sacrificed 1,000 burnt offerings on it.

⁷That night God appeared to Solomon and said, "What do you want? Ask, and I will give it to you!"

⁸Solomon replied to God, "You showed faithful love to David, my father, and now you have made me king in his place. ⁹O Lord God, please continue to keep your promise to David my father, for you have made me king over a people as numerous as the dust of the earth! ¹⁰Give me the wisdom and knowledge to lead them properly, for who could possibly govern this great people of yours?"

¹¹God said to Solomon, "Because your greatest desire is to help your people, and you did not ask for wealth, riches, fame, or even the death of your enemies or a long life, but rather you asked for wisdom and knowledge to properly govern my people—¹²I will certainly give you the wisdom and knowledge you requested. But I will also give you wealth, riches, and fame such as no other king has had before you or will ever have in the future!"

¹³Then Solomon returned to Jerusalem from the Tabernacle at the place of worship in Gibeon, and he reigned over Israel.

~ 2 Chronicles 1:5-13

God's holiness overcomes

When God visited the temple, His holy fire consumed the building. God's glorious appearance was so awe-inspiring that everyone fell face down and praised God respectfully. God is a consuming fire. He is holy. Nobody can keep standing in His presence.

[1]When Solomon finished praying, fire flashed down from heaven and burned up the burnt offerings and sacrifices, and the glorious presence of the LORD filled the Temple. [2]The priests could not enter the Temple of the LORD because the glorious presence of the LORD filled it. [3]When all the people of Israel saw the fire coming down and the glorious presence of the LORD filling the Temple, they fell face down on the ground and worshiped and praised the LORD, saying,

"He is good! His faithful love endures forever!"

[4]Then the king and all the people offered sacrifices to the LORD. [5]King Solomon offered a sacrifice of 22,000 cattle and 120,000 sheep and goats. And so the king and all the people dedicated the Temple of God. [6]The priests took their assigned positions, and so did the Levites who were singing, "His faithful love endures forever!" They accompanied the singing with music from the instruments King David had made for praising the LORD. Across from the Levites, the priests blew the trumpets, while all Israel stood.

[8]For the next seven days Solomon and all Israel celebrated the Festival of Shelters. A large congregation had gathered from as far away as Lebo-hamath in the north and the Brook of Egypt in the south.

~ 2 Chronicles 7:1-6, 8

Dependent on God

King Asa depended on God throughout his life. Therefore, on the day that a million soldiers attacked his land, in his anxiety, he placed all his hope in God. The Lord mercifully came to his rescue. In dark times God's light is visible.

⁹Once an Ethiopian named Zerah attacked Judah with an army of 1,000,000 men and 300 chariots. They advanced to the town of Mareshah, ¹⁰so Asa deployed his armies for battle in the valley north of Mareshah. ¹¹Then Asa cried out to the LORD his God, "O LORD, no one but you can help the powerless against the mighty! Help us, O LORD our God, for we trust in you alone. It is in your name that we have come against this vast horde. O LORD, you are our God; do not let mere men prevail against you!"

¹²So the LORD defeated the Ethiopians in the presence of Asa and the army of Judah, and the enemy fled. ¹³Asa and his army pursued them as far as Gerar, and so many Ethiopians fell that they were unable to rally. They were destroyed by the LORD and his army, and the army of Judah carried off a vast amount of plunder.

¹⁴While they were at Gerar, they attacked all the towns in that area, and terror from the LORD came upon the people there. As a result, a vast amount of plunder was taken from these towns, too. ¹⁵They also attacked the camps of herdsmen and captured many sheep, goats, and camels before finally returning to Jerusalem.

~ 2 Chronicles 14:9-15

Against the stream

Four hundred against one – this was Micaiah's position when he had to prophesy for King Ahab and Jehoshaphat. Four hundred false prophets predicted victories, but Micaiah did not. True prophets sometimes prophesy against the stream.

[17]"Didn't I tell you?" the king of Israel exclaimed to Jehoshaphat. "He never prophesies anything but trouble for me."

[18]Then Micaiah continued, "Listen to what the LORD says! I saw the LORD sitting on his throne with all the armies of heaven around him, on his right and on his left. [19]And the LORD said, 'Who can entice King Ahab of Israel to go into battle against Ramoth-gilead so he can be killed?'

"There were many suggestions, [20]and finally a spirit approached the LORD and said, 'I can do it!'

"'How will you do this?' the LORD asked.

[21]"And the spirit replied, 'I will go out and inspire all of Ahab's prophets to speak lies.'

"'You will succeed,' said the LORD. 'Go ahead and do it.'

[22]"So you see, the LORD has put a lying spirit in the mouths of your prophets. For the LORD has pronounced your doom."

[23]Then Zedekiah son of Kenaanah walked up to Micaiah and slapped him across the face. "Since when did the Spirit of the LORD leave me to speak to you?" he demanded.

[24]And Micaiah replied, "You will find out soon enough when you are trying to hide in some secret room!"

[25]"Arrest him!" the king of Israel ordered. "Take him back to Amon, the governor of the city, and to my son Joash. [26]Give them this order from the king: 'Put this man in prison, and feed him nothing but bread and water until I return safely from the battle!'"

~ 2 Chronicles 18:17-26

Know your place

Uzziah's biggest sin was probably that he didn't know his place. He became so important in his own eyes that he thought he had the right to do the priests' work himself. Mistake! Kings should be kings, and priests should be priests.

[16]But when he had become powerful, he also became proud, which led to his downfall. He sinned against the LORD his God by entering the sanctuary of the LORD's Temple and personally burning incense on the incense altar. [17]Azariah the high priest went in after him with eighty other priests of the LORD, all brave men. [18]They confronted King Uzziah and said, "It is not for you, Uzziah, to burn incense to the LORD. That is the work of the priests alone, the descendants of Aaron who are set apart for this work. Get out of the sanctuary, for you have sinned. The LORD God will not honor you for this!"

[19]Uzziah, who was holding an incense burner, became furious. But as he was standing there raging at the priests before the incense altar in the LORD's Temple, leprosy suddenly broke out on his forehead. [20]When Azariah the high priest and all the other priests saw the leprosy, they rushed him out. And the king himself was eager to get out because the LORD had struck him. [21]So King Uzziah had leprosy until the day he died. He lived in isolation in a separate house, for he was excluded from the Temple of the LORD. His son Jotham was put in charge of the royal palace, and he governed the people of the land.

[22]The rest of the events of Uzziah's reign, from beginning to end, are recorded by the prophet Isaiah son of Amoz. [23]When Uzziah died, he was buried with his ancestors; his grave was in a nearby burial field belonging to the kings, for the people said, "He had leprosy." And his son Jotham became the next king.

~ 2 Chronicles 26:16-23

Mercy for a godless person

Manasseh reigned for fifty-five years. The largest part of his reign was filled with godlessness. His conversion as a prisoner of war in Babylon changed his mind. Afterwards he openly lived out his remorse by serving the Lord wholeheartedly when he returned to Jerusalem.

[10]The Lord spoke to Manasseh and his people, but they ignored all his warnings. [11]So the Lord sent the commanders of the Assyrian armies, and they took Manasseh prisoner. They put a ring through his nose, bound him in bronze chains, and led him away to Babylon. [12]But while in deep distress, Manasseh sought the Lord his God and sincerely humbled himself before the God of his ancestors. [13]And when he prayed, the Lord listened to him and was moved by his request. So the Lord brought Manasseh back to Jerusalem and to his kingdom. Then Manasseh finally realized that the Lord alone is God!

[14]After this Manasseh rebuilt the outer wall of the City of David, from west of the Gihon Spring in the Kidron Valley to the Fish Gate, and continuing around the hill of Ophel. He built the wall very high. And he stationed his military officers in all of the fortified towns of Judah. [15]Manasseh also removed the foreign gods and the idol from the Lord's Temple. He tore down all the altars he had built on the hill where the Temple stood and all the altars that were in Jerusalem, and he dumped them outside the city. [16]Then he restored the altar of the Lord and sacrificed peace offerings and thanksgiving offerings on it. He also encouraged the people of Judah to worship the Lord, the God of Israel. [17]However, the people still sacrificed at the pagan shrines, though only to the Lord their God.

~ 2 Chronicles 33:10-17

Rebuilding the temple

After the Judean exiles' return from imprisonment in Babylon they immediately started rebuilding the temple in the fifth century BC. Their hardship did not stand in the way of their calling to do God's work.

⁷Then the people hired masons and carpenters and bought cedar logs from the people of Tyre and Sidon, paying them with food, wine, and olive oil. The logs were brought down from the Lebanon mountains and floated along the coast of the Mediterranean Sea to Joppa, for King Cyrus had given permission for this.

⁸The construction of the Temple of God began in midspring, during the second year after they arrived in Jerusalem. The work force was made up of everyone who had returned from exile, including Zerubbabel son of Shealtiel, Jeshua son of Jehozadak and his fellow priests, and all the Levites. The Levites who were twenty years old or older were put in charge of rebuilding the LORD's Temple. ⁹The workers at the Temple of God were supervised by Jeshua with his sons and relatives, and Kadmiel and his sons, all descendants of Hodaviah. They were helped in this task by the Levites of the family of Henadad.

¹⁰When the builders completed the foundation of the LORD's Temple, the priests put on their robes and took their places to blow their trumpets. And the Levites, descendants of Asaph, clashed their cymbals to praise the LORD, just as King David had prescribed. ¹¹With praise and thanks, they sang this song to the LORD: "He is so good! His faithful love for Israel endures forever!" Then all the people gave a great shout, praising the LORD because the foundation of the LORD's Temple had been laid.

~ Ezra 3:7-11

Resistance

The building of God's temple came to a halt. Fortunately King Darius, the new world leader, rescued the Jews. The result was that the temple rose again! God's people once again had a symbolic earthly sanctuary where they could serve Him.

[7]Do not disturb the construction of the Temple of God. Let it be rebuilt on its original site, and do not hinder the governor of Judah and the elders of the Jews in their work.

[12]May the God who has chosen the city of Jerusalem as the place to honor his name destroy any king or nation that violates this command and destroys this Temple.

"I, Darius, have issued this decree. Let it be obeyed with all diligence."

[13]Tattenai, governor of the province west of the Euphrates River, and Shethar-bozenai and their colleagues complied at once with the command of King Darius. [14]So the Jewish elders continued their work, and they were greatly encouraged by the preaching of the prophets Haggai and Zechariah son of Iddo. The Temple was finally finished, as had been commanded by the God of Israel and decreed by Cyrus, Darius, and Artaxerxes, the kings of Persia. [15]The Temple was completed on March 12, during the sixth year of King Darius's reign.

[16]The Temple of God was then dedicated with great joy by the people of Israel, the priests, the Levites, and the rest of the people who had returned from exile. [17]During the dedication ceremony for the Temple of God, 100 young bulls, 200 rams, and 400 male lambs were sacrificed. And 12 male goats were presented as a sin offering for the twelve tribes of Israel. [18]Then the priests and Levites were divided into their various divisions to serve at the Temple of God in Jerusalem, as prescribed in the Book of Moses.

~ Ezra 6:7, 12-18

Onward to God

Ezra the scribe and the people returned to Jerusalem to teach God's will to the Israelites living there. Without the necessary knowledge of God and His Word, people go to rack and ruin. Without the right teachers God's people stay in the dark.

[15]I assembled the exiles at the Ahava Canal, and we camped there for three days while I went over the lists of the people and the priests who had arrived. I found that not one Levite had volunteered to come along. [16]So I sent for Eliezer, Ariel, Shemaiah, Elnathan, Jarib, Elnathan, Nathan, Zechariah, and Meshullam, who were leaders of the people. I also sent for Joiarib and Elnathan, who were men of discernment. [17]I sent them to Iddo, the leader of the Levites at Casiphia, to ask him and his relatives and the Temple servants to send us ministers for the Temple of God at Jerusalem.

[18]Since the gracious hand of our God was on us, they sent us a man named Sherebiah, along with eighteen of his sons and brothers. He was a very astute man and a descendant of Mahli, who was a descendant of Levi son of Israel. [19]They also sent Hashabiah, together with Jeshaiah from the descendants of Merari, and twenty of his sons and brothers, [20]and 220 Temple servants. The Temple servants were assistants to the Levites—a group of Temple workers first instituted by King David and his officials. They were all listed by name.

[21]And there by the Ahava Canal, I gave orders for all of us to fast and humble ourselves before our God. We prayed that he would give us a safe journey and protect us, our children, and our goods as we traveled.

~ Ezra 8:15-21

Expat with a heart

Nehemiah was an emigrant in Persia. He was the king's cupbearer and advisor. When he heard that his people lived shamefully in Jerusalem, it broke his heart. He reported for duty then and there.

¹In late autumn, in the month of Kislev, in the twentieth year of King Artaxerxes' reign, I was at the fortress of Susa. ²Hanani, one of my brothers, came to visit me with some other men who had just arrived from Judah. I asked them about the Jews who had returned there from captivity and about how things were going in Jerusalem. ³They said to me, "Things are not going well for those who returned to the province of Judah. They are in great trouble and disgrace. The wall of Jerusalem has been torn down, and the gates have been destroyed by fire."

⁴When I heard this, I sat down and wept. In fact, for days I mourned, fasted, and prayed to the God of heaven. ⁵Then I said, "O LORD, God of heaven, the great and awesome God who keeps his covenant of unfailing love with those who love him and obey his commands, ⁶listen to my prayer! Look down and see me praying night and day for your people Israel. I confess that we have sinned against you. Yes, even my own family and I have sinned!

⁸"Please remember what you told your servant Moses: 'If you are unfaithful to me, I will scatter you among the nations. ⁹But if you return to me and obey my commands and live by them, then even if you are exiled to the ends of the earth, I will bring you back to the place I have chosen for my name to be honored.' ¹⁰"The people you rescued by your great power and strong hand are your servants. ¹¹O Lord, please hear my prayer! Listen to the prayers of those of us who delight in honoring you. Please grant me success today by making the king favorable to me. Put it into his heart to be kind to me."

~ Nehemiah 1:1-6, 8-11

Keep it in your heart

You don't always have to bear your heart. Nehemiah did not announce all his plans when he returned to Jerusalem. He first looked things through carefully. When he was sure that he acted according to God's will, he shared his vision with the people.

11So I arrived in Jerusalem. Three days later, 12I slipped out during the night, taking only a few others with me. I had not told anyone about the plans God had put in my heart for Jerusalem. We took no pack animals with us except the donkey I was riding. 13After dark I went out through the Valley Gate, past the Jackal's Well, and over to the Dung Gate to inspect the broken walls and burned gates. 14Then I went to the Fountain Gate and to the King's Pool, but my donkey couldn't get through the rubble. 15So, though it was still dark, I went up the Kidron Valley instead, inspecting the wall before I turned back and entered again at the Valley Gate.

16The city officials did not know I had been out there or what I was doing, for I had not yet said anything to anyone about my plans. I had not yet spoken to the Jewish leaders—the priests, the nobles, the officials, or anyone else in the administration. 17But now I said to them, "You know very well what trouble we are in. Jerusalem lies in ruins, and its gates have been destroyed by fire. Let us rebuild the wall of Jerusalem and end this disgrace!" 18Then I told them about how the gracious hand of God had been on me, and about my conversation with the king.

They replied at once, "Yes, let's rebuild the wall!" So they began the good work.

~ Nehemiah 2:11-18

Resistance does not mean God is absent

Hardship is not a sign that God has abandoned you. Ask Nehemiah. He and his people were within God's will. Therefore his opponent was furious and resisted their work. It is an art to hold on to your vision and calling in such times.

¹Sanballat was very angry when he learned that we were rebuilding the wall. He flew into a rage and mocked the Jews, ²saying in front of his friends and the Samarian army officers, "What does this bunch of poor, feeble Jews think they're doing? Do they think they can build the wall in a single day by just offering a few sacrifices? Do they actually think they can make something of stones from a rubbish heap—and charred ones at that?"

³Tobiah the Ammonite, who was standing beside him, remarked, "That stone wall would collapse if even a fox walked along the top of it!"

⁴Then I prayed, "Hear us, our God, for we are being mocked. May their scoffing fall back on their own heads, and may they themselves become captives in a foreign land! ⁵Do not ignore their guilt. Do not blot out their sins, for they have provoked you to anger here in front of the builders."

⁶At last the wall was completed to half its height around the entire city, for the people had worked with enthusiasm.

⁷But when Sanballat and Tobiah and the Arabs, Ammonites, and Ashdodites heard that the work was going ahead and that the gaps in the wall of Jerusalem were being repaired, they were furious. ⁸They all made plans to come and fight against Jerusalem and throw us into confusion. ⁹But we prayed to our God and guarded the city day and night to protect ourselves.

~ Nehemiah 4:1-9

Walk upright for God's Word

Nehemiah's wall building had far-reaching results. It made God's people walk proud and upright again. God's Law also echoed loudly in their midst. This happens when spiritual leaders with vision do what God placed in their hearts.

¹In October, when the Israelites had settled in their towns, ⁸ː¹all the people assembled with a unified purpose at the square just inside the Water Gate. They asked Ezra the scribe to bring out the Book of the Law of Moses, which the LORD had given for Israel to obey.

²So on October 8 Ezra the priest brought the Book of the Law before the assembly, which included the men and women and all the children old enough to understand. ³He faced the square just inside the Water Gate from early morning until noon and read aloud to everyone who could understand. All the people listened closely to the Book of the Law. ⁴Ezra the scribe stood on a high wooden platform that had been made for the occasion. To his right stood Mattithiah, Shema, Anaiah, Uriah, Hilkiah, and Maaseiah. To his left stood Pedaiah, Mishael, Malkijah, Hashum, Hashbaddanah, Zechariah, and Meshullam. ⁵Ezra stood on the platform in full view of all the people. When they saw him open the book, they all rose to their feet.

⁶Then Ezra praised the LORD, the great God, and all the people chanted, "Amen! Amen!" as they lifted their hands. Then they bowed down and worshiped the LORD with their faces to the ground. ⁷The Levites—Jeshua, Bani, Sherebiah, Jamin, Akkub, Shabbethai, Hodiah, Maaseiah, Kelita, Azariah, Jozabad, Hanan, and Pelaiah—then instructed the people in the Law while everyone remained in their places. ⁸They read from the Book of the Law of God and clearly explained the meaning of what was being read, helping the people understand each passage.

~ Nehemiah 8:1-8

Commitment is concrete

Nehemiah's reforms were far more than skin-deep. It resulted in God's people placing not only their transgressions at His feet, but also forming concrete commitments with God. Their lives changed completely. Their faith touched ground again.

²⁸Then the rest of the people—the priests, Levites, gatekeepers, singers, Temple servants, and all who had separated themselves from the pagan people of the land in order to obey the Law of God, together with their wives, sons, daughters, and all who were old enough to understand—²⁹joined their leaders and bound themselves with an oath. They swore a curse on themselves if they failed to obey the Law of God as issued by his servant Moses. They solemnly promised to carefully follow all the commands, regulations, and decrees of the LORD our Lord:

³⁰"We promise not to let our daughters marry the pagan people of the land, and not to let our sons marry their daughters.

³¹"We also promise that if the people of the land should bring any merchandise or grain to be sold on the Sabbath or on any other holy day, we will refuse to buy it. Every seventh year we will let our land rest, and we will cancel all debts owed to us.

³²"In addition, we promise to obey the command to pay the annual Temple tax of one-eighth of an ounce of silver for the care of the Temple of our God. ³³This will provide for the Bread of the Presence; for the regular grain offerings and burnt offerings; for the offerings on the Sabbaths, the new moon celebrations, and the annual festivals; for the holy offerings; and for the sin offerings to make atonement for Israel. It will provide for everything necessary for the work of the Temple of our God.

~ Nehemiah 10:28-33

God works between the lines

The book of Esther takes place in the Persian Empire when Ahasuerus, or Xerxes as he was known, was the king (486-465 BC). Although this book never refers directly to God, it tells how God intervenes in human circumstances all the time. He also works between the lines.

¹These events happened in the days of King Xerxes, who reigned over 127 provinces stretching from India to Ethiopia. ²At that time Xerxes ruled his empire from his royal throne at the fortress of Susa. ³In the third year of his reign, he gave a banquet for all his nobles and officials. He invited all the military officers of Persia and Media as well as the princes and nobles of the provinces. ⁴The celebration lasted 180 days—a tremendous display of the opulent wealth of his empire and the pomp and splendor of his majesty.

⁵When it was all over, the king gave a banquet for all the people, from the greatest to the least, who were in the fortress of Susa. It lasted for seven days and was held in the courtyard of the palace garden. ⁶The courtyard was beautifully decorated with white cotton curtains and blue hangings, which were fastened with white linen cords and purple ribbons to silver rings embedded in marble pillars. Gold and silver couches stood on a mosaic pavement of porphyry, marble, mother-of-pearl, and other costly stones.

⁷Drinks were served in gold goblets of many designs, and there was an abundance of royal wine, reflecting the king's generosity. ⁸By edict of the king, no limits were placed on the drinking, for the king had instructed all his palace officials to serve each man as much as he wanted.

~ Esther 1:1-8

The first Miss World in God's service

Esther won the greatest beauty contest of her time ... and also the king's heart! God even uses such talents to make His will triumph. He places such people in key positions from where they can influence others. God doesn't need a lot of people to do His work – only the right ones!

[15]Esther was the daughter of Abihail, who was Mordecai's uncle. (Mordecai had adopted his younger cousin Esther.) When it was Esther's turn to go to the king, she accepted the advice of Hegai, the eunuch in charge of the harem. She asked for nothing except what he suggested, and she was admired by everyone who saw her.

[16]Esther was taken to King Xerxes at the royal palace in early winter of the seventh year of his reign. [17]And the king loved Esther more than any of the other young women. He was so delighted with her that he set the royal crown on her head and declared her queen instead of Vashti. [18]To celebrate the occasion, he gave a great banquet in Esther's honor for all his nobles and officials, declaring a public holiday for the provinces and giving generous gifts to everyone.

[19]Even after all the young women had been transferred to the second harem and Mordecai had become a palace official, [20]Esther continued to keep her family background and nationality a secret. She was still following Mordecai's directions, just as she did when she lived in his home.

~ Esther 2:15-20

Destined for a time like this

One of the key Scripture verses in Esther is chapter 4:14 where Esther's uncle, Mordecai, told her that she perhaps became queen for a time like that. God sends the right people in difficult times to be His bright lights. In times like these they shine like lights in the dark.

¹⁰Then Esther told Hathach to go back and relay this message to Mordecai: ¹¹"All the king's officials and even the people in the provinces know that anyone who appears before the king in his inner court without being invited is doomed to die unless the king holds out his gold scepter. And the king has not called for me to come to him for thirty days." ¹²So Hathach gave Esther's message to Mordecai.

¹³Mordecai sent this reply to Esther: "Don't think for a moment that because you're in the palace you will escape when all other Jews are killed. ¹⁴If you keep quiet at a time like this, deliverance and relief for the Jews will arise from some other place, but you and your relatives will die. Who knows if perhaps you were made queen for just such a time as this?"

¹⁵Then Esther sent this reply to Mordecai: ¹⁶"Go and gather together all the Jews of Susa and fast for me. Do not eat or drink for three days, night or day. My maids and I will do the same. And then, though it is against the law, I will go in to see the king. If I must die, I must die." ¹⁷So Mordecai went away and did everything as Esther had ordered him.

~ Esther 4:10-17

What goes around comes around

Haman's plans to kill the Jews boomeranged. To celebrate this victory, the Jews started Purim. Esther's uncle, Mordecai, even became second in command of Persia. What a godly intervention in a desperate situation.

²³So the Jews accepted Mordecai's proposal and adopted this annual custom. ²⁴Haman son of Hammedatha the Agagite, the enemy of the Jews, had plotted to crush and destroy them on the date determined by casting lots (the lots were called *purim*). ²⁵But when Esther came before the king, he issued a decree causing Haman's evil plot to backfire, and Haman and his sons were impaled on a sharpened pole. ²⁶That is why this celebration is called Purim, because it is the ancient word for casting lots.

So because of Mordecai's letter and because of what they had experienced, ²⁷the Jews throughout the realm agreed to inaugurate this tradition and to pass it on to their descendants and to all who became Jews. They declared they would never fail to celebrate these two prescribed days at the appointed time each year. ²⁸These days would be remembered and kept from generation to generation and celebrated by every family throughout the provinces and cities of the empire. This Festival of Purim would never cease to be celebrated among the Jews, nor would the memory of what happened ever die out among their descendants.

²⁹Then Queen Esther, the daughter of Abihail, along with Mordecai the Jew, wrote another letter putting the queen's full authority behind Mordecai's letter to establish the Festival of Purim.

~ Esther 9:23-29

On the testing field

Job's piousness did not impress the devil. Therefore he challenged God to take everything away from Job. But when Job lost all his possessions and his children, his hand still remained shakily in God's. He knew that hardship was not a ruler to measure God's distance from you.

¹One day the members of the heavenly court came again to present themselves before the LORD, and the Accuser, Satan, came with them. ²"Where have you come from?" the LORD asked Satan.

Satan answered the LORD, "I have been patrolling the earth, watching everything that's going on."

³Then the LORD asked Satan, "Have you noticed my servant Job? He is the finest man in all the earth. He is blameless—a man of complete integrity. He fears God and stays away from evil. And he has maintained his integrity, even though you urged me to harm him without cause."

⁴Satan replied to the LORD, "Skin for skin! A man will give up everything he has to save his life. ⁵But reach out and take away his health, and he will surely curse you to your face!"

⁶"All right, do with him as you please," the LORD said to Satan. "But spare his life." ⁷So Satan left the LORD's presence, and he struck Job with terrible boils from head to foot.

⁸Job scraped his skin with a piece of broken pottery as he sat among the ashes. ⁹His wife said to him, "Are you still trying to maintain your integrity? Curse God and die."

¹⁰But Job replied, "You talk like a foolish woman. Should we accept only good things from the hand of God and never anything bad?" So in all this, Job said nothing wrong.

~ Job 2:1-10

Arm Wrestling with God

Piousness doesn't mean just accepting everything blindly. Therefore, Job dared to differ from God and his friends' explanation for the reasons of his suffering. Job knew that God didn't punish His children by sending hardship their way.

¹Then Job spoke again:

²"If my misery could be weighed and my troubles be put on the scales, ³they would outweigh all the sands of the sea. That is why I spoke impulsively.

⁴For the Almighty has struck me down with his arrows. Their poison infects my spirit. God's terrors are lined up against me.

⁵Don't I have a right to complain? Don't wild donkeys bray when they find no grass, and oxen bellow when they have no food?

⁶Don't people complain about unsalted food? Does anyone want the tasteless white of an egg?

⁷My appetite disappears when I look at it; I gag at the thought of eating it!

⁸"Oh, that I might have my request, that God would grant my desire.

⁹I wish he would crush me. I wish he would reach out his hand and kill me.

¹⁰At least I can take comfort in this: Despite the pain,
I have not denied the words of the Holy One.

¹¹But I don't have the strength to endure. I have nothing to live for.

¹²Do I have the strength of a stone? Is my body made of bronze?

¹³No, I am utterly helpless, without any chance of success.

~ Job 6:1-13

Beware of false declarers

Job's friends, Eliphaz, Bildad and Zophar, had many different explanations for Job's hardship. Bildad said that Job's children sinned against God and died (see Job 8:4). Job refused to accept it and still called on God. He kept on taking his doubts to God. That was his secret.

¹Then Job spoke again: ²"You people really know everything, don't you? And when you die, wisdom will die with you! ³Well, I know a few things myself—and you're no better than I am. Who doesn't know these things you've been saying? ⁴Yet my friends laugh at me, for I call on God and expect an answer. I am a just and blameless man, yet they laugh at me. ⁵People who are at ease mock those in trouble. They give a push to people who are stumbling. ⁶But robbers are left in peace, and those who provoke God live in safety—though God keeps them in his power.

⁷"Just ask the animals, and they will teach you. Ask the birds of the sky, and they will tell you. ⁸Speak to the earth, and it will instruct you. Let the fish in the sea speak to you. ⁹For they all know that my disaster has come from the hand of the LORD. ¹⁰For the life of every living thing is in his hand, and the breath of every human being. ¹¹The ear tests the words it hears just as the mouth distinguishes between foods. ¹²Wisdom belongs to the aged, and understanding to the old. ¹³"But true wisdom and power are found in God; counsel and understanding are his. ¹⁴What he destroys cannot be rebuilt. When he puts someone in prison, there is no escape. ¹⁵If he holds back the rain, the earth becomes a desert. If he releases the waters, they flood the earth. ¹⁶Yes, strength and wisdom are his; deceivers and deceived are both in his power.

~ Job 12:1-16

God is inexplicably present

Even when Job could not understand anything about God's behavior, he still called on God. It was as if Job asked God to manage his situation. Despite all Job's hurt, God remained his Redeemer. Job knew he would see God!

¹³They savored it, holding it long in their mouths. ¹⁴But suddenly the food in their bellies turns sour, a poisonous venom in their stomach. ¹⁵They will vomit the wealth they swallowed. God won't let them keep it down. ¹⁶They will suck the poison of cobras. The viper will kill them. ¹⁷They will never again enjoy streams of olive oil or rivers of milk and honey. ¹⁸They will give back everything they worked for. Their wealth will bring them no joy. ¹⁹For they oppressed the poor and left them destitute. They foreclosed on their homes. ²⁰They were always greedy and never satisfied. Nothing remains of all the things they dreamed about.

²¹Nothing is left after they finish gorging themselves. Therefore, their prosperity will not endure. ²²"In the midst of plenty, they will run into trouble and be overcome by misery.

²³May God give them a bellyful of trouble. May God rain down his anger upon them. ²⁴When they try to escape an iron weapon, a bronze-tipped arrow will pierce them. ²⁵The arrow is pulled from their back, and the arrowhead glistens with blood. The terrors of death are upon them. ²⁶Their treasures will be thrown into deepest darkness. A wildfire will devour their goods, consuming all they have left. ²⁷The heavens will reveal their guilt, and the earth will testify against them.

²⁸A flood will sweep away their house. God's anger will descend on them in torrents. ²⁹This is the reward that God gives the wicked. It is the inheritance decreed by God."

~ Job 20:13-29

APRIL

Journey through Creation

When God eventually answered Job, He didn't give any rational answers or explanations for Job's suffering. On the contrary, God took His servant on a journey through Creation. He showed Job His omnipotence and His love for Creation. All of a sudden Job's questions stopped.

¹"Do you know when the wild goats give birth? Have you watched as deer are born in the wild?

²Do you know how many months they carry their young? Are you aware of the time of their delivery?

³They crouch down to give birth to their young and deliver their offspring.

²²It laughs at fear and is unafraid. It does not run from the sword.

²³The arrows rattle against it, and the spear and javelin flash.

²⁴It paws the ground fiercely and rushes forward into battle when the ram's horn blows.

²⁵It snorts at the sound of the horn. It senses the battle in the distance. It quivers at the captain's commands and the noise of battle.

²⁶"Is it your wisdom that makes the hawk soar and spread its wings toward the south?

²⁷Is it at your command that the eagle rises to the heights to make its nest?

²⁸It lives on the cliffs, making its home on a distant, rocky crag.

²⁹From there it hunts its prey, keeping watch with piercing eyes.

³⁰Its young gulp down blood. Where there's a carcass, there you'll find it."

~ Job 39:1-3, 22-30

God is the answer

That well-known saying, "You will understand some-day," does not count in Job's situation. Job did not get explanations for his suffering from God, but he met God in new ways. God does not owe us expla-nations for our hardship. But He lets every sincere seeker find Him.

¹Then Job replied to the LORD:

²"I know that you can do anything, and no one can stop you.

³You asked, 'Who is this that questions my wisdom with such ignorance?' It is I—and I was talking about things I knew nothing about, things far too wonderful for me.

⁴You said, 'Listen and I will speak! I have some questions for you, and you must answer them.'

⁵I had only heard about you before, but now I have seen you with my own eyes.

⁶I take back everything I said, and I sit in dust and ashes to show my repentance."

⁷After the LORD had finished speaking to Job, he said to El-iphaz the Temanite: "I am angry with you and your two friends, for you have not spoken accurately about me, as my servant Job has. ⁸So take seven bulls and seven rams and go to my servant Job and offer a burnt offering for yourselves. My ser-vant Job will pray for you, and I will accept his prayer on your behalf. I will not treat you as you deserve, for you have not spo-ken accurately about me, as my servant Job has." ⁹So Eliphaz the Temanite, Bildad the Shuhite, and Zophar the Naamathite did as the LORD commanded them, and the LORD accepted Job's prayer.

¹⁰When Job prayed for his friends, the LORD restored his for-tunes. In fact, the LORD gave him twice as much as before!

~ Job 42:1-10

It goes well

God's definition of "it goes well" is totally different than ours. According to Him it goes well with us if we don't spend all our time in godless people's presence, but rather find our joy in His Word. Then the floodgates of heavenly blessing open up above our heads.

¹Oh, the joys of those who do not follow the advice of the wicked, or stand around with sinners, or join in with mockers.

²But they delight in the law of the LORD, meditating on it day and night.

³They are like trees planted along the riverbank, bearing fruit each season. Their leaves never wither, and they prosper in all they do.

⁴But not the wicked! They are like worthless chaff, scattered by the wind.

⁵They will be condemned at the time of judgment. Sinners will have no place among the godly.

⁶For the LORD watches over the path of the godly, but the path of the wicked leads to destruction.

~ Psalm 1

I love You

We often speak about obeying God. But we seldom say out loud to God that we love Him. We should learn from David. He was not ashamed to profess his love for God out loud, and that he trusted God in times of danger.

For the choir director: A psalm of David, the servant of the LORD. He sang this song to the LORD on the day the LORD rescued him from all his enemies and from Saul. He sang:

¹I love you, LORD; you are my strength. ²The LORD is my rock, my fortress, and my savior; my God is my rock, in whom I find protection. He is my shield, the power that saves me, and my place of safety. ³I called on the LORD, who is worthy of praise, and he saved me from my enemies. ⁴The ropes of death entangled me; floods of destruction swept over me.

⁵The grave wrapped its ropes around me; death laid a trap in my path. ⁶But in my distress I cried out to the LORD; yes, I prayed to my God for help. He heard me from his sanctuary; my cry to him reached his ears. ⁷Then the earth quaked and trembled. The foundations of the mountains shook; they quaked because of his anger.

¹⁸They attacked me at a moment when I was in distress, but the LORD supported me. ¹⁹He led me to a place of safety; he rescued me because he delights in me. ²⁰The LORD rewarded me for doing right; he restored me because of my innocence. ²¹For I have kept the ways of the LORD; I have not turned from my God to follow evil. ²²I have followed all his regulations; I have never abandoned his decrees. ²³I am blameless before God; I have kept myself from sin. ²⁴The LORD rewarded me for doing right. He has seen my innocence. ²⁵To the faithful you show yourself faithful; to those with integrity you show integrity.

~ Psalm 18:1-7, 18-25

I have all that I need

Everyone knows Psalm 23. The second part of verse 1 which says, "I have all that I need," is not that well known – meaning only a few of us live it out. Perhaps this happens because we don't fully understand the fact that we are completely dependent on our Shepherd's care.

¹The LORD is my shepherd; I have all that I need.

²He lets me rest in green meadows; he leads me beside peaceful streams.

³He renews my strength. He guides me along right paths, bringing honor to his name.

⁴Even when I walk through the darkest valley, I will not be afraid, for you are close beside me. Your rod and your staff protect and comfort me.

⁵You prepare a feast for me in the presence of my enemies. You honor me by anointing my head with oil. My cup overflows with blessings.

⁶Surely your goodness and unfailing love will pursue me all the days of my life, and I will live in the house of the LORD forever.

~ Psalm 23

Life is short

Life is short. It passes quickly. The psalmist knew this all too well. Therefore his prayer that life should be spent in God's presence. God was his only hope during his time on earth. From God alone he expected help and salvation from his enemies.

¹I said to myself, "I will watch what I do and not sin in what I say. I will hold my tongue when the ungodly are around me."

²But as I stood there in silence—not even speaking of good things—the turmoil within me grew worse.

³The more I thought about it, the hotter I got, igniting a fire of words:

⁴"LORD, remind me how brief my time on earth will be. Remind me that my days are numbered—how fleeting my life is.

⁵You have made my life no longer than the width of my hand. My entire lifetime is just a moment to you; at best, each of us is but a breath."

⁶We are merely moving shadows, and all our busy rushing ends in nothing. We heap up wealth, not knowing who will spend it.

⁷And so, Lord, where do I put my hope? My only hope is in you.

⁸Rescue me from my rebellion. Do not let fools mock me.

⁹I am silent before you; I won't say a word, for my punishment is from you.

¹⁰But please stop striking me! I am exhausted by the blows from your hand.

~ Psalm 39:1-10

Take it away

After David's sin with Bathsheba, he went public with it. In Psalm 51 he shared it honestly with God. He pleaded that God would start over with him, and give him another chance.

³For I recognize my rebellion; it haunts me day and night. ⁴Against you, and you alone, have I sinned; I have done what is evil in your sight. You will be proved right in what you say, and your judgment against me is just.

⁵For I was born a sinner—yes, from the moment my mother conceived me. ⁶But you desire honesty from the womb, teaching me wisdom even there. ⁷Purify me from my sins, and I will be clean; wash me, and I will be whiter than snow. ⁸Oh, give me back my joy again; you have broken me—now let me rejoice.

⁹Don't keep looking at my sins. Remove the stain of my guilt. ¹⁰Create in me a clean heart, O God. Renew a loyal spirit within me. ¹¹Do not banish me from your presence, and don't take your Holy Spirit from me. ¹²Restore to me the joy of your salvation, and make me willing to obey you. ¹³Then I will teach your ways to rebels, and they will return to you. ¹⁴Forgive me for shedding blood, O God who saves; then I will joyfully sing of your forgiveness. ¹⁵Unseal my lips, O Lord, that my mouth may praise you. ¹⁶You do not desire a sacrifice, or I would offer one. You do not want a burnt offering. ¹⁷The sacrifice you desire is a broken spirit. You will not reject a broken and repentant heart, O God.

¹⁸Look with favor on Zion and help her; rebuild the walls of Jerusalem. ¹⁹Then you will be pleased with sacrifices offered in the right spirit—with burnt offerings and whole burnt offerings. Then bulls will again be sacrificed on your altar.

~ Psalm 51:3-19

To thirst for God

That deeper thirst for God never goes away. The longer you walk in His way, the more you yearn for His presence. This deep yearning lets not only your heart, but also your entire being, call out to God. Are you aware of it?

A psalm of David, regarding a time when David was in the wilderness of Judah.

¹O God, you are my God; I earnestly search for you. My soul thirsts for you; my whole body longs for you in this parched and weary land where there is no water.

²I have seen you in your sanctuary and gazed upon your power and glory.

³Your unfailing love is better than life itself; how I praise you!

⁴I will praise you as long as I live, lifting up my hands to you in prayer.

⁵You satisfy me more than the richest feast. I will praise you with songs of joy.

⁶I lie awake thinking of you, meditating on you through the night.

⁷Because you are my helper, I sing for joy in the shadow of your wings.

⁸I cling to you; your strong right hand holds me securely.

⁹But those plotting to destroy me will come to ruin. They will go down into the depths of the earth.

¹⁰They will die by the sword and become the food of jackals.

¹¹But the king will rejoice in God. All who trust in him will praise him, while liars will be silenced.

~ Psalm 63

Faith against the stream

To have faith against the stream is not easy. Asaph wondered about God. But he discovered God's goodness in His sanctuary. God never abandons His children – especially not in times of crises.

[1]Truly God is good to Israel, to those whose hearts are pure. [2]But as for me, I almost lost my footing. My feet were slipping, and I was almost gone. [3]For I envied the proud when I saw them prosper despite their wickedness. [4]They seem to live such painless lives; their bodies are so healthy and strong. [5]They don't have troubles like other people; they're not plagued with problems like everyone else. [6]They wear pride like a jeweled necklace and clothe themselves with cruelty. [7]These fat cats have everything their hearts could ever wish for! [8]They scoff and speak only evil; in their pride they seek to crush others. [9]They boast against the very heavens, and their words strut throughout the earth. [10]And so the people are dismayed and confused, drinking in all their words. [11]"What does God know?" they ask. "Does the Most High even know what's happening?" [12]Look at these wicked people—enjoying a life of ease while their riches multiply.

[21]Then I realized that my heart was bitter, and I was all torn up inside. [22]I was so foolish and ignorant—I must have seemed like a senseless animal to you. [23]Yet I still belong to you; you hold my right hand. [24]You guide me with your counsel, leading me to a glorious destiny. [25]Whom have I in heaven but you? I desire you more than anything on earth. [26]My health may fail, and my spirit may grow weak, but God remains the strength of my heart; he is mine forever. [27]Those who desert him will perish, for you destroy those who abandon you. [28]But as for me, how good it is to be near God! I have made the Sovereign LORD my shelter, and I will tell everyone about the wonderful things you do.

~ Psalm 73:1-12, 21-28

The Almighty protects

God is a shelter for His children. He does not guarantee a problem-free life, but He does guarantee His presence in the midst of the storm. He is on duty during the worst crisis. We are never alone. When the storms rage we can run to Him.

¹Those who live in the shelter of the Most High will find rest in the shadow of the Almighty. ²This I declare about the LORD: He alone is my refuge, my place of safety; he is my God, and I trust him. ³For he will rescue you from every trap and protect you from deadly disease. ⁴He will cover you with his feathers. He will shelter you with his wings. His faithful promises are your armor and protection. ⁵Do not be afraid of the terrors of the night, nor the arrow that flies in the day. ⁶Do not dread the disease that stalks in darkness, nor the disaster that strikes at midday. ⁷Though a thousand fall at your side, though ten thousand are dying around you, these evils will not touch you. ⁸Just open your eyes, and see how the wicked are punished.

⁹If you make the LORD your refuge, if you make the Most High your shelter, ¹⁰no evil will conquer you; no plague will come near your home. ¹¹For he will order his angels to protect you wherever you go. ¹²They will hold you up with their hands so you won't even hurt your foot on a stone. ¹³You will trample upon lions and cobras; you will crush fierce lions and serpents under your feet!

¹⁴The LORD says, "I will rescue those who love me. I will protect those who trust in my name. ¹⁵When they call on me, I will answer; I will be with them in trouble. I will rescue and honor them. ¹⁶I will reward them with a long life and give them my salvation."

~ Psalm 91

Sing and praise for life

Praising God must be on our lips for life. Why? Because He is merciful. He cares for us. He removes our transgressions light years away from us. He touches us with His healing hand when we are sick. Therefore we may never forget His good deeds.

¹Let all that I am praise the LORD; with my whole heart, I will praise his holy name. ²Let all that I am praise the LORD; may I never forget the good things he does for me. ³He forgives all my sins and heals all my diseases. ⁴He redeems me from death and crowns me with love and tender mercies. ⁵He fills my life with good things. My youth is renewed like the eagle's! ⁶The LORD gives righteousness and justice to all who are treated unfairly. ⁷He revealed his character to Moses and his deeds to the people of Israel. ⁸The LORD is compassionate and merciful, slow to get angry and filled with unfailing love. ⁹He will not constantly accuse us, nor remain angry forever. ¹⁰He does not punish us for all our sins; he does not deal harshly with us, as we deserve. ¹¹For his unfailing love toward those who fear him is as great as the height of the heavens above the earth. ¹²He has removed our sins as far from us as the east is from the west. ¹³The LORD is like a father to his children, tender and compassionate to those who fear him. ¹⁴For he knows how weak we are; he remembers we are only dust. ¹⁵Our days on earth are like grass; like wildflowers, we bloom and die. ¹⁶The wind blows, and we are gone—as though we had never been here. ¹⁷But the love of the LORD remains forever with those who fear him. His salvation extends to the children's children ¹⁸of those who are faithful to his covenant, of those who obey his commandments!

~ Psalm 103:1-18

God's words taste like honey

God's words are sweet like honey. How do you eat it? By loving and obeying His commands, and by meditating on His Word. In this way the Word will come into your heart and will change your life.

89Your eternal word, O LORD, stands firm in heaven. 90Your faithfulness extends to every generation, as enduring as the earth you created. 91Your regulations remain true to this day, for everything serves your plans. 92If your instructions hadn't sustained me with joy, I would have died in my misery. 93I will never forget your commandments, for by them you give me life.

97Oh, how I love your instructions! I think about them all day long. 98Your commands make me wiser than my enemies, for they are my constant guide. 99Yes, I have more insight than my teachers, for I am always thinking of your laws. 100I am even wiser than my elders, for I have kept your commandments. 101I have refused to walk on any evil path, so that I may remain obedient to your word. 102I haven't turned away from your regulations, for you have taught me well. 103How sweet your words taste to me; they are sweeter than honey. 104Your commandments give me understanding; no wonder I hate every false way of life.

105Your word is a lamp to guide my feet and a light for my path. 106I've promised it once, and I'll promise it again: I will obey your righteous regulations. 107I have suffered much, O LORD; restore my life again as you promised. 108LORD, accept my offering of praise, and teach me your regulations. 109My life constantly hangs in the balance, but I will not stop obeying your instructions. 110The wicked have set their traps for me, but I will not turn from your commandments. 111Your laws are my treasure; they are my heart's delight. 112I am determined to keep your decrees to the very end.

~ Psalm 119:89-93, 97-112

Is everything wasted, or not?

If God is not on the scene, everything is wasted. If He is not the Builder, the builders labor in vain. Unless He guards a city, the guards try and maintain law and order in vain. Therefore, God deserves the place of honor everywhere.

¹Unless the LORD builds a house, the work of the builders is wasted. Unless the LORD protects a city, guarding it with sentries will do no good.

²It is useless for you to work so hard from early morning until late at night, anxiously working for food to eat; for God gives rest to his loved ones.

³Children are a gift from the LORD; they are a reward from him.

⁴Children born to a young man are like arrows in a warrior's hands.

⁵How joyful is the man whose quiver is full of them! He will not be put to shame when he confronts his accusers at the city gates.

~ Psalm 127

A musical symphony

God's praise is colorful. Worshiping Him requires many voices, sounds, and musical instruments. God's colorful grace asks a joyful, symphonic response from our side. Let us praise God enthusiastically, continually, joyfully, and wholeheartedly. Let our lives become a symphony in His honor.

¹Praise the LORD!

Praise God in his sanctuary; praise him in his mighty heaven!

²Praise him for his mighty works; praise his unequaled greatness!

³Praise him with a blast of the ram's horn; praise him with the lyre and harp!

⁴Praise him with the tambourine and dancing; praise him with strings and flutes!

⁵Praise him with a clash of cymbals; praise him with loud clanging cymbals.

⁶Let everything that breathes sing praises to the LORD!

Praise the LORD!

~ Psalm 150

Wisdom has a starting point

The wisdom in Proverbs is not just a few detached verses or nice sayings. It is the result of the wisdom tradition started in the time of David and Solomon to teach young people the right principles.

¹These are the proverbs of Solomon, David's son, king of Israel.

²Their purpose is to teach people wisdom and discipline, to help them understand the insights of the wise. ³Their purpose is to teach people to live disciplined and successful lives, to help them do what is right, just, and fair. ⁴These proverbs will give insight to the simple, knowledge and discernment to the young. ⁵Let the wise listen to these proverbs and become even wiser. Let those with understanding receive guidance ⁶by exploring the meaning in these proverbs and parables, the words of the wise and their riddles.

⁷Fear of the LORD is the foundation of true knowledge, but fools despise wisdom and discipline.

²⁰Wisdom shouts in the streets. She cries out in the public square. ²¹She calls to the crowds along the main street, to those gathered in front of the city gate: ²²"How long, you simpletons, will you insist on being simpleminded? How long will you mockers relish your mocking? How long will you fools hate knowledge?

²³Come and listen to my counsel. I'll share my heart with you and make you wise. ²⁴"I called you so often, but you wouldn't come. I reached out to you, but you paid no attention. ²⁵You ignored my advice and rejected the correction I offered. ²⁶So I will laugh when you are in trouble! I will mock you when disaster overtakes you

~ Proverbs 1:1-7, 20-26

Do not postpone good deeds

Proverbs is about wisdom. Wise people know what is right because they place God first. They know when to speak and when to keep quiet. They also know that helping others may never be postponed. The right time is always here and now.

²¹My child, don't lose sight of common sense and discernment. Hang on to them, ²²for they will refresh your soul. They are like jewels on a necklace.

²³They keep you safe on your way, and your feet will not stumble. ²⁴You can go to bed without fear; you will lie down and sleep soundly.

²⁵You need not be afraid of sudden disaster or the destruction that comes upon the wicked, ²⁶for the Lord is your security. He will keep your foot from being caught in a trap.

²⁷Do not withhold good from those who deserve it when it's in your power to help them. ²⁸If you can help your neighbor now, don't say, "Come back tomorrow, and then I'll help you."

²⁹Don't plot harm against your neighbor, for those who live nearby trust you. ³⁰Don't pick a fight without reason, when no one has done you harm.

³¹Don't envy violent people or copy their ways.

³²Such wicked people are detestable to the Lord, but he offers his friendship to the godly.

³³The Lord curses the house of the wicked, but he blesses the home of the upright. ³⁴The Lord mocks the mockers but is gracious to the humble. ³⁵The wise inherit honor, but fools are put to shame!

~ Proverbs 3:21-35

Words are medicine and weapons

Wise people know the power and danger of words. Well-intentioned words that bless and serve others are like good medicine. Demeaning words are like weapons of mass destruction. Therefore, wise people rather keep quiet than to gossip. Gossips only give away secrets that cause harm.

⁹With their words, the godless destroy their friends, but knowledge will rescue the righteous.

¹⁰The whole city celebrates when the godly succeed; they shout for joy when the wicked die.

¹¹Upright citizens are good for a city and make it prosper, but the talk of the wicked tears it apart.

¹²It is foolish to belittle one's neighbor; a sensible person keeps quiet.

¹³A gossip goes around telling secrets, but those who are trustworthy can keep a confidence.

¹⁴Without wise leadership, a nation falls; there is safety in having many advisers.

¹⁵There's danger in putting up security for a stranger's debt; it's safer not to guarantee another person's debt.

¹⁶A gracious woman gains respect, but ruthless men gain only wealth.

¹⁷Your kindness will reward you, but your cruelty will destroy you.

¹⁸Evil people get rich for the moment, but the reward of the godly will last.

¹⁹Godly people find life; evil people find death.

²⁰The LORD detests people with crooked hearts, but he delights in those with integrity.

~ Proverbs 11:9-20

Laziness causes poverty

Rather poor than a fraud. Sluggards are even too lazy to eat their food. Therefore, they suffer. No wonder Proverbs calls on us to work hard. Being able to work is a gift from God. Wise people do it to honor God, and in this way care for their families.

[17]If you help the poor, you are lending to the LORD—and he will repay you! [18]Discipline your children while there is hope. Otherwise you will ruin their lives. [19]Hot-tempered people must pay the penalty. If you rescue them once, you will have to do it again. [20]Get all the advice and instruction you can, so you will be wise the rest of your life. [21]You can make many plans, but the LORD's purpose will prevail. [22]Loyalty makes a person attractive. It is better to be poor than dishonest. [23]Fear of the LORD leads to life, bringing security and protection from harm. [24]Lazy people take food in their hand but don't even lift it to their mouth. [25]If you punish a mocker, the simpleminded will learn a lesson; if you correct the wise, they will be all the wiser. [26]Children who mistreat their father or chase away their mother are an embarrassment and a public disgrace. [27]If you stop listening to instruction, my child, you will turn your back on knowledge. [28]A corrupt witness makes a mockery of justice; the mouth of the wicked gulps down evil. [29]Punishment is made for mockers, and the backs of fools are made to be beaten.

~ Proverbs 19:17-29

The right words at the right time

The art to say the right words at the right time is a characteristic of wisdom. Knowing when to say what, can be a living blessing to others. The right words can calm anger. Soft-spoken words wipe hostility out.

¹¹Timely advice is lovely, like golden apples in a silver basket.

¹²To one who listens, valid criticism is like a gold earring or other gold jewelry.

¹³Trustworthy messengers refresh like snow in summer. They revive the spirit of their employer.

¹⁴A person who promises a gift but doesn't give it is like clouds and wind that bring no rain.

¹⁵Patience can persuade a prince, and soft speech can break bones.

¹⁶Do you like honey? Don't eat too much, or it will make you sick!

¹⁷Don't visit your neighbors too often, or you will wear out your welcome.

¹⁸Telling lies about others is as harmful as hitting them with an ax, wounding them with a sword, or shooting them with a sharp arrow.

¹⁹Putting confidence in an unreliable person in times of trouble is like chewing with a broken tooth or walking on a lame foot.

²⁰Singing cheerful songs to a person with a heavy heart is like taking someone's coat in cold weather or pouring vinegar in a wound.

²¹If your enemies are hungry, give them food to eat. If they are thirsty, give them water to drink.

²²You will heap burning coals of shame on their heads, and the LORD will reward you.

~ Proverbs 25:11-22

Do not brag

Bragging is irritating. Even worse, it is a sign of foolishness. Therefore Proverbs calls on us not to be too full of ourselves. Listening to the reprimands of wise people is just as clever. It leads to a life that honors God and fills others' lives with happiness.

¹Don't brag about tomorrow, since you don't know what the day will bring.

²Let someone else praise you, not your own mouth—a stranger, not your own lips.

³A stone is heavy and sand is weighty, but the resentment caused by a fool is even heavier.

⁴Anger is cruel, and wrath is like a flood, but jealousy is even more dangerous.

⁵An open rebuke is better than hidden love!

⁶Wounds from a sincere friend are better than many kisses from an enemy.

⁷A person who is full refuses honey, but even bitter food tastes sweet to the hungry.

⁸A person who strays from home is like a bird that strays from its nest.

⁹The heartfelt counsel of a friend is as sweet as perfume and incense.

¹⁰Never abandon a friend—either yours or your father's. When disaster strikes, you won't have to ask your brother for assistance. It's better to go to a neighbor than to a brother who lives far away.

¹¹Be wise, my child, and make my heart glad. Then I will be able to answer my critics.

¹²A prudent person foresees danger and takes precautions. The simpleton goes blindly on and suffers the consequences.

~ Proverbs 27:1-12

Chasing after the wind

Chasing wind is meaningless. You can't catch it. Therefore the author of Ecclesiastes is cynical about a lot of things people keep themselves busy with – like chasing manmade wisdom and pleasure. Only the things that come from God is worthwhile.

[12]I, the Teacher, was king of Israel, and I lived in Jerusalem. [13]I devoted myself to search for understanding and to explore by wisdom everything being done under heaven. I soon discovered that God has dealt a tragic existence to the human race. [14]I observed everything going on under the sun, and really, it is all meaningless—like chasing the wind.

[15]What is wrong cannot be made right.

What is missing cannot be recovered.

[16]I said to myself, "Look, I am wiser than any of the kings who ruled in Jerusalem before me. I have greater wisdom and knowledge than any of them." [17]So I set out to learn everything from wisdom to madness and folly. But I learned firsthand that pursuing all this is like chasing the wind.

[18]The greater my wisdom, the greater my grief. To increase knowledge only increases sorrow.

2[24]So I decided there is nothing better than to enjoy food and drink and to find satisfaction in work. Then I realized that these pleasures are from the hand of God. [25]For who can eat or enjoy anything apart from him? [26]God gives wisdom, knowledge, and joy to those who please him. But if a sinner becomes wealthy, God takes the wealth away and gives it to those who please him. This, too, is meaningless—like chasing the wind.

~ Ecclesiastes 1:12-18, 2:24-26

Fewer words, please

Count your words when you talk to God. Use fewer words and be sincere and humble. Remember you are in the presence of the Almighty God when you pray. Know your place. Too many words can land you in trouble with Him.

[1]As you enter the house of God, keep your ears open and your mouth shut. It is evil to make mindless offerings to God. [2]Don't make rash promises, and don't be hasty in bringing matters before God. After all, God is in heaven, and you are here on earth. So let your words be few.

[3]Too much activity gives you restless dreams; too many words make you a fool.

[4]When you make a promise to God, don't delay in following through, for God takes no pleasure in fools. Keep all the promises you make to him. [5]It is better to say nothing than to make a promise and not keep it.

~ Ecclesiastes 5:1-5

To understand God
is to not understand

The author of Ecclesiastes says in chapter 8:17, "I realized that no one can discover everything God is doing under the sun." No one can comprehend what goes on under the sun. Rational thoughts and logical explanations will not bring you to God. Only faith will.

[11]When a crime is not punished quickly, people feel it is safe to do wrong. [12]But even though a person sins a hundred times and still lives a long time, I know that those who fear God will be better off. [13]The wicked will not prosper, for they do not fear God. Their days will never grow long like the evening shadows.

[14]And this is not all that is meaningless in our world. In this life, good people are often treated as though they were wicked, and wicked people are often treated as though they were good. This is so meaningless!

[15]So I recommend having fun, because there is nothing better for people in this world than to eat, drink, and enjoy life. That way they will experience some happiness along with all the hard work God gives them under the sun.

[16]In my search for wisdom and in my observation of people's burdens here on earth, I discovered that there is ceaseless activity, day and night. [17]I realized that no one can discover everything God is doing under the sun. Not even the wisest people discover everything, no matter what they claim.

~ Ecclesiastes 8:11-17

Do as you please, as long as you place God first

The author of Ecclesiastes says to enjoy the days of your youth. Find pleasure in what you do each day. But remember one thing: "You must give an account to God of everything you do." Therefore, place Him first. To live healthy is to live right.

⁷Light is sweet; how pleasant to see a new day dawning.

⁸When people live to be very old, let them rejoice in every day of life. But let them also remember there will be many dark days. Everything still to come is meaningless.

⁹Young people, it's wonderful to be young! Enjoy every minute of it. Do everything you want to do; take it all in. But remember that you must give an account to God for everything you do. ¹⁰So refuse to worry, and keep your body healthy. But remember that youth, with a whole life before you, is meaningless.

12¹Don't let the excitement of youth cause you to forget your Creator. Honor him in your youth before you grow old and say, "Life is not pleasant anymore." ²Remember him before the light of the sun, moon, and stars is dim to your old eyes, and rain clouds continually darken your sky.

¹⁰The Teacher sought to find just the right words to express truths clearly.

¹¹The words of the wise are like cattle prods—painful but helpful. Their collected sayings are like a nail-studded stick with which a shepherd drives the sheep.

¹²But, my child, let me give you some further advice: Be careful, for writing books is endless, and much study wears you out.

¹³That's the whole story. Here now is my final conclusion: Fear God and obey his commands, for this is everyone's duty. ¹⁴God will judge us for everything we do, including every secret thing, whether good or bad.

~ Ecclesiastes 11:7-12:2, 10-14

Sing about love

Song of Songs is not an allegorical book about the Lord and the church. It is a book about the love between a wife and a husband. Song of Songs praises the beauty and excitement of love. It tells about the beauty and mystery of love for one another, which is a gift from God.

¹This is Solomon's song of songs, more wonderful than any other.

²Kiss me and kiss me again, for your love is sweeter than wine.

³How fragrant your cologne; your name is like its spreading fragrance. No wonder all the young women love you!

⁴Take me with you; come, let's run! The king has brought me into his bedroom.

How happy we are for you, O king. We praise your love even more than wine. How right they are to adore you.

⁵I am dark but beautiful, O women of Jerusalem—dark as the tents of Kedar, dark as the curtains of Solomon's tents.

⁶Don't stare at me because I am dark—the sun has darkened my skin. My brothers were angry with me; they forced me to care for their vineyards, so I couldn't care for myself—my own vineyard.

¹²The king is lying on his couch, enchanted by the fragrance of my perfume.

¹³My lover is like a sachet of myrrh lying between my breasts.

¹⁴He is like a bouquet of sweet henna blossoms from the vineyards of En-gedi.

~ Song of Songs 1:1-6, 12-14

Love makes your heart beat

The warmth of love between husband and wife is not taboo in religious circles. The love for your spouse that sends the blood rushing through your veins and makes your head spin, is what Song of Songs is all about. It is colorful songs of praise about the beauty of love.

¹²Let us get up early and go to the vineyards to see if the grapevines have budded, if the blossoms have opened, and if the pomegranates have bloomed. There I will give you my love.

¹³There the mandrakes give off their fragrance, and the finest fruits are at our door, new delights as well as old, which I have saved for you, my lover.

8¹Oh, I wish you were my brother, who nursed at my mother's breasts. Then I could kiss you no matter who was watching, and no one would criticize me.

²I would bring you to my childhood home, and there you would teach me. I would give you spiced wine to drink, my sweet pomegranate wine.

³Your left arm would be under my head, and your right arm would embrace me.

⁴Promise me, O women of Jerusalem, not to awaken love until the time is right.

⁵Who is this sweeping in from the desert, leaning on her lover? I aroused you under the apple tree, where your mother gave you birth, where in great pain she delivered you.

⁶Place me like a seal over your heart, like a seal on your arm. For love is as strong as death, its jealousy as enduring as the grave. Love flashes like fire, the brightest kind of flame.

⁷Many waters cannot quench love, nor can rivers drown it. If a man tried to buy love with all his wealth, his offer would be utterly scorned.

~ Song of Songs 7:12-8:7

Be ashamed about your mistakes

The Book of Isaiah is connected to the prophet who acted during the time of four kings of Judah. During this time he exposed the sins of the Lord's people. Things were so bad that the people would be ashamed if they had to hear it again. Therefore the necessity to convert.

[16]Wash yourselves and be clean! Get your sins out of my sight. Give up your evil ways.

[17]Learn to do good. Seek justice. Help the oppressed. Defend the cause of orphans. Fight for the rights of widows.

[18]"Come now, let's settle this," says the LORD. "Though your sins are like scarlet, I will make them as white as snow. Though they are red like crimson, I will make them as white as wool.

[29]You will be ashamed of your idol worship in groves of sacred oaks. You will blush because you worshiped in gardens dedicated to idols.

[30]You will be like a great tree with withered leaves, like a garden without water.

[31]The strongest among you will disappear like straw; their evil deeds will be the spark that sets it on fire. They and their evil works will burn up together, and no one will be able to put out the fire.

~ Isaiah 1:16-18, 29-31

Coals for your lips

When God called Isaiah there was one problem – his lips were filthy. But God had the answer – a burning coal from His altar. It is a cure for all foolish words. The fire of God's altar brought new life for His prophet, and for all other people.

¹It was in the year King Uzziah died that I saw the Lord. He was sitting on a lofty throne, and the train of his robe filled the Temple. ²Attending him were mighty seraphim, each having six wings. With two wings they covered their faces, with two they covered their feet, and with two they flew. ³They were calling out to each other,

"Holy, holy, holy is the LORD of Heaven's Armies! The whole earth is filled with his glory!"

⁴Their voices shook the Temple to its foundations, and the entire building was filled with smoke.

⁵Then I said, "It's all over! I am doomed, for I am a sinful man. I have filthy lips, and I live among a people with filthy lips. Yet I have seen the King, the LORD of Heaven's Armies."

⁶Then one of the seraphim flew to me with a burning coal he had taken from the altar with a pair of tongs. ⁷He touched my lips with it and said, "See, this coal has touched your lips. Now your guilt is removed, and your sins are forgiven."

⁸Then I heard the Lord asking, "Whom should I send as a messenger to this people? Who will go for us?"

I said, "Here I am. Send me."

⁹And he said, "Yes, go, and say to this people, 'Listen carefully, but do not understand. Watch closely, but learn nothing.'"

~ Isaiah 6:1-9

God's greatness
knows no boundaries

God is not only a national God. He does not only care for Israel. When He rises, His glory is known worldwide. Then everybody, near and far, will see His power and might. Everybody in the whole world will tremble. Who can keep standing before God?

⁷But now your brave warriors weep in public. Your ambassadors of peace cry in bitter disappointment.

⁸Your roads are deserted; no one travels them anymore. The Assyrians have broken their peace treaty and care nothing for the promises they made before witnesses. They have no respect for anyone.

⁹The land of Israel wilts in mourning. Lebanon withers with shame. The plain of Sharon is now a wilderness. Bashan and Carmel have been plundered.

¹⁰But the Lord says: "Now I will stand up. Now I will show my power and might.

¹¹You Assyrians produce nothing but dry grass and stubble. Your own breath will turn to fire and consume you.

¹²Your people will be burned up completely, like thornbushes cut down and tossed in a fire.

¹³Listen to what I have done, you nations far away! And you that are near, acknowledge my might!"

¹⁴The sinners in Jerusalem shake with fear. Terror seizes the godless. "Who can live with this devouring fire?" they cry. "Who can survive this all-consuming fire?"

¹⁵Those who are honest and fair, who refuse to profit by fraud, who stay far away from bribes, who refuse to listen to those who plot murder, who shut their eyes to all enticement to do wrong—¹⁶these are the ones who will dwell on high. The rocks of the mountains will be their fortress. Food will be supplied to them, and they will have water in abundance.

~ Isaiah 33:7-16

Sing when God intervenes

When Isaiah brought King Hezekiah the bad news that he was going to die, the king prayed for mercy. God healed him. In answer to this Hezekiah sang a song of praise. This is how you thank God for intervening in your life. Then it is celebration time – time to sing and dance.

[11]I said, "Never again will I see the LORD GOD while still in the land of the living. Never again will I see my friends or be with those who live in this world.

[12]My life has been blown away like a shepherd's tent in a storm. It has been cut short, as when a weaver cuts cloth from a loom. Suddenly, my life was over.

[13]I waited patiently all night, but I was torn apart as though by lions. Suddenly, my life was over.

[14]Delirious, I chattered like a swallow or a crane, and then I moaned like a mourning dove. My eyes grew tired of looking to heaven for help. I am in trouble, Lord. Help me!"

[15]But what could I say? For he himself sent this sickness. Now I will walk humbly throughout my years because of this anguish I have felt.

[16]Lord, your discipline is good, for it leads to life and health. You restore my health and allow me to live!

[17]Yes, this anguish was good for me, for you have rescued me from death and forgiven all my sins.

[18]For the dead cannot praise you; they cannot raise their voices in praise. Those who go down to the grave can no longer hope in your faithfulness.

[19]Only the living can praise you as I do today. Each generation tells of your faithfulness to the next.

~ Isaiah 38:11-19

May

Comfort at last

God's words of comfort to His weary people were not idle. On the contrary, His words introduced a new highway of grace. His words were also about the coming of God's salvation. Just open your ears and listen. Start walking on God's highway of grace and live!

³Listen! It's the voice of someone shouting, "Clear the way through the wilderness for the Lord! Make a straight highway through the wasteland for our God!

⁴Fill in the valleys, and level the mountains and hills. Straighten the curves, and smooth out the rough places.

⁵Then the glory of the Lord will be revealed, and all people will see it together. The Lord has spoken!"

⁶A voice said, "Shout!" I asked, "What should I shout?" "Shout that people are like the grass. Their beauty fades as quickly as the flowers in a field.

⁷The grass withers and the flowers fade beneath the breath of the Lord. And so it is with people.

⁸The grass withers and the flowers fade, but the word of our God stands forever."

⁹O Zion, messenger of good news, shout from the mountaintops! Shout it louder, O Jerusalem. Shout, and do not be afraid. Tell the towns of Judah, "Your God is coming!"

¹⁰Yes, the Sovereign Lord is coming in power. He will rule with a powerful arm. See, he brings his reward with him as he comes.

¹¹He will feed his flock like a shepherd. He will carry the lambs in his arms, holding them close to his heart. He will gently lead the mother sheep with their young.

~ Isaiah 40:3-11

Ridiculous!

To carve an idol out of a dead tree stump and to worship it is stupid. No, it's actually ridiculous. Even so, millions of people worship the work of their hands, even today. Idolatry is alive and well, unless you choose to call its bluff and decide to worship the true God instead.

¹²The blacksmith stands at his forge to make a sharp tool, pounding and shaping it with all his might. His work makes him hungry and weak. It makes him thirsty and faint.

¹³Then the wood-carver measures a block of wood and draws a pattern on it. He works with chisel and plane and carves it into a human figure. He gives it human beauty and puts it in a little shrine.

¹⁴He cuts down cedars; he selects the cypress and the oak; he plants the pine in the forest to be nourished by the rain.

¹⁵Then he uses part of the wood to make a fire. With it he warms himself and bakes his bread. Then—yes, it's true—he takes the rest of it and makes himself a god to worship! He makes an idol and bows down in front of it!

¹⁶He burns part of the tree to roast his meat and to keep himself warm. He says, "Ah, that fire feels good."

¹⁷Then he takes what's left and makes his god: a carved idol! He falls down in front of it, worshiping and praying to it. "Rescue me!" he says. "You are my god!"

¹⁸Such stupidity and ignorance! Their eyes are closed, and they cannot see. Their minds are shut, and they cannot think.

~ Isaiah 44:12-18

Something to sing about

Isaiah 49 speaks about God rescuing weak and defenseless people. People who thought that God had abandoned them found out that that was not true. God will never disown His children, just like a good mother will never forget her children. Our names are written on the palms of God's hands.

[11]And I will make my mountains into level paths for them. The highways will be raised above the valleys. [12]See, my people will return from far away, from lands to the north and west, and from as far south as Egypt."

[13]Sing for joy, O heavens! Rejoice, O earth! Burst into song, O mountains! For the LORD has comforted his people and will have compassion on them in their suffering.

[14]Yet Jerusalem says, "The LORD has deserted us; the Lord has forgotten us." [15]"Never! Can a mother forget her nursing child? Can she feel no love for the child she has borne? But even if that were possible, I would not forget you! [16]See, I have written your name on the palms of my hands. Always in my mind is a picture of Jerusalem's walls in ruins. [17]Soon your descendants will come back, and all who are trying to destroy you will go away. [18]Look around you and see, for all your children will come back to you. As surely as I live," says the LORD, "they will be like jewels or bridal ornaments for you to display.

[25]But the LORD says, "The captives of warriors will be released, and the plunder of tyrants will be retrieved. For I will fight those who fight you, and I will save your children.

[26]I will feed your enemies with their own flesh. They will be drunk with rivers of their own blood. All the world will know that I, the LORD, am your Savior and your Redeemer, the Mighty One of Israel."

~ Isaiah 49:11-18, 25-26

The messenger of good news

Listen carefully to the feet of those who bring God's good news to you. Good news will soon pour from their lips that will surround your life with heavenly blessing. Since the days of Isaiah this is precisely how God's Good News has reached the world.

¹Wake up, wake up, O Zion! Clothe yourself with strength. Put on your beautiful clothes, O holy city of Jerusalem, for unclean and godless people will enter your gates no longer.

²Rise from the dust, O Jerusalem. Sit in a place of honor. Remove the chains of slavery from your neck, O captive daughter of Zion.

⁷How beautiful on the mountains are the feet of the messenger who brings good news, the good news of peace and salvation, the news that the God of Israel reigns!

⁸The watchmen shout and sing with joy, for before their very eyes they see the LORD returning to Jerusalem.

⁹Let the ruins of Jerusalem break into joyful song, for the LORD has comforted his people. He has redeemed Jerusalem.

¹⁰The LORD has demonstrated his holy power before the eyes of all the nations. All the ends of the earth will see the victory of our God.

¹¹Get out! Get out and leave your captivity, where everything you touch is unclean. Get out of there and purify yourselves, you who carry home the sacred objects of the LORD.

¹²You will not leave in a hurry, running for your lives. For the LORD will go ahead of you; yes, the God of Israel will protect you from behind.

~ Isaiah 52:1-2, 7-12

A free transaction

Nothing in life is free, except for God's grace. God freely gives of His goodness. He freely gives heavenly wine and milk to those who thirst. Simply accept it by faith and live. Obey God and join in the heavenly feast.

¹"Is anyone thirsty? Come and drink—even if you have no money! Come, take your choice of wine or milk—it's all free!

²Why spend your money on food that does not give you strength? Why pay for food that does you no good? Listen to me, and you will eat what is good. You will enjoy the finest food.

³"Come to me with your ears wide open. Listen, and you will find life. I will make an everlasting covenant with you. I will give you all the unfailing love I promised to David.

⁴See how I used him to display my power among the peoples. I made him a leader among the nations.

⁵You also will command nations you do not know, and peoples unknown to you will come running to obey, because I, the LORD your God, the Holy One of Israel, have made you glorious."

⁶Seek the LORD while you can find him. Call on him now while he is near.

⁷Let the wicked change their ways and banish the very thought of doing wrong. Let them turn to the LORD that he may have mercy on them. Yes, turn to our God, for he will forgive generously.

⁸"My thoughts are nothing like your thoughts," says the LORD. "And my ways are far beyond anything you could imagine.

⁹For just as the heavens are higher than the earth, so my ways are higher than your ways and my thoughts higher than your thoughts."

~ Isaiah 55:1-9

Neither deaf nor helpless

Our God is not helpless, neither is He deaf. It's human sinfulness that sometimes blocks the path between Him and us. We create the interference on the line of communication to heaven from our side. The solution: confession and obedience to the living God!

¹Listen! The LORD's arm is not too weak to save you, nor is his ear too deaf to hear you call. ²It's your sins that have cut you off from God. Because of your sins, he has turned away and will not listen anymore. ³Your hands are the hands of murderers, and your fingers are filthy with sin. Your lips are full of lies, and your mouth spews corruption. ⁴No one cares about being fair and honest. The people's lawsuits are based on lies. They conceive evil deeds and then give birth to sin.

¹²For our sins are piled up before God and testify against us. Yes, we know what sinners we are.

¹³We know we have rebelled and have denied the LORD. We have turned our backs on our God. We know how unfair and oppressive we have been, carefully planning our deceitful lies.

¹⁴Our courts oppose the righteous, and justice is nowhere to be found. Truth stumbles in the streets, and honesty has been outlawed.

¹⁵Yes, truth is gone, and anyone who renounces evil is attacked. The LORD looked and was displeased to find there was no justice.

¹⁶He was amazed to see that no one intervened to help the oppressed. So he himself stepped in to save them with his strong arm, and his justice sustained him.

¹⁷He put on righteousness as his body armor and placed the helmet of salvation on his head. He clothed himself with a robe of vengeance and wrapped himself in a cloak of divine passion.

~ Isaiah 59:1-4, 12-17

Long acquainted with God

Jeremiah was one of the great prophets in Israel. For over forty years He preached God's will under the most difficult circumstances imaginable. During his time Jerusalem was besieged by the Babylonians and Jeremiah was often scorned. But his perseverance stems from his calling which came long before his birth. How have you been called?

⁴The Lord gave me this message:

⁵"I knew you before I formed you in your mother's womb. Before you were born I set you apart and appointed you as my prophet to the nations."

⁶"O Sovereign Lord," I said, "I can't speak for you! I'm too young!"

⁷The Lord replied, "Don't say, 'I'm too young,' for you must go wherever I send you and say whatever I tell you. ⁸And don't be afraid of the people, for I will be with you and will protect you. I, the Lord, have spoken!" ⁹Then the Lord reached out and touched my mouth and said,

"Look, I have put my words in your mouth!

¹⁰Today I appoint you to stand up against nations and kingdoms. Some you must uproot and tear down, destroy and overthrow. Others you must build up and plant."

¹⁷"Get up and prepare for action. Go out and tell them everything I tell you to say. Do not be afraid of them, or I will make you look foolish in front of them.

¹⁸For see, today I have made you strong like a fortified city that cannot be captured, like an iron pillar or a bronze wall. You will stand against the whole land—the kings, officials, priests, and people of Judah."

~ Jeremiah 1:4-10, 17-18

Beware of false prophets

During Jeremiah's years of prophetic service, he encountered many false prophets. What distinguishes them? Well, they usually speak empty words and false messages of comfort. God's messengers always have the courage, when necessary, to swim upstream. They don't play around with God's grace.

⁴"Jeremiah, say to the people, 'This is what the Lord says: "'When people fall down, don't they get up again? When they discover they're on the wrong road, don't they turn back?

⁵Then why do these people stay on their self-destructive path? Why do the people of Jerusalem refuse to turn back? They cling tightly to their lies and will not turn around.

⁶I listen to their conversations and don't hear a word of truth. Is anyone sorry for doing wrong? Does anyone say, "What a terrible thing I have done"? No! All are running down the path of sin as swiftly as a horse galloping into battle!

⁷Even the stork that flies across the sky knows the time of her migration, as do the turtledove, the swallow, and the crane. They all return at the proper time each year. But not my people! They do not know the Lord's laws. ⁸"'How can you say, "We are wise because we have the word of the Lord," when your teachers have twisted it by writing lies? ⁹These wise teachers will fall into the trap of their own foolishness, for they have rejected the word of the Lord. Are they so wise after all?

¹¹They offer superficial treatments for my people's mortal wound. They give assurances of peace when there is no peace. ¹²Are they ashamed of these disgusting actions? Not at all—they don't even know how to blush! Therefore, they will lie among the slaughtered. They will be brought down when I punish them, says the Lord.

~ Jeremiah 8:4-9, 11-12

No deserters in God's service

Sometimes things get too much, even for big names like Jeremiah. But then, after his deluge of complaints to God he is told that he doesn't have the right to one-sidedly revoke his prophetic calling. Follow God on His conditions, or not at all.

¹⁵Then I said, "LORD, you know what's happening to me. Please step in and help me. Punish my persecutors! Please give me time; don't let me die young. It's for your sake that I am suffering.

¹⁶When I discovered your words, I devoured them. They are my joy and my heart's delight, for I bear your name, O LORD God of Heaven's Armies.

¹⁷I never joined the people in their merry feasts. I sat alone because your hand was on me. I was filled with indignation at their sins.

¹⁸Why then does my suffering continue? Why is my wound so incurable? Your help seems as uncertain as a seasonal brook, like a spring that has gone dry."

¹⁹This is how the LORD responds: "If you return to me, I will restore you so you can continue to serve me. If you speak good words rather than worthless ones, you will be my spokesman. You must influence them; do not let them influence you!

²⁰They will fight against you like an attacking army, but I will make you as secure as a fortified wall of bronze. They will not conquer you, for I am with you to protect and rescue you. I, the LORD, have spoken!

²¹Yes, I will certainly keep you safe from these wicked men. I will rescue you from their cruel hands."

~ Jeremiah 15:15-21

Hope in the midst of despair

There was much rejoicing when God told His exiled people that He would return them to their own land. God Himself removes people's grief. He removes obstacles from their path. He dried the tears of Rachel and her descendants. And He continues to do this – even today.

¹⁵This is what the LORD says: "A cry is heard in Ramah—deep anguish and bitter weeping. Rachel weeps for her children, refusing to be comforted—for her children are gone."

¹⁶But now this is what the LORD says: "Do not weep any longer, for I will reward you," says the LORD. "Your children will come back to you from the distant land of the enemy.

¹⁷There is hope for your future," says the LORD. "Your children will come again to their own land.

¹⁸I have heard Israel saying, 'You disciplined me severely, like a calf that needs training for the yoke. Turn me again to you and restore me, for you alone are the LORD my God.

¹⁹I turned away from God, but then I was sorry. I kicked myself for my stupidity! I was thoroughly ashamed of all I did in my younger days.'

²⁰"Is not Israel still my son, my darling child?" says the LORD. "I often have to punish him, but I still love him. That's why I long for him and surely will have mercy on him.

²¹Set up road signs; put up guideposts. Mark well the path by which you came. Come back again, my virgin Israel; return to your towns here."

~ Jeremiah 31:15-21

In an empty cistern

Jeremiah was a persona non grata in the time of King Zedekiah. The result was that he was thrown into a pit which apparently was also used as a toilet. But this didn't break his spirit. God's people are not defeated by such setbacks.

¹Now Shephatiah son of Mattan, Gedaliah son of Pashhur, Jehucal son of Shelemiah, and Pashhur son of Malkijah heard what Jeremiah had been telling the people. He had been saying, ²"This is what the LORD says: 'Everyone who stays in Jerusalem will die from war, famine, or disease, but those who surrender to the Babylonians will live. Their reward will be life. They will live!' ³The LORD also says: 'The city of Jerusalem will certainly be handed over to the army of the king of Babylon, who will capture it.'"

⁴So these officials went to the king and said, "Sir, this man must die! That kind of talk will undermine the morale of the few fighting men we have left, as well as that of all the people. This man is a traitor!"

⁵King Zedekiah agreed. "All right," he said. "Do as you like. I can't stop you."

⁶So the officials took Jeremiah from his cell and lowered him by ropes into an empty cistern in the prison yard. It belonged to Malkijah, a member of the royal family. There was no water in the cistern, but there was a thick layer of mud at the bottom, and Jeremiah sank down into it.

~ Jeremiah 38:1-6

No peaceful retirement

Jeremiah was not granted a peaceful retirement at the end of his life. On the contrary; he was carried off into exile by the Israelites who fled to Egypt. Even so, he didn't waver to clearly declare God's Word in a strange land.

¹When Jeremiah had finished giving this message from the LORD their God to all the people, ²Azariah son of Hoshaiah and Johanan son of Kareah and all the other proud men said to Jeremiah, "You lie! The LORD our God hasn't forbidden us to go to Egypt! ³Baruch son of Neriah has convinced you to say this, because he wants us to stay here and be killed by the Babylonians or be carried off into exile."

⁴So Johanan and the other guerrilla leaders and all the people refused to obey the LORD's command to stay in Judah. ⁵Johanan and the other leaders took with them all the people who had returned from the nearby countries to which they had fled. ⁶In the crowd were men, women, and children, the king's daughters, and all those whom Nebuzaradan, the captain of the guard, had left with Gedaliah. The prophet Jeremiah and Baruch were also included. ⁷The people refused to obey the voice of the LORD and went to Egypt, going as far as the city of Tahpanhes.

⁸Then at Tahpanhes, the LORD gave another message to Jeremiah.

~ Jeremiah 43:1-8

God's mercies never cease

Lamentations was written on the Israelites' return from exile to their beloved Jerusalem. They mourned the chaos and destruction in their once renowned city. They felt abandoned, lonely, bitter and hopeless. Yet even so, God is present in the midst of hopelessness.

¹⁸I cry out, "My splendor is gone! Everything I had hoped for from the LORD is lost!" ¹⁹The thought of my suffering and homelessness is bitter beyond words. ²⁰I will never forget this awful time, as I grieve over my loss. ²¹Yet I still dare to hope when I remember this: ²²The faithful love of the LORD never ends! His mercies never cease.

²³Great is his faithfulness; his mercies begin afresh each morning. ²⁴I say to myself, "The LORD is my inheritance; therefore, I will hope in him!" ²⁵The LORD is good to those who depend on him, to those who search for him. ²⁶So it is good to wait quietly for salvation from the LORD. ²⁷And it is good for people to submit at an early age to the yoke of his discipline: ²⁸Let them sit alone in silence beneath the LORD's demands. ²⁹Let them lie face down in the dust, for there may be hope at last. ³⁰Let them turn the other cheek to those who strike them and accept the insults of their enemies.

³¹For no one is abandoned by the Lord forever. ³²Though he brings grief, he also shows compassion because of the greatness of his unfailing love. ³³For he does not enjoy hurting people or causing them sorrow.

³⁷Who can command things to happen without the Lord's permission? ³⁸Does not the Most High send both calamity and good?

~ Lamentations 3:18-33, 37-38

Lord, please remember us!

When the Israelites lost their pride and human dignity and even felt that God had abandoned them, they reminded God of their lot. They pleaded with Him to step in and change their situation. Fortunately the New Testament teaches us that Jesus is Immanuel – God with us.

¹²Our princes are being hanged by their thumbs, and our elders are treated with contempt.

¹³Young men are led away to work at millstones, and boys stagger under heavy loads of wood.

¹⁴The elders no longer sit in the city gates; the young men no longer dance and sing.

¹⁵Joy has left our hearts; our dancing has turned to mourning.

¹⁶The garlands have fallen from our heads. Weep for us because we have sinned.

¹⁷Our hearts are sick and weary, and our eyes grow dim with tears.

¹⁸For Jerusalem is empty and desolate, a place haunted by jackals.

¹⁹But LORD, you remain the same forever! Your throne continues from generation to generation.

²⁰Why do you continue to forget us? Why have you abandoned us for so long?

²¹Restore us, O LORD, and bring us back to you again! Give us back the joys we once had!

²²Or have you utterly rejected us? Are you angry with us still?

~ Lamentations 5:12-22

A vision of hope in captivity

Ezekiel, a contemporary of Jeremiah, was also captured along with the Judean exiles and carried off to Babylon. The Lord spoke to him in a great vision one day at the Kebar River. There, in a foreign country, he saw the glory of the Lord. That's why he fell to the ground, face down before the Lord.

¹On July 31 of my thirtieth year, while I was with the Judean exiles beside the Kebar River in Babylon, the heavens were opened and I saw visions of God.

²²Spread out above them was a surface like the sky, glittering like crystal. ²³Beneath this surface the wings of each living being stretched out to touch the others' wings, and each had two wings covering its body. ²⁴As they flew, their wings sounded to me like waves crashing against the shore or like the voice of the Almighty or like the shouting of a mighty army. When they stopped, they let down their wings. ²⁵As they stood with wings lowered, a voice spoke from beyond the crystal surface above them.

²⁶Above this surface was something that looked like a throne made of blue lapis lazuli. And on this throne high above was a figure whose appearance resembled a man. ²⁷From what appeared to be his waist up, he looked like gleaming amber, flickering like a fire. And from his waist down, he looked like a burning flame, shining with splendor. ²⁸All around him was a glowing halo, like a rainbow shining in the clouds on a rainy day. This is what the glory of the LORD looked like to me. When I saw it, I fell face down on the ground, and I heard someone's voice speaking to me.

~ Ezekiel 1:1, 22-28

God's holiness
can not be profaned

On September 17 in the year 592 BC Ezekiel had a vision in a foreign country that transported him to Jerusalem where he saw an idol standing in the temple. God was greatly angered at this because He does not allow His name to be mocked. He has been, and will forever be, the Most Holy.

¹Then on September 17, during the sixth year of King Jehoiachin's captivity, while the leaders of Judah were in my home, the Sovereign LORD took hold of me. ²I saw a figure that appeared to be a man. From what appeared to be his waist down, he looked like a burning flame. From the waist up he looked like gleaming amber. ³He reached out what seemed to be a hand and took me by the hair. Then the Spirit lifted me up into the sky and transported me to Jerusalem in a vision from God. I was taken to the north gate of the inner courtyard of the Temple, where there is a large idol that has made the LORD very jealous. ⁴Suddenly, the glory of the God of Israel was there, just as I had seen it before in the valley.

⁵Then the LORD said to me, "Son of man, look toward the north." So I looked, and there to the north, beside the entrance to the gate near the altar, stood the idol that had made the LORD so jealous.

⁶"Son of man," he said, "do you see what they are doing? Do you see the detestable sins the people of Israel are committing to drive me from my Temple? But come, and you will see even more detestable sins than these!" ⁷Then he brought me to the door of the Temple courtyard, where I could see a hole in the wall.

~ Ezekiel 8:1-7

False spokesmen

The Lord does not tolerate religious games where people make as if He has spoken to them, while actually they are just imagining things. Ezekiel warns us to guard against such falsities. Find your truth and comfort in the Word, not in self-appointed spokesmen.

¹Then this message came to me from the LORD: ²"Son of man, prophesy against the false prophets of Israel who are inventing their own prophecies. Say to them, 'Listen to the word of the LORD. ³This is what the Sovereign LORD says: What sorrow awaits the false prophets who are following their own imaginations and have seen nothing at all!'

⁴"O people of Israel, these prophets of yours are like jackals digging in the ruins. ⁵They have done nothing to repair the breaks in the walls around the nation. They have not helped it to stand firm in battle on the day of the LORD. ⁶Instead, they have told lies and made false predictions. They say, 'This message is from the LORD,' even though the LORD never sent them. And yet they expect him to fulfill their prophecies! ⁷Can your visions be anything but false if you claim, 'This message is from the LORD,' when I have not even spoken to you?

⁸"Therefore, this is what the Sovereign LORD says: Because what you say is false and your visions are a lie, I will stand against you, says the Sovereign LORD. ⁹I will raise my fist against all the prophets who see false visions and make lying predictions, and they will be banished from the community of Israel. I will blot their names from Israel's record books, and they will never again set foot in their own land. Then you will know that I am the Sovereign LORD."

~ Ezekiel 13:1-9

The sins of the parents

**God makes it clear that He never punishes child-
ren for their parents' mistakes. It is a myth that if
parents eat sour grapes (do wrong things); their
children's mouths will pucker at the taste (that the
children will have to pay for their parents' sins).**

[1]Then another message came to me from the LORD: [2]"Why do
you quote this proverb concerning the land of Israel: 'The parents have eaten sour grapes, but their children's mouths pucker
at the taste'? [3]As surely as I live, says the Sovereign LORD, you
will not quote this proverb anymore in Israel. [4]For all people are
mine to judge—both parents and children alike. And this is my
rule: The person who sins is the one who will die.

[5]"Suppose a certain man is righteous and does what is just
and right. [6]He does not feast in the mountains before Israel's
idols or worship them. He does not commit adultery or have
intercourse with a woman during her menstrual period. [7]He is
a merciful creditor, not keeping the items given as security by
poor debtors. He does not rob the poor but instead gives food
to the hungry and provides clothes for the needy. [8]He grants
loans without interest, stays away from injustice, is honest and
fair when judging others, [9]and faithfully obeys my decrees and
regulations. Anyone who does these things is just and will surely live, says the Sovereign LORD.

[10]"But suppose that man has a son who grows up to be a
robber or murderer and refuses to do what is right.

[13]He lends money at excessive interest. Should such a sinful person live? No! He must die and must take full blame."

~ Ezekiel 18:1-10, 13

Watchman for the Lord

When the Lord appoints you as a watchman for His people, it's your job to sound the alarm bells when danger threatens. If you don't, you are guilty. This is what God told Ezekiel. Every watchman stands up for God's cause and must warn the people when danger approaches. You and I must do the same.

¹Once again a message came to me from the LORD: ²"Son of man, give your people this message: 'When I bring an army against a country, the people of that land choose one of their own to be a watchman. ³When the watchman sees the enemy coming, he sounds the alarm to warn the people. ⁴Then if those who hear the alarm refuse to take action, it is their own fault if they die. ⁵They heard the alarm but ignored it, so the responsibility is theirs. If they had listened to the warning, they could have saved their lives. ⁶But if the watchman sees the enemy coming and doesn't sound the alarm to warn the people, he is responsible for their captivity. They will die in their sins, but I will hold the watchman responsible for their deaths.'

⁷"Now, son of man, I am making you a watchman for the people of Israel. Therefore, listen to what I say and warn them for me. ⁸If I announce that some wicked people are sure to die and you fail to tell them to change their ways, then they will die in their sins, and I will hold you responsible for their deaths. ⁹But if you warn them to repent and they don't repent, they will die in their sins, but you will have saved yourself."

~ Ezekiel 33:1-9

Dead bones live

We are all familiar with Ezekiel 37. What an amazing chapter about the Spirit making dry bones live again. God specializes in bringing the dead back to life. Such miracles take place when His Spirit is at work.

¹The LORD took hold of me, and I was carried away by the Spirit of the LORD to a valley filled with bones. ²He led me all around among the bones that covered the valley floor. They were scattered everywhere across the ground and were completely dried out. ³Then he asked me, "Son of man, can these bones become living people again?" "O Sovereign LORD," I replied, "you alone know the answer to that."

⁴Then he said to me, "Speak a prophetic message to these bones and say, 'Dry bones, listen to the word of the LORD! ⁵This is what the Sovereign LORD says: Look! I am going to put breath into you and make you live again! ⁶I will put flesh and muscles on you and cover you with skin. I will put breath into you, and you will come to life. Then you will know that I am the LORD.'"

⁷So I spoke this message, just as he told me. Suddenly as I spoke, there was a rattling noise all across the valley. The bones of each body came together and attached themselves as complete skeletons. ⁸Then as I watched, muscles and flesh formed over the bones. Then skin formed to cover their bodies, but they still had no breath in them.

⁹Then he said to me, "Speak a prophetic message to the winds, son of man. Speak a prophetic message and say, 'This is what the Sovereign LORD says: Come, O breath, from the four winds! Breathe into these dead bodies so they may live again.'"

¹⁰So I spoke the message as he commanded me, and breath came into their bodies. They all came to life and stood up on their feet—a great army.

~ Ezekiel 37:1-10

Man of God in a foreign country

Daniel was God's greatest hero in a strange land. Daniel and his friends didn't waver when they had to shine God's light. Their lives are real examples of the living God's presence in a far country.

[11]Daniel spoke with the attendant who had been appointed by the chief of staff to look after Daniel, Hananiah, Mishael, and Azariah. [12]"Please test us for ten days on a diet of vegetables and water," Daniel said. [13]"At the end of the ten days, see how we look compared to the other young men who are eating the king's food. Then make your decision in light of what you see." [14]The attendant agreed to Daniel's suggestion and tested them for ten days.

[15]At the end of the ten days, Daniel and his three friends looked healthier and better nourished than the young men who had been eating the food assigned by the king. [16]So after that, the attendant fed them only vegetables instead of the food and wine provided for the others.

[17]God gave these four young men an unusual aptitude for understanding every aspect of literature and wisdom. And God gave Daniel the special ability to interpret the meanings of visions and dreams.

[18]When the training period ordered by the king was completed, the chief of staff brought all the young men to King Nebuchadnezzar. [19]The king talked with them, and no one impressed him as much as Daniel, Hananiah, Mishael, and Azariah. So they entered the royal service. [20]Whenever the king consulted them in any matter requiring wisdom and balanced judgment, he found them ten times more capable than any of the magicians and enchanters in his entire kingdom.

~ Daniel 1:11-20

Dream good dreams

We know Daniel as the interpreter of dreams. He could interpret even the most complex dreams of Nebuchadnezzar, even when it didn't necessarily mean good news. This is exactly what God's people should be doing today – they should be speaking and living the truth, even though it might not be popular.

²⁴Then Daniel went in to see Arioch, whom the king had ordered to execute the wise men of Babylon. Daniel said to him, "Don't kill the wise men. Take me to the king, and I will tell him the meaning of his dream."

²⁵Arioch quickly took Daniel to the king and said, "I have found one of the captives from Judah who will tell the king the meaning of his dream!"

²⁶The king said to Daniel (also known as Belteshazzar), "Is this true? Can you tell me what my dream was and what it means?"

²⁷Daniel replied, "There are no wise men, enchanters, magicians, or fortune-tellers who can reveal the king's secret. ²⁸But there is a God in heaven who reveals secrets, and he has shown King Nebuchadnezzar what will happen in the future. Now I will tell you your dream and the visions you saw as you lay on your bed.

²⁹"While Your Majesty was sleeping, you dreamed about coming events. He who reveals secrets has shown you what is going to happen. ³⁰And it is not because I am wiser than anyone else that I know the secret of your dream, but because God wants you to understand what was in your heart."

~ Daniel 2:24-30

Heavenly graffiti

When God began to write on the king's wall, the fat was in the fire. Daniel made it clear that the king did not measure up on God's heavenly scale. God's scale is very accurate – after all, He has all the facts about every one of us at His disposal.

[18]Your Majesty, the Most High God gave sovereignty, majesty, glory, and honor to your predecessor, Nebuchadnezzar.

[20]But when his heart and mind were puffed up with arrogance, he was brought down from his royal throne and stripped of his glory.

[22]"You are his successor, O Belshazzar, and you knew all this, yet you have not humbled yourself. [23]For you have proudly defied the Lord of heaven and have had these cups from his Temple brought before you. You and your nobles and your wives and concubines have been drinking wine from them while praising gods of silver, gold, bronze, iron, wood, and stone— gods that neither see nor hear nor know anything at all. But you have not honored the God who gives you the breath of life and controls your destiny! [24]So God has sent this hand to write this message.

[25]"This is the message that was written: MENE, MENE, TEKEL, and PARSIN. [26]This is what these words mean: *Mene* means 'numbered'—God has numbered the days of your reign and has brought it to an end. [27]*Tekel* means 'weighed'—you have been weighed on the balances and have not measured up. [28]*Parsin* means 'divided'—your kingdom has been divided and given to the Medes and Persians."

[29]Then at Belshazzar's command, Daniel was dressed in purple robes, a gold chain was hung around his neck, and he was proclaimed the third highest ruler in the kingdom. [30]That very night Belshazzar, the Babylonian king, was killed.

~ Daniel 5:18, 20, 22-30

What about a lion
in a den of Daniels?

Daniel in the lions' den is a lion tamer. But actually, the true lion tamer is the One who was with Daniel. Maybe it's because His name is also the Lion of Judah. When this Lion is among the Daniels, the scale always tips in heaven's favor.

[19]Very early the next morning, the king got up and hurried out to the lions' den. [20]When he got there, he called out in anguish, "Daniel, servant of the living God! Was your God, whom you serve so faithfully, able to rescue you from the lions?"

[21]Daniel answered, "Long live the king! [22]My God sent his angel to shut the lions' mouths so that they would not hurt me, for I have been found innocent in his sight. And I have not wronged you, Your Majesty."

[23]The king was overjoyed and ordered that Daniel be lifted from the den. Not a scratch was found on him, for he had trusted in his God.

[24]Then the king gave orders to arrest the men who had maliciously accused Daniel. He had them thrown into the lions' den, along with their wives and children. The lions leaped on them and tore them apart before they even hit the floor of the den.

[25]Then King Darius sent this message to the people of every race and nation and language throughout the world: "Peace and prosperity to you!

[26]"I decree that everyone throughout my kingdom should tremble with fear before the God of Daniel.

For he is the living God, and he will endure forever. His kingdom will never be destroyed, and his rule will never end.

[27]He rescues and saves his people; he performs miraculous signs and wonders in the heavens and on earth. He has rescued Daniel from the power of the lions."

~ Daniel 6:19-27

God's foreign paths

Hosea prophesied to the ten tribes shortly before they were destroyed by the Assyrians in 722 BC. One of his most challenging tasks as a prophet was to marry the prostitute Gomer. This marriage was symbolic of Israel's unfaithfulness to God. But it also illustrates God's faithfulness to His people despite their sins.

⁶Soon Gomer became pregnant again and gave birth to a daughter. And the LORD said to Hosea, "Name your daughter Lo-ruhamah—'Not loved'—for I will no longer show love to the people of Israel or forgive them. ⁷But I will show love to the people of Judah. I will free them from their enemies—not with weapons and armies or horses and charioteers, but by my power as the LORD their God."

⁸After Gomer had weaned Lo-ruhamah, she again became pregnant and gave birth to a second son. ⁹And the LORD said, "Name him Lo-ammi—'Not my people'—for Israel is not my people, and I am not their God.

¹⁰"Yet the time will come when Israel's people will be like the sands of the seashore—too many to count! Then, at the place where they were told, 'You are not my people,' it will be said, 'You are children of the living God.' ¹¹Then the people of Judah and Israel will unite together. They will choose one leader for themselves, and they will return from exile together. What a day that will be—the day of Jezreel—when God will again plant his people in his land."

~ Hosea 1:6-11

Healer!

God is not a destroyer. He is a Savior and a Healer. With Him there is always a new beginning. With Him there is always another chance, even if it is the thousandth one. This is what Hosea told the sick people of God. Yet, they never did fully understand the extent of their mortal illness.

¹"Come, let us return to the Lord. He has torn us to pieces; now he will heal us. He has injured us; now he will bandage our wounds.

²In just a short time he will restore us, so that we may live in his presence.

³Oh, that we might know the Lord! Let us press on to know him. He will respond to us as surely as the arrival of dawn or the coming of rains in early spring."

⁴"O Israel and Judah, what should I do with you?" asks the Lord. "For your love vanishes like the morning mist and disappears like dew in the sunlight.

⁵I sent my prophets to cut you to pieces—to slaughter you with my words, with judgments as inescapable as light.

⁶I want you to show love, not offer sacrifices. I want you to know me more than I want burnt offerings.

⁷But like Adam, you broke my covenant and betrayed my trust."

~ Hosea 6:1-7

Endless love

Hosea 11 is a classic passage about God's love for His people. No, not just love, but unselfish, unconditional and limitless love. Like a parent, God cared for Israel from babyhood. And for this reason He did not abandon them in their time of need.

¹"When Israel was a child, I loved him, and I called my son out of Egypt.

²But the more I called to him, the farther he moved from me, offering sacrifices to the images of Baal and burning incense to idols.

³I myself taught Israel how to walk, leading him along by the hand. But he doesn't know or even care that it was I who took care of him.

⁴I led Israel along with my ropes of kindness and love. I lifted the yoke from his neck, and I myself stooped to feed him.

⁵"But since my people refuse to return to me, they will return to Egypt and will be forced to serve Assyria.

⁶War will swirl through their cities; their enemies will crash through their gates. They will destroy them, trapping them in their own evil plans.

⁷For my people are determined to desert me. They call me the Most High, but they don't truly honor me.

⁸"Oh, how can I give you up, Israel? How can I let you go? How can I destroy you like Admah or demolish you like Zeboiim? My heart is torn within me, and my compassion overflows.

⁹No, I will not unleash my fierce anger. I will not completely destroy Israel, for I am God and not a mere mortal. I am the Holy One living among you, and I will not come to destroy."

~ Hosea 11:1-9

Young and old will receive God's Spirit

Joel 2 tells of God's great promise to send His Spirit. The good news was that everyone would share in His coming, both young and old alike. The old men would suddenly dream godly dreams and the young men would have visions of God's great and new acts. At Pentecost this promise came true.

[25]The LORD says, "I will give you back what you lost to the swarming locusts, the hopping locusts, the stripping locusts, and the cutting locusts. It was I who sent this great destroying army against you.

[26]Once again you will have all the food you want, and you will praise the LORD your God, who does these miracles for you. Never again will my people be disgraced.

[27]Then you will know that I am among my people Israel, that I am the LORD your God, and there is no other. Never again will my people be disgraced.

[28]"Then, after doing all those things, I will pour out my Spirit upon all people. Your sons and daughters will prophesy. Your old men will dream dreams, and your young men will see visions.

[29]In those days I will pour out my Spirit even on servants—men and women alike.

[30]And I will cause wonders in the heavens and on the earth—blood and fire and columns of smoke.

[31]The sun will become dark, and the moon will turn blood red before that great and terrible day of the LORD arrives.

[32]But everyone who calls on the name of the LORD will be saved, for some on Mount Zion in Jerusalem will escape, just as the LORD has said. These will be among the survivors whom the LORD has called.

~ Joel 2:25-32

Sheep farmer becomes prophet

Amos was a prophet who was sent from the Southern Kingdom to the Northern Kingdom to make God's will known to them. Amos wasn't a professional religious worker, he was a sheep farmer. How marvelous is God's goodness that He uses ordinary people so powerfully in His service.

¹This message was given to Amos, a shepherd from the town of Tekoa in Judah. He received this message in visions two years before the earthquake, when Uzziah was king of Judah and Jeroboam II, the son of Jehoash, was king of Israel.

²This is what he saw and heard: "The LORD's voice will roar from Zion and thunder from Jerusalem! The lush pastures of the shepherds will dry up; the grass on Mount Carmel will wither and die."

³This is what the LORD says: "The people of Damascus have sinned again and again, and I will not let them go unpunished! They beat down my people in Gilead as grain is threshed with iron sledges.

⁴So I will send down fire on King Hazael's palace, and the fortresses of King Ben-hadad will be destroyed.

⁵I will break down the gates of Damascus and slaughter the people in the valley of Aven. I will destroy the ruler in Beth-eden, and the people of Aram will go as captives to Kir," says the LORD.

⁶This is what the LORD says: "The people of Gaza have sinned again and again, and I will not let them go unpunished! They sent whole villages into exile, selling them as slaves to Edom.

⁷So I will send down fire on the walls of Gaza, and all its fortresses will be destroyed.

~ Amos 1:1-7

God notices injustice

God notices when the poor and weak are entrapped by the powers in authority. It breaks His heart. That is why He sent Amos to protest and to be a voice for the silent. Social injustice always screams against heaven. Add your voice and act in favor of the defenseless ones.

6Come back to the Lord and live! Otherwise, he will roar through Israel like a fire, devouring you completely. Your gods in Bethel won't be able to quench the flames.

7You twist justice, making it a bitter pill for the oppressed. You treat the righteous like dirt.

8It is the Lord who created the stars, the Pleiades and Orion. He turns darkness into morning and day into night. He draws up water from the oceans and pours it down as rain on the land. The Lord is his name! 9With blinding speed and power he destroys the strong, crushing all their defenses. 10How you hate honest judges! How you despise people who tell the truth!

11You trample the poor, stealing their grain through taxes and unfair rent. Therefore, though you build beautiful stone houses, you will never live in them. Though you plant lush vineyards, you will never drink wine from them. 12For I know the vast number of your sins and the depth of your rebellions. You oppress good people by taking bribes and deprive the poor of justice in the courts. 13So those who are smart keep their mouths shut, for it is an evil time.

14Do what is good and run from evil so that you may live! Then the Lord God of Heaven's Armies will be your helper, just as you have claimed. 15Hate evil and love what is good; turn your courts into true halls of justice. Perhaps even yet the Lord God of Heaven's Armies will have mercy on the remnant of his people.

~ Amos 5:6-15

Don't wish for the day of the Lord

Israel were wrong to wish for the Day of the Lord to appear. Why? Because it will be a day of judgment and darkness. People who appear holy, but mock God can expect nothing good on that day. The only thing that will stand are hearts that are repentant and remorseful.

[18] What sorrow awaits you who say, "If only the day of the Lord were here!" You have no idea what you are wishing for. That day will bring darkness, not light.

[19] In that day you will be like a man who runs from a lion— only to meet a bear. Escaping from the bear, he leans his hand against a wall in his house—and he's bitten by a snake.

[20] Yes, the day of the Lord will be dark and hopeless, without a ray of joy or hope.

[21] "I hate all your show and pretense—the hypocrisy of your religious festivals and solemn assemblies.

[22] I will not accept your burnt offerings and grain offerings. I won't even notice all your choice peace offerings.

[23] Away with your noisy hymns of praise! I will not listen to the music of your harps.

[24] Instead, I want to see a mighty flood of justice, an endless river of righteous living.

[25] "Was it to me you were bringing sacrifices and offerings during the forty years in the wilderness, Israel? [26] No, you served your pagan gods—Sakkuth your king god and Kaiwan your star god—the images you made for yourselves. [27] So I will send you into exile, to a land east of Damascus," says the Lord, whose name is the God of Heaven's Armies.

~ Amos 5:18-27

JUNE

True prophets are scarce

"Get out of here, you prophet!" These were the king's words to Amos because his prophecy was so shocking and challenging. Prophets who pronounce heavenly wisdom so eloquently in earthly language are scarce. It's easy to be a conformist, but it's not so easy to be God's mouthpiece.

¹¹He is saying, 'Jeroboam will soon be killed, and the people of Israel will be sent away into exile.'"

¹²Then Amaziah sent orders to Amos: "Get out of here, you prophet! Go on back to the land of Judah, and earn your living by prophesying there! ¹³Don't bother us with your prophecies here in Bethel. This is the king's sanctuary and the national place of worship!"

¹⁴But Amos replied, "I'm not a professional prophet, and I was never trained to be one. I'm just a shepherd, and I take care of sycamore-fig trees. ¹⁵But the LORD called me away from my flock and told me, 'Go and prophesy to my people in Israel.' ¹⁶Now then, listen to this message from the LORD:

"You say, 'Don't prophesy against Israel. Stop preaching against my people.'

¹⁷But this is what the LORD says: 'Your wife will become a prostitute in this city, and your sons and daughters will be killed. Your land will be divided up, and you yourself will die in a foreign land. And the people of Israel will certainly become captives in exile, far from their homeland.'"

~ Amos 7:11-17

Ripe for punishment

It is sad that people can become as ripe for God's punishment as a basket of fruit. This is exactly what happened to Israel. They robbed the poor and broke God's commandments and then expected mercy. But only a heart-felt conversion is enough for God.

¹Then the Sovereign LORD showed me another vision. In it I saw a basket filled with ripe fruit. ²"What do you see, Amos?" he asked. I replied, "A basket full of ripe fruit." Then the LORD said, "Like this fruit, Israel is ripe for punishment! I will not delay their punishment again.

³In that day the singing in the Temple will turn to wailing. Dead bodies will be scattered everywhere. They will be carried out of the city in silence. I, the Sovereign LORD, have spoken!"

⁴Listen to this, you who rob the poor and trample down the needy! ⁵You can't wait for the Sabbath day to be over and the religious festivals to end so you can get back to cheating the helpless. You measure out grain with dishonest measures and cheat the buyer with dishonest scales. ⁶And you mix the grain you sell with chaff swept from the floor. Then you enslave poor people for one piece of silver or a pair of sandals.

⁷Now the LORD has sworn this oath by his own name, the Pride of Israel: "I will never forget the wicked things you have done! ⁸The earth will tremble for your deeds, and everyone will mourn. The ground will rise like the Nile River at floodtime; it will heave up, then sink again.

⁹"In that day," says the Sovereign LORD, "I will make the sun go down at noon and darken the earth while it is still day. ¹⁰I will turn your celebrations into times of mourning and your singing into weeping. You will wear funeral clothes and shave your heads to show your sorrow—as if your only son had died. How very bitter that day will be!"

~ Amos 8:1-10

A worldwide God

Obadiah's prophetic words were not only for the tribes of Judah and Benjamin; God is international and universal. God sees what the nations are doing. Their sins shout against heaven. For this reason He reveals His will to all the nations.

[11]When they were invaded, you stood aloof, refusing to help them. Foreign invaders carried off their wealth and cast lots to divide up Jerusalem, but you acted like one of Israel's enemies.

[12]"You should not have gloated when they exiled your relatives to distant lands. You should not have rejoiced when the people of Judah suffered such misfortune. You should not have spoken arrogantly in that terrible time of trouble.

[13]You should not have plundered the land of Israel when they were suffering such calamity. You should not have gloated over their destruction when they were suffering such calamity. You should not have seized their wealth when they were suffering such calamity.

[14]You should not have stood at the crossroads, killing those who tried to escape. You should not have captured the survivors and handed them over in their terrible time of trouble.

[15]"The day is near when I, the Lord, will judge all godless nations! As you have done to Israel, so it will be done to you. All your evil deeds will fall back on your own heads.

[16]Just as you swallowed up my people on my holy mountain, so you and the surrounding nations will swallow the punishment I pour out on you. Yes, all you nations will drink and stagger and disappear from history."

~ Obadiah v. 11-16

Deserters in God's service

Fugitives don't only try to flee from other people, but they sometimes also try to flee from God, as was the case with Jonah. God wanted him to go to Nineveh, but he headed to Tarshish. Yet God caught up with him in the midst of a storm because it is impossible to escape a heavenly calling.

¹The LORD gave this message to Jonah son of Amittai: ²"Get up and go to the great city of Nineveh. Announce my judgment against it because I have seen how wicked its people are."

³But Jonah got up and went in the opposite direction to get away from the LORD. He went down to the port of Joppa, where he found a ship leaving for Tarshish. He bought a ticket and went on board, hoping to escape from the LORD by sailing to Tarshish.

⁴But the LORD hurled a powerful wind over the sea, causing a violent storm that threatened to break the ship apart.

⁷Then the crew cast lots to see which of them had offended the gods and caused the terrible storm. When they did this, the lots identified Jonah as the culprit. ⁸"Why has this awful storm come down on us?" they demanded. "Who are you? What is your line of work? What country are you from? What is your nationality?"

⁹Jonah answered, "I am a Hebrew, and I worship the LORD, the God of heaven, who made the sea and the land."

~ Jonah 1:1-4, 7-9

When in need, pray

Prayer is not supposed to be a spare wheel, but rather the steering wheel of our lives. But sometimes we learn to pray quickly in times of need. Ask Jonah. The good news is that God is gracious. He even hears those spare-wheel prayers and offers help in times of need.

¹Then Jonah prayed to the Lord his God from inside the fish. ²He said, "I cried out to the Lord in my great trouble, and he answered me. I called to you from the land of the dead, and Lord, you heard me!

³You threw me into the ocean depths, and I sank down to the heart of the sea. The mighty waters engulfed me; I was buried beneath your wild and stormy waves.

⁴Then I said, 'O Lord, you have driven me from your presence. Yet I will look once more toward your holy Temple.'

⁵"I sank beneath the waves, and the waters closed over me. Seaweed wrapped itself around my head.

⁶I sank down to the very roots of the mountains. I was imprisoned in the earth, whose gates lock shut forever. But you, O Lord my God, snatched me from the jaws of death!

⁷As my life was slipping away, I remembered the Lord. And my earnest prayer went out to you in your holy Temple.

⁸Those who worship false gods turn their backs on all God's mercies.

⁹But I will offer sacrifices to you with songs of praise, and I will fulfill all my vows. For my salvation comes from the Lord alone."

¹⁰Then the Lord ordered the fish to spit Jonah out onto the beach.

~ Jonah 2:1-10

God can change His plans

Who said that God's plans are cast in stone? When the Ninevites heard that they were going to be destroyed within forty days, they came to repentance. God there and then decided not to punish them. God is gracious and He willingly postpones or cancels sentences.

¹Then the LORD spoke to Jonah a second time: ²"Get up and go to the great city of Nineveh, and deliver the message I have given you."

³This time Jonah obeyed the LORD's command and went to Nineveh, a city so large that it took three days to see it all. ⁴On the day Jonah entered the city, he shouted to the crowds: "Forty days from now Nineveh will be destroyed!" ⁵The people of Nineveh believed God's message, and from the greatest to the least, they declared a fast and put on burlap to show their sorrow.

⁶When the king of Nineveh heard what Jonah was saying, he stepped down from his throne and took off his royal robes. He dressed himself in burlap and sat on a heap of ashes. ⁷Then the king and his nobles sent this decree throughout the city:

"No one, not even the animals from your herds and flocks, may eat or drink anything at all. ⁸People and animals alike must wear garments of mourning, and everyone must pray earnestly to God. They must turn from their evil ways and stop all their violence. ⁹Who can tell? Perhaps even yet God will change his mind and hold back his fierce anger from destroying us."

¹⁰When God saw what they had done and how they had put a stop to their evil ways, he changed his mind and did not carry out the destruction he had threatened.

~ Jonah 3

God shows more mercy than His prophets

Jonah was furious when God showed mercy to the Gentiles living in Nineveh. He couldn't accept the fact that God could forgive people who looked, spoke and thought different to him. Hence, his small rebellion against heaven. But God then reminded His stubborn prophet that He is in the business of showing grace.

⁴The LORD replied, "Is it right for you to be angry about this?"

⁵Then Jonah went out to the east side of the city and made a shelter to sit under as he waited to see what would happen to the city. ⁶And the LORD God arranged for a leafy plant to grow there, and soon it spread its broad leaves over Jonah's head, shading him from the sun. This eased his discomfort, and Jonah was very grateful for the plant.

⁷But God also arranged for a worm! The next morning at dawn the worm ate through the stem of the plant so that it withered away. ⁸And as the sun grew hot, God arranged for a scorching east wind to blow on Jonah. The sun beat down on his head until he grew faint and wished to die. "Death is certainly better than living like this!" he exclaimed.

⁹Then God said to Jonah, "Is it right for you to be angry because the plant died?"

"Yes," Jonah retorted, "even angry enough to die!"

¹⁰Then the LORD said, "You feel sorry about the plant, though you did nothing to put it there. It came quickly and died quickly. ¹¹But Nineveh has more than 120,000 people living in spiritual darkness, not to mention all the animals. Shouldn't I feel sorry for such a great city?"

~ Jonah 4:4-11

He is coming

Micah said that God is coming. But His coming will not be safe, predictable or controllable. God's appearance will be a day of terror. God's coming will be shocking for those who thought they had God figured out. No one can do that.

³Look! The LORD is coming! He leaves his throne in heaven and tramples the heights of the earth.

⁴The mountains melt beneath his feet and flow into the valleys like wax in a fire, like water pouring down a hill.

⁵And why is this happening? Because of the rebellion of Israel—yes, the sins of the whole nation. Who is to blame for Israel's rebellion? Samaria, its capital city! Where is the center of idolatry in Judah? In Jerusalem, its capital!

⁶"So I, the LORD, will make the city of Samaria a heap of ruins. Her streets will be plowed up for planting vineyards. I will roll the stones of her walls into the valley below, exposing her foundations.

⁷All her carved images will be smashed. All her sacred treasures will be burned. These things were bought with the money earned by her prostitution, and they will now be carried away to pay prostitutes elsewhere."

⁸Therefore, I will mourn and lament. I will walk around barefoot and naked. I will howl like a jackal and moan like an owl.

⁹For my people's wound is too deep to heal. It has reached into Judah, even to the gates of Jerusalem.

~ Micah 1:3-9

God sees the plans of evildoers

It doesn't help to think out evil plans at night. God knows about your plans. He reads the evildoers' thoughts and knows their plans. Their exploitation of the defenseless and weak disgusts Him. You and I must therefore protest against such injustice in His name.

¹What sorrow awaits you who lie awake at night, thinking up evil plans. You rise at dawn and hurry to carry them out, simply because you have the power to do so.

²When you want a piece of land, you find a way to seize it. When you want someone's house, you take it by fraud and violence. You cheat a man of his property, stealing his family's inheritance.

³But this is what the LORD says: "I will reward your evil with evil; you won't be able to pull your neck out of the noose. You will no longer walk around proudly, for it will be a terrible time."

⁴In that day your enemies will make fun of you by singing this song of despair about you: "We are finished, completely ruined! God has confiscated our land, taking it from us. He has given our fields to those who betrayed us."

⁵Others will set your boundaries then, and the LORD's people will have no say in how the land is divided.

⁶"Don't say such things," the people respond. "Don't prophesy like that. Such disasters will never come our way!"

⁷Should you talk that way, O family of Israel? Will the LORD's Spirit have patience with such behavior? If you would do what is right, you would find my words comforting.

~ Micah 2:1-7

Know the difference between right and wrong

The Lord says that the leaders of the people must know the difference between right and wrong and apply it. Otherwise injustice wins. Otherwise wickedness triumphs. God is seeking a society where justice reigns on all levels. He doesn't tolerate things like corruption and fraud.

[1]I said, "Listen, you leaders of Israel! You are supposed to know right from wrong, [2]but you are the very ones who hate good and love evil. You skin my people alive and tear the flesh from their bones.

[3]Yes, you eat my people's flesh, strip off their skin, and break their bones. You chop them up like meat for the cooking pot.

[4]Then you beg the LORD for help in times of trouble! Do you really expect him to answer? After all the evil you have done, he won't even look at you!"

[5]This is what the LORD says: "You false prophets are leading my people astray! You promise peace for those who give you food, but you declare war on those who refuse to feed you.

[6]Now the night will close around you, cutting off all your visions. Darkness will cover you, putting an end to your predictions. The sun will set for you prophets, and your day will come to an end. [7]Then you seers will be put to shame, and you fortune-tellers will be disgraced. And you will cover your faces because there is no answer from God."

[8]But as for me, I am filled with power—with the Spirit of the LORD. I am filled with justice and strength to boldly declare Israel's sin and rebellion.

~ Micah 3:1-8

When the mountains turn against you

Creation is not dead. Micah reminded Israel that God would call the mountains in as witnesses of their unfaithfulness. God's creation is alive. Creation praises and glorifies Him. In the end it's only people who are the big troublemakers.

¹Listen to what the Lord is saying: "Stand up and state your case against me. Let the mountains and hills be called to witness your complaints.

²And now, O mountains, listen to the Lord's complaint! He has a case against his people. He will bring charges against Israel.

³"O my people, what have I done to you? What have I done to make you tired of me? Answer me!

⁴For I brought you out of Egypt and redeemed you from slavery. I sent Moses, Aaron, and Miriam to help you.

⁵Don't you remember, my people, how King Balak of Moab tried to have you cursed and how Balaam son of Beor blessed you instead? And remember your journey from Acacia Grove to Gilgal, when I, the Lord, did everything I could to teach you about my faithfulness."

⁶What can we bring to the Lord? What kind of offerings should we give him? Should we bow before God with offerings of yearling calves?

⁷Should we offer him thousands of rams and ten thousand rivers of olive oil? Should we sacrifice our firstborn children to pay for our sins?

⁸No, O people, the Lord has told you what is good, and this is what he requires of you: to do what is right, to love mercy, and to walk humbly with your God.

~ Micah 6:1-8

God's compassionate heart

God's heart breaks when people walk away from Him. He wants them to be close to Him at all costs. He therefore announces that He will lead them back and that they will again see His might. In this way all the nations of the world will see that He is almighty.

[14]O Lord, protect your people with your shepherd's staff; lead your flock, your special possession. Though they live alone in a thicket on the heights of Mount Carmel, let them graze in the fertile pastures of Bashan and Gilead as they did long ago.

[15]"Yes," says the Lord, "I will do mighty miracles for you, like those I did when I rescued you from slavery in Egypt."

[16]All the nations of the world will stand amazed at what the Lord will do for you. They will be embarrassed at their feeble power. They will cover their mouths in silent awe, deaf to everything around them.

[17]Like snakes crawling from their holes, they will come out to meet the Lord our God. They will fear him greatly, trembling in terror at his presence.

[18]Where is another God like you, who pardons the guilt of the remnant, overlooking the sins of his special people? You will not stay angry with your people forever, because you delight in showing unfailing love.

[19]Once again you will have compassion on us. You will trample our sins under your feet and throw them into the depths of the ocean!

[20]You will show us your faithfulness and unfailing love as you promised to our ancestors Abraham and Jacob long ago.

~ Micah 7:14-20

Be loyal

Stabbing others in the back is not part of a life of faith. God seeks sincerity and loyalty. This is the message from God that the people received through Nahum. God's opposition must step aside and His followers must step closer with great respect. God expects His followers' lives to bear witness of His goodness and favor.

¹This message concerning Nineveh came as a vision to Nahum, who lived in Elkosh.

²The LORD is a jealous God, filled with vengeance and rage. He takes revenge on all who oppose him and continues to rage against his enemies!

³The LORD is slow to get angry, but his power is great, and he never lets the guilty go unpunished. He displays his power in the whirlwind and the storm. The billowing clouds are the dust beneath his feet.

⁴At his command the oceans dry up, and the rivers disappear. The lush pastures of Bashan and Carmel fade, and the green forests of Lebanon wither.

⁵In his presence the mountains quake, and the hills melt away; the earth trembles, and its people are destroyed.

⁶Who can stand before his fierce anger? Who can survive his burning fury? His rage blazes forth like fire, and the mountains crumble to dust in his presence.

⁷The LORD is good, a strong refuge when trouble comes. He is close to those who trust in him.

⁸But he will sweep away his enemies in an overwhelming flood. He will pursue his foes into the darkness of night.

~ Nahum 1:1-8

A complaining prophet

Habakkuk was a complaining prophet. He poured out no less than two great complaints before God in his prophetic book. He begged God to step in and end all the people's injustice and disobedience. How did God respond? Well, He was about to do amazing things.

¹This is the message that the prophet Habakkuk received in a vision. ²How long, O LORD, must I call for help? But you do not listen! "Violence is everywhere!" I cry, but you do not come to save. ³Must I forever see these evil deeds? Why must I watch all this misery? Wherever I look, I see destruction and violence. I am surrounded by people who love to argue and fight. ⁴The law has become paralyzed, and there is no justice in the courts. The wicked far outnumber the righteous, so that justice has become perverted. The LORD's Reply

⁵The LORD replied, "Look around at the nations; look and be amazed! For I am doing something in your own day, something you wouldn't believe even if someone told you about it.

⁶I am raising up the Babylonians, a cruel and violent people. They will march across the world and conquer other lands.

⁷They are notorious for their cruelty and do whatever they like.

⁸Their horses are swifter than cheetahs and fiercer than wolves at dusk. Their charioteers charge from far away. Like eagles, they swoop down to devour their prey.

¹⁰They scoff at kings and princes and scorn all their fortresses. They simply pile ramps of earth against their walls and capture them!

¹¹They sweep past like the wind and are gone. But they are deeply guilty,

~ Habakkuk 1:1-8, 10-11

Prayer is a song

Habakkuk prayed, or more accurately, he sang. Singing in the Lord's presence is also prayer. To sing is to talk to God. It might even be true that we pray with more focus and sincerity when we do it melodiously. Habakkuk brought His deepest need to God in song.

¹This prayer was sung by the prophet Habakkuk:

²I have heard all about you, LORD. I am filled with awe by your amazing works. In this time of our deep need, help us again as you did in years gone by. And in your anger, remember your mercy.

³I see God moving across the deserts from Edom, the Holy One coming from Mount Paran. His brilliant splendor fills the heavens, and the earth is filled with his praise. ⁴His coming is as brilliant as the sunrise. Rays of light flash from his hands, where his awesome power is hidden. ⁵Pestilence marches before him; plague follows close behind. ⁶When he stops, the earth shakes. When he looks, the nations tremble. He shatters the everlasting mountains and levels the eternal hills. He is the Eternal One! ⁷I see the people of Cushan in distress, and the nation of Midian trembling in terror.

⁸Was it in anger, LORD, that you struck the rivers and parted the sea? Were you displeased with them? No, you were sending your chariots of salvation!

⁹You brandished your bow and your quiver of arrows. You split open the earth with flowing rivers.

¹⁰The mountains watched and trembled. Onward swept the raging waters. The mighty deep cried out, lifting its hands to the LORD.

¹¹The sun and moon stood still in the sky as your brilliant arrows flew and your glittering spear flashed.

~ Habakkuk 3:1-11

Be still

Be still before the Sovereign Lord. He seeks quiet, humble people who speak without using words. He seeks people who are sincere and lowly before Him. He seeks people who have learnt how to bow low and acknowledge that He alone is God.

⁷Stand in silence in the presence of the Sovereign LORD, for the awesome day of the LORD's judgment is near. The LORD has prepared his people for a great slaughter and has chosen their executioners.

⁸"On that day of judgment," says the LORD, "I will punish the leaders and princes of Judah and all those following pagan customs.

⁹Yes, I will punish those who participate in pagan worship ceremonies, and those who fill their masters' houses with violence and deceit.

¹⁰"On that day," says the LORD, "a cry of alarm will come from the Fish Gate and echo throughout the New Quarter of the city. And a great crash will sound from the hills.

¹¹Wail in sorrow, all you who live in the market area, for all the merchants and traders will be destroyed.

¹²"I will search with lanterns in Jerusalem's darkest corners to punish those who sit complacent in their sins. They think the LORD will do nothing to them, either good or bad.

¹³So their property will be plundered, their homes will be ransacked. They will build new homes but never live in them. They will plant vineyards but never drink wine from them.

~ Zephaniah 1:7-13

Turn around

Zephaniah was a prophet during the time of King Josiah, the great reformer. His preaching and the prophecies of his contemporary, Jeremiah, contributed to the people's new spirit of dedication to the living God. God doesn't need a great number of people to bring about change, He only needs sincere ones.

¹Gather together—yes, gather together, you shameless nation.

²Gather before judgment begins, before your time to repent is blown away like chaff. Act now, before the fierce fury of the LORD falls and the terrible day of the LORD's anger begins.

³Seek the LORD, all who are humble, and follow his commands. Seek to do what is right and to live humbly. Perhaps even yet the LORD will protect you—protect you from his anger on that day of destruction.

⁴Gaza and Ashkelon will be abandoned, Ashdod and Ekron torn down.

⁵And what sorrow awaits you Philistines who live along the coast and in the land of Canaan, for this judgment is against you, too! The LORD will destroy you until not one of you is left.

⁶The Philistine coast will become a wilderness pasture, a place of shepherd camps and enclosures for sheep and goats.

⁷The remnant of the tribe of Judah will pasture there. They will rest at night in the abandoned houses in Ashkelon. For the LORD their God will visit his people in kindness and restore their prosperity again.

~ Zephaniah 2:1-7

The faithful few

God knows that there will always be a small group of people who will remain obedient to Him. They will remain obedient till the end. They are the ones who stand alone at their posts in the trenches of the faith. Such people bring great honor to God's name.

[8]Therefore, be patient," says the LORD. "Soon I will stand and accuse these evil nations. For I have decided to gather the kingdoms of the earth and pour out my fiercest anger and fury on them. All the earth will be devoured by the fire of my jealousy.

[9]"Then I will purify the speech of all people, so that everyone can worship the LORD together. [10]My scattered people who live beyond the rivers of Ethiopia will come to present their offerings. [11]On that day you will no longer need to be ashamed, for you will no longer be rebels against me. I will remove all proud and arrogant people from among you. There will be no more haughtiness on my holy mountain. [12]Those who are left will be the lowly and humble, for it is they who trust in the name of the LORD. [13]The remnant of Israel will do no wrong; they will never tell lies or deceive one another. They will eat and sleep in safety, and no one will make them afraid."

[14]Sing, O daughter of Zion; shout aloud, O Israel! Be glad and rejoice with all your heart, O daughter of Jerusalem! [15]For the LORD will remove his hand of judgment and will disperse the armies of your enemy. And the LORD himself, the King of Israel, will live among you! At last your troubles will be over, and you will never again fear disaster.

[16]On that day the announcement to Jerusalem will be, "Cheer up, Zion! Don't be afraid! [17]For the LORD your God is living among you. He is a mighty savior. He will take delight in you with gladness. With his love, he will calm all your fears. He will rejoice over you with joyful songs."

~ Zephaniah 3:8-17

Fast and effective

Haggai is surely one of the most successful prophets in Israel. Through four sermons given over four months he moves God's people to start rebuilding the temple. God's prophet first exposes the people's self-centeredness and then motivates them to unconditional devotion to their Lord.

¹On August 29 of the second year of King Darius's reign, the LORD gave a message through the prophet Haggai to Zerubbabel son of Shealtiel, governor of Judah, and to Jeshua son of Jehozadak, the high priest.

²"This is what the LORD of Heaven's Armies says: The people are saying, 'The time has not yet come to rebuild the house of the LORD.'"

³Then the LORD sent this message through the prophet Haggai: ⁴"Why are you living in luxurious houses while my house lies in ruins? ⁵This is what the LORD of Heaven's Armies says: Look at what's happening to you! ⁶You have planted much but harvest little. You eat but are not satisfied. You drink but are still thirsty. You put on clothes but cannot keep warm. Your wages disappear as though you were putting them in pockets filled with holes!

⁷"This is what the LORD of Heaven's Armies says: Look at what's happening to you! ⁸Now go up into the hills, bring down timber, and rebuild my house. Then I will take pleasure in it and be honored, says the LORD. ⁹You hoped for rich harvests, but they were poor. And when you brought your harvest home, I blew it away. Why? Because my house lies in ruins, says the LORD of Heaven's Armies, while all of you are busy building your own fine houses.

~ Haggai 1:1-9

Place God first,
then miracles will happen

Haggai's four candid sermons move an entire nation to step into action and rebuild God's temple. They hear that God will reveal His power anew and will cause the nations that threaten them to fall. God did this because He is gracious toward His people.

¹Then on October 17 of that same year, the LORD sent another message through the prophet Haggai. ²"Say this to Zerubbabel son of Shealtiel, governor of Judah, and to Jeshua son of Jehozadak, the high priest, and to the remnant of God's people there in the land: ³'Does anyone remember this house—this Temple—in its former splendor? How, in comparison, does it look to you now? It must seem like nothing at all! ⁴But now the LORD says: Be strong, Zerubbabel. Be strong, Jeshua son of Jehozadak, the high priest. Be strong, all you people still left in the land. And now get to work, for I am with you, says the LORD of Heaven's Armies. ⁵My Spirit remains among you, just as I promised when you came out of Egypt. So do not be afraid.'

⁶"For this is what the LORD of Heaven's Armies says: In just a little while I will again shake the heavens and the earth, the oceans and the dry land. ⁷I will shake all the nations, and the treasures of all the nations will be brought to this Temple. I will fill this place with glory, says the LORD of Heaven's Armies. ⁸The silver is mine, and the gold is mine, says the LORD of Heaven's Armies. ⁹The future glory of this Temple will be greater than its past glory, says the LORD of Heaven's Armies. And in this place I will bring peace. I, the LORD of Heaven's Armies, have spoken!"

~ Haggai 2:1-9

Turn back to God

God asked for a change in the physical position of His people when He asked them to turn around. They must acknowledge Him and run back to His gracious arms. God asks for repentance and obedience. He asks for hearts that are like clay in His mighty hands. Such people will receive grace upon grace.

[1]In November of the second year of King Darius's reign, the LORD gave this message to the prophet Zechariah son of Berekiah and grandson of Iddo:

[2]"I, the LORD, was very angry with your ancestors. [3]Therefore, say to the people, 'This is what the LORD of Heaven's Armies says: Return to me, and I will return to you, says the LORD of Heaven's Armies.' [4]Don't be like your ancestors who would not listen or pay attention when the earlier prophets said to them, 'This is what the LORD of Heaven's Armies says: Turn from your evil ways, and stop all your evil practices.'

[5]"Where are your ancestors now? They and the prophets are long dead. [6]But everything I said through my servants the prophets happened to your ancestors, just as I said. As a result, they repented and said, 'We have received what we deserved from the LORD of Heaven's Armies. He has done what he said he would do.'"

~ Zechariah 1:1-6

Satan loses

Zechariah is one of the great visionary prophets of Israel in the time of King Darius of Persia. He saw among other things how Satan accused Jeshua the high priest. But he also saw how God stood up for His children. Satan does not have the final say about us.

¹Then the angel showed me Jeshua the high priest standing before the angel of the LORD. The Accuser, Satan, was there at the angel's right hand, making accusations against Jeshua. ²And the LORD said to Satan, "I, the LORD, reject your accusations, Satan. Yes, the LORD, who has chosen Jerusalem, rebukes you. This man is like a burning stick that has been snatched from the fire."

³Jeshua's clothing was filthy as he stood there before the angel. ⁴So the angel said to the others standing there, "Take off his filthy clothes." And turning to Jeshua he said, "See, I have taken away your sins, and now I am giving you these fine new clothes."

⁵Then I said, "They should also place a clean turban on his head." So they put a clean priestly turban on his head and dressed him in new clothes while the angel of the LORD stood by.

⁶Then the angel of the LORD spoke very solemnly to Jeshua and said, ⁷"This is what the LORD of Heaven's Armies says: If you follow my ways and carefully serve me, then you will be given authority over my Temple and its courtyards. I will let you walk among these others standing here.

⁸"Listen to me, O Jeshua the high priest, and all you other priests. You are symbols of things to come. Soon I am going to bring my servant, the Branch.

~ Zechariah 3:1-8

Just pleasing yourself?

How often do our religious activities concern ourselves rather than God? This is what Zechariah accused the priests of. All their religious feasts were just there to honor themselves and not God. This is why they, and we, should come to repentance.

¹On December 7 of the fourth year of King Darius's reign, another message came to Zechariah from the LORD. ²The people of Bethel had sent Sharezer and Regemmelech, along with their attendants, to seek the LORD's favor. ³They were to ask this question of the prophets and the priests at the Temple of the LORD of Heaven's Armies: "Should we continue to mourn and fast each summer on the anniversary of the Temple's destruction, as we have done for so many years?"

⁴The LORD of Heaven's Armies sent me this message in reply: ⁵"Say to all your people and your priests, 'During these seventy years of exile, when you fasted and mourned in the summer and in early autumn, was it really for me that you were fasting? ⁶And even now in your holy festivals, aren't you eating and drinking just to please yourselves? ⁷Isn't this the same message the LORD proclaimed through the prophets in years past when Jerusalem and the towns of Judah were bustling with people, and the Negev and the foothills of Judah were well populated?'"

⁸Then this message came to Zechariah from the LORD: ⁹"This is what the LORD of Heaven's Armies says: Judge fairly, and show mercy and kindness to one another. ¹⁰Do not oppress widows, orphans, foreigners, and the poor. And do not scheme against each other."

~ Zechariah 7:1-10

The King is coming

Zechariah 9 tells of the king who is coming to save his people. He is humble and comes riding on a donkey. And yet, this king is mighty and great. No wonder that the New Testament writers applied these words to Jesus. He is indeed our King.

⁹Rejoice, O people of Zion! Shout in triumph, O people of Jerusalem! Look, your king is coming to you. He is righteous and victorious, yet he is humble, riding on a donkey—riding on a donkey's colt. ¹⁰I will remove the battle chariots from Israel and the warhorses from Jerusalem. I will destroy all the weapons used in battle, and your king will bring peace to the nations. His realm will stretch from sea to sea and from the Euphrates River to the ends of the earth.

¹¹Because of the covenant I made with you, sealed with blood, I will free your prisoners from death in a waterless dungeon. ¹²Come back to the place of safety, all you prisoners who still have hope! I promise this very day that I will repay two blessings for each of your troubles. ¹³Judah is my bow, and Israel is my arrow. Jerusalem is my sword, and like a warrior, I will brandish it against the Greeks.

¹⁴The LORD will appear above his people; his arrows will fly like lightning! The Sovereign LORD will sound the ram's horn and attack like a whirlwind from the southern desert. ¹⁵The LORD of Heaven's Armies will protect his people, and they will defeat their enemies by hurling great stones. They will shout in battle as though drunk with wine. They will be filled with blood like a bowl, drenched with blood like the corners of the altar.

¹⁶On that day the LORD their God will rescue his people, just as a shepherd rescues his sheep. They will sparkle in his land like jewels in a crown. ¹⁷How wonderful and beautiful they will be!

~ Zechariah 9:9-17

God's people have a future

God promises His people that He is going to do great things. Zechariah proclaims that God will remove all the idols from the land. He will also make sure that the prophets are sincere and will not mislead the people through their false words.

¹"On that day a fountain will be opened for the dynasty of David and for the people of Jerusalem, a fountain to cleanse them from all their sins and impurity.

²"And on that day," says the LORD of Heaven's Armies, "I will erase idol worship throughout the land, so that even the names of the idols will be forgotten. I will remove from the land both the false prophets and the spirit of impurity that came with them. ³If anyone continues to prophesy, his own father and mother will tell him, 'You must die, for you have prophesied lies in the name of the LORD.' And as he prophesies, his own father and mother will stab him.

⁴"On that day people will be ashamed to claim the prophetic gift. No one will pretend to be a prophet by wearing prophet's clothes.

⁷"Awake, O sword, against my shepherd, the man who is my partner," says the LORD of Heaven's Armies. "Strike down the shepherd, and the sheep will be scattered, and I will turn against the lambs.

⁸Two-thirds of the people in the land will be cut off and die," says the LORD. "But one-third will be left in the land.

⁹I will bring that group through the fire and make them pure. I will refine them like silver and purify them like gold. They will call on my name, and I will answer them. I will say, 'These are my people,' and they will say, 'The LORD is our God.'"

~ Zechariah 13:1-4, 7-9

I love you

The Lord says that "I have always loved you." What an opening statement to a book of the Bible! Malachi can't wait to reveal God's heart. God loves His people. But the people often doubt it. How tragic that people so easily reject God's goodness.

¹This is the message that the LORD gave to Israel through the prophet Malachi.

²"I have always loved you," says the LORD.

But you retort, "Really? How have you loved us?"

And the LORD replies, "This is how I showed my love for you: I loved your ancestor Jacob, ³but I rejected his brother, Esau, and devastated his hill country. I turned Esau's inheritance into a desert for jackals." ⁴Esau's descendants in Edom may say, "We have been shattered, but we will rebuild the ruins."

But the LORD of Heaven's Armies replies, "They may try to rebuild, but I will demolish them again. Their country will be known as 'The Land of Wickedness,' and their people will be called 'The People with Whom the LORD Is Forever Angry.' ⁵When you see the destruction for yourselves, you will say, 'Truly, the LORD's greatness reaches far beyond Israel's borders!'"

⁶The LORD of Heaven's Armies says to the priests: "A son honors his father, and a servant respects his master. If I am your father and master, where are the honor and respect I deserve? You have shown contempt for my name!

"But you ask, 'How have we ever shown contempt for your name?'

⁷"You have shown contempt by offering defiled sacrifices on my altar.

"Then you ask, 'How have we defiled the sacrifices?'

"You defile them by saying the altar of the LORD deserves no respect.

~ Malachi 1:1-7

Unfaithfulness doesn't work

It is impossible to be unfaithful in your marriage and think that you will remain in God's favor. God sees through such hypocrisy. This is what Malachi had to say to all the unfaithful men in Israel. God seeks holy marriages and faithful spouses.

¹³Here is another thing you do. You cover the LORD's altar with tears, weeping and groaning because he pays no attention to your offerings and doesn't accept them with pleasure. ¹⁴You cry out, "Why doesn't the LORD accept my worship?" I'll tell you why! Because the LORD witnessed the vows you and your wife made when you were young. But you have been unfaithful to her, though she remained your faithful partner, the wife of your marriage vows.

¹⁵Didn't the LORD make you one with your wife? In body and spirit you are his. And what does he want? Godly children from your union. So guard your heart; remain loyal to the wife of your youth. ¹⁶"For I hate divorce!" says the LORD, the God of Israel. "To divorce your wife is to overwhelm her with cruelty," says the LORD of Heaven's Armies. "So guard your heart; do not be unfaithful to your wife."

¹⁷You have wearied the LORD with your words.

"How have we wearied him?" you ask.

You have wearied him by saying that all who do evil are good in the LORD's sight, and he is pleased with them. You have wearied him by asking, "Where is the God of justice?"

~ Malachi 2:13-17

Don't rob God

The Lord says that not to give your full financial offering to the Lord is to rob heaven. He also says that we must test Him by giving generously and then see if He does not open the windows of heaven for us.

⁶"I am the LORD, and I do not change. That is why you descendants of Jacob are not already destroyed. ⁷Ever since the days of your ancestors, you have scorned my decrees and failed to obey them. Now return to me, and I will return to you," says the LORD of Heaven's Armies.

"But you ask, 'How can we return when we have never gone away?'

⁸"Should people cheat God? Yet you have cheated me!

"But you ask, 'What do you mean? When did we ever cheat you?'

"You have cheated me of the tithes and offerings due to me. ⁹You are under a curse, for your whole nation has been cheating me. ¹⁰Bring all the tithes into the storehouse so there will be enough food in my Temple. If you do," says the LORD of Heaven's Armies, "I will open the windows of heaven for you. I will pour out a blessing so great you won't have enough room to take it in! Try it! Put me to the test! ¹¹Your crops will be abundant, for I will guard them from insects and disease. Your grapes will not fall from the vine before they are ripe," says the LORD of Heaven's Armies. ¹²"Then all nations will call you blessed, for your land will be such a delight," says the LORD of Heaven's Armies.

~ Malachi 3:6-12

The day that will burn

God's great day is coming. Malachi says that it is a day that will burn like a furnace. Who will remain standing? Only those who are pure in heart and conduct. On that day those who humbly serve the Lord will shine like stars in God's hand.

¹The LORD of Heaven's Armies says, "The day of judgment is coming, burning like a furnace. On that day the arrogant and the wicked will be burned up like straw. They will be consumed—roots, branches, and all.

²"But for you who fear my name, the Sun of Righteousness will rise with healing in his wings. And you will go free, leaping with joy like calves let out to pasture. ³On the day when I act, you will tread upon the wicked as if they were dust under your feet," says the LORD of Heaven's Armies.

⁴"Remember to obey the Law of Moses, my servant—all the decrees and regulations that I gave him on Mount Sinai for all Israel.

⁵"Look, I am sending you the prophet Elijah before the great and dreadful day of the LORD arrives. ⁶His preaching will turn the hearts of fathers to their children, and the hearts of children to their fathers. Otherwise I will come and strike the land with a curse."

~ Malachi 4:1-6

The Child is coming

How surprisingly different is the arrival of God's Child on earth. He comes in a strange, if not shocking, manner. It takes an angel to convince Joseph of the true facts. Yet, this is how God's Son prefers to make Himself known. Even today, He is still way out of the box!

[18]This is how Jesus the Messiah was born. His mother, Mary, was engaged to be married to Joseph. But before the marriage took place, while she was still a virgin, she became pregnant through the power of the Holy Spirit. [19]Joseph, her fiancé, was a good man and did not want to disgrace her publicly, so he decided to break the engagement quietly.

[20]As he considered this, an angel of the Lord appeared to him in a dream. "Joseph, son of David," the angel said, "do not be afraid to take Mary as your wife. For the child within her was conceived by the Holy Spirit. [21]And she will have a son, and you are to name him Jesus, for he will save his people from their sins."

[22]All of this occurred to fulfill the Lord's message through his prophet:

[23]"Look! The virgin will conceive a child! She will give birth to a son, and they will call him Immanuel, which means 'God is with us.'"

[24]When Joseph woke up, he did as the angel of the Lord commanded and took Mary as his wife. [25]But he did not have sexual relations with her until her son was born. And Joseph named him Jesus.

~ Matthew 1:18-25

JULY

Clear the road

Road builders are important people because without them we wouldn't be able to travel. John the Baptist was Jesus' road builder. It was his job to make the Messiah's path straight and even. John also explains the instructions to every potential traveler. He says that you must be converted before you can travel on Christ's road.

[1]In those days John the Baptist came to the Judean wilderness and began preaching. His message was, [2]"Repent of your sins and turn to God, for the Kingdom of Heaven is near."

[3]The prophet Isaiah was speaking about John when he said, "He is a voice shouting in the wilderness, 'Prepare the way for the LORD's coming! Clear the road for him!'"

[4]John's clothes were woven from coarse camel hair, and he wore a leather belt around his waist. For food he ate locusts and wild honey. [5]People from Jerusalem and from all of Judea and all over the Jordan Valley went out to see and hear John. [6]And when they confessed their sins, he baptized them in the Jordan River.

[7]But when he saw many Pharisees and Sadducees coming to watch him baptize, he denounced them. "You brood of snakes!" he exclaimed. "Who warned you to flee God's coming wrath? [8]Prove by the way you live that you have repented of your sins and turned to God."

~ Matthew 3:1-8

The world champion

Jesus and the devil confronted each other in the desert and Jesus won all four rounds. Jesus is not only the world champion, but the champion of the universe. All power in heaven and on earth is His. Christ is in control – not the devil.

¹Then Jesus was led by the Spirit into the wilderness to be tempted there by the devil. ²For forty days and forty nights he fasted and became very hungry. ³During that time the devil came and said to him, "If you are the Son of God, tell these stones to become loaves of bread."

⁴But Jesus told him, "No! The Scriptures say, 'People do not live by bread alone, but by every word that comes from the mouth of God.'"

⁵Then the devil took him to the holy city, Jerusalem, to the highest point of the Temple, ⁶and said, "If you are the Son of God, jump off! For the Scriptures say, 'He will order his angels to protect you. And they will hold you up with their hands so you won't even hurt your foot on a stone.'"

⁷Jesus responded, "The Scriptures also say, 'You must not test the Lord your God.'"

⁸Next the devil took him to the peak of a very high mountain and showed him all the kingdoms of the world and their glory. ⁹"I will give it all to you," he said, "if you will kneel down and worship me."

¹⁰"Get out of here, Satan," Jesus told him. "For the Scriptures say, 'You must worship the Lord your God and serve only him.'"

¹¹Then the devil went away, and angels came and took care of Jesus.

~ Matthew 4:1-11

Sermon on the Mount

The Sermon on the Mount is the new law for God's kingdom. Jesus teaches us that relationships win in God's kingdom, even your relationship with your enemies. You must walk the second mile for them and turn the other cheek. You must love your enemies.

[38]"You have heard the law that says the punishment must match the injury: 'An eye for an eye, and a tooth for a tooth.' [39]But I say, do not resist an evil person! If someone slaps you on the right cheek, offer the other cheek also. [40]If you are sued in court and your shirt is taken from you, give your coat, too. [41]If a soldier demands that you carry his gear for a mile, carry it two miles. [42]Give to those who ask, and don't turn away from those who want to borrow.

[43]"You have heard the law that says, 'Love your neighbor' and hate your enemy. [44]But I say, love your enemies! Pray for those who persecute you! [45]In that way, you will be acting as true children of your Father in heaven. For he gives his sunlight to both the evil and the good, and he sends rain on the just and the unjust alike. [46]If you love only those who love you, what reward is there for that? Even corrupt tax collectors do that much. [47]If you are kind only to your friends, how are you different from anyone else? Even pagans do that. [48]But you are to be perfect, even as your Father in heaven is perfect."

~ Matthew 5:38-48

Celebrate

How can you fast at a wedding? It's a time to celebrate. The heavenly Groom is here. Jesus is among us. This is reason enough to rejoice and be glad. It is a time to pour out the new wine and put on new heavenly garments. Get dressed and share in the celebration.

¹⁴One day the disciples of John the Baptist came to Jesus and asked him, "Why don't your disciples fast like we do and the Pharisees do?"

¹⁵Jesus replied, "Do wedding guests mourn while celebrating with the groom? Of course not. But someday the groom will be taken away from them, and then they will fast.

¹⁶"Besides, who would patch old clothing with new cloth? For the new patch would shrink and rip away from the old cloth, leaving an even bigger tear than before.

¹⁷"And no one puts new wine into old wineskins. For the old skins would burst from the pressure, spilling the wine and ruining the skins. New wine is stored in new wineskins so that both are preserved."

~ Matthew 9:14-17

Peace in the midst of unrest

It is wrong to think that Jesus wants to be everybody's best friend and tries to keep the whole world happy. To follow Him is costly. Think carefully, following Him is not a popular choice today; yet it is the only right choice to make.

[34]"Don't imagine that I came to bring peace to the earth! I came not to bring peace, but a sword.

[35]'I have come to set a man against his father, a daughter against her mother, and a daughter-in-law against her mother-in-law. [36]Your enemies will be right in your own household!'

[37]"If you love your father or mother more than you love me, you are not worthy of being mine; or if you love your son or daughter more than me, you are not worthy of being mine. [38]If you refuse to take up your cross and follow me, you are not worthy of being mine. [39]If you cling to your life, you will lose it; but if you give up your life for me, you will find it.

[40]"Anyone who receives you receives me, and anyone who receives me receives the Father who sent me. [41]If you receive a prophet as one who speaks for God, you will be given the same reward as a prophet. And if you receive righteous people because of their righteousness, you will be given a reward like theirs. [42]And if you give even a cup of cold water to one of the least of my followers, you will surely be rewarded."

~ Matthew 10:34-42

Walking on water

Jesus was among storms more often than in safe harbors. He effortlessly walked on water. His purpose? To find and save those who are drowning. Your mission? To walk toward the storm with Jesus. There, in the midst of the storm, you are safe with Him.

25About three o'clock in the morning Jesus came toward them, walking on the water. 26When the disciples saw him walking on the water, they were terrified. In their fear, they cried out, "It's a ghost!"

27But Jesus spoke to them at once. "Don't be afraid," he said. "Take courage. I am here!"

28Then Peter called to him, "Lord, if it's really you, tell me to come to you, walking on the water."

29"Yes, come," Jesus said.

So Peter went over the side of the boat and walked on the water toward Jesus. 30But when he saw the strong wind and the waves, he was terrified and began to sink. "Save me, Lord!" he shouted.

31Jesus immediately reached out and grabbed him. "You have so little faith," Jesus said. "Why did you doubt me?"

32When they climbed back into the boat, the wind stopped.

33Then the disciples worshiped him. "You really are the Son of God!" they exclaimed.

~ Matthew 14:25-33

The rich young man

The rich young man's problem was his wealth. It blocked his path to God's heart. He had to learn to give it away, but he couldn't. He let the opportunity of a lifetime slip through his fingers. Please don't make the same mistake.

¹⁶Someone came to Jesus with this question: "Teacher, what good deed must I do to have eternal life?"

¹⁷"Why ask me about what is good?" Jesus replied. "There is only One who is good. But to answer your question—if you want to receive eternal life, keep the commandments."

¹⁸"Which ones?" the man asked.

And Jesus replied: "'You must not murder. You must not commit adultery. You must not steal. You must not testify falsely. ¹⁹Honor your father and mother. Love your neighbor as yourself.'"

²⁰"I've obeyed all these commandments," the young man replied. "What else must I do?"

²¹Jesus told him, "If you want to be perfect, go and sell all your possessions and give the money to the poor, and you will have treasure in heaven. Then come, follow me." ²²But when the young man heard this, he went away sad, for he had many possessions.

²³Then Jesus said to his disciples, "I tell you the truth, it is very hard for a rich person to enter the Kingdom of Heaven. ²⁴I'll say it again—it is easier for a camel to go through the eye of a needle than for a rich person to enter the Kingdom of God!"

~ Matthew 19:16-24

Keep your suitcase packed

My grandma always used to say that we must keep our suitcase packed and ready, because the Lord can come and fetch us at any time. Jesus emphasizes how unexpected His Second Coming will be in Matthew 24-25. We don't know when He will return, so our only preparation for it is to live holy lives.

¹"Then the Kingdom of Heaven will be like ten bridesmaids who took their lamps and went to meet the bridegroom. ²Five of them were foolish, and five were wise. ³The five who were foolish didn't take enough olive oil for their lamps, ⁴but the other five were wise enough to take along extra oil. ⁵When the bridegroom was delayed, they all became drowsy and fell asleep. ⁶"At midnight they were roused by the shout, 'Look, the bridegroom is coming! Come out and meet him!'

⁷"All the bridesmaids got up and prepared their lamps. ⁸Then the five foolish ones asked the others, 'Please give us some of your oil because our lamps are going out.'

⁹"But the others replied, 'We don't have enough for all of us. Go to a shop and buy some for yourselves.'

¹⁰"But while they were gone to buy oil, the bridegroom came. Then those who were ready went in with him to the marriage feast, and the door was locked. ¹¹Later, when the other five bridesmaids returned, they stood outside, calling, 'Lord! Lord! Open the door for us!'

¹²"But he called back, 'Believe me, I don't know you!'

¹³"So you, too, must keep watch! For you do not know the day or hour of my return."

~ Matthew 25:1-13

Put God's will first

While Jesus sweated drops of blood in Gethsemane, God's will was the most important thing to Him. For Him it was all about God, even though it meant His own suffering and death. Submitting to God is the only way to salvation. If Jesus had not put God's will first, we would all still be trapped in darkness.

36 Jesus went with them to the olive grove called Gethsemane, and he said, "Sit here while I go over there to pray." 37 He took Peter and Zebedee's two sons, James and John, and he became anguished and distressed. 38 He told them, "My soul is crushed with grief to the point of death. Stay here and keep watch with me."

39 He went on a little farther and bowed with his face to the ground, praying, "My Father! If it is possible, let this cup of suffering be taken away from me. Yet I want your will to be done, not mine."

40 Then he returned to the disciples and found them asleep. He said to Peter, "Couldn't you watch with me even one hour? 41 Keep watch and pray, so that you will not give in to temptation. For the spirit is willing, but the body is weak!"

42 Then Jesus left them a second time and prayed, "My Father! If this cup cannot be taken away unless I drink it, your will be done."

~ Matthew 26:36-42

The sun stopped shining

As Jesus died on the cross, the sun lost all its strength. Out of the blue, God switched the sun off. How could the sun keep shining when the Son of Righteousness was dying on Golgotha? How could there be light as Jesus took the sins of the world upon Himself?

⁴⁵At noon, darkness fell across the whole land until three o'clock. ⁴⁶At about three o'clock, Jesus called out with a loud voice, *"Eli, Eli, lema sabachthani?"* which means "My God, my God, why have you abandoned me?"

⁴⁷Some of the bystanders misunderstood and thought he was calling for the prophet Elijah. ⁴⁸One of them ran and filled a sponge with sour wine, holding it up to him on a reed stick so he could drink. ⁴⁹But the rest said, "Wait! Let's see whether Elijah comes to save him."

⁵⁰Then Jesus shouted out again, and he released his spirit. ⁵¹At that moment the curtain in the sanctuary of the Temple was torn in two, from top to bottom. The earth shook, rocks split apart, ⁵²and tombs opened. The bodies of many godly men and women who had died were raised from the dead. ⁵³They left the cemetery after Jesus' resurrection, went into the holy city of Jerusalem, and appeared to many people.

⁵⁴The Roman officer and the other soldiers at the crucifixion were terrified by the earthquake and all that had happened. They said, "This man truly was the Son of God!"

⁵⁵And many women who had come from Galilee with Jesus to care for him were watching from a distance. ⁵⁶Among them were Mary Magdalene, Mary (the mother of James and Joseph), and the mother of James and John, the sons of Zebedee.

~ Matthew 27:45-56

Jesus is with us

Jesus' last earthly words, as recorded by Matthew, ended on a high note. He announced His permanent presence with us. Jesus has not left us. The resurrected Jesus is present with His church at all times. This is reason to be joyful and celebrate.

¹¹As the women were on their way, some of the guards went into the city and told the leading priests what had happened. ¹²A meeting with the elders was called, and they decided to give the soldiers a large bribe. ¹³They told the soldiers, "You must say, 'Jesus' disciples came during the night while we were sleeping, and they stole his body.' ¹⁴If the governor hears about it, we'll stand up for you so you won't get in trouble."

¹⁵So the guards accepted the bribe and said what they were told to say. Their story spread widely among the Jews, and they still tell it today.

¹⁶Then the eleven disciples left for Galilee, going to the mountain where Jesus had told them to go. ¹⁷When they saw him, they worshiped him—but some of them doubted!

¹⁸Jesus came and told his disciples, "I have been given all authority in heaven and on earth. ¹⁹Therefore, go and make disciples of all the nations, baptizing them in the name of the Father and the Son and the Holy Spirit. ²⁰Teach these new disciples to obey all the commands I have given you. And be sure of this: I am with you always, even to the end of the age."

~ Matthew 28:11-20

Newsflash!

A newsflash immediately attracts people's attention. It means that you are going to hear, see or read something important. Mark 1:1 is a heavenly newsflash. It begins with the good news that Jesus Christ has come to us. The Son of God has appeared to save us.

¹This is the Good News about Jesus the Messiah, the Son of God. It began ²just as the prophet Isaiah had written:

"Look, I am sending my messenger ahead of you, and he will prepare your way. ³He is a voice shouting in the wilderness, 'Prepare the way for the Lᴏʀᴅ's coming! Clear the road for him!'"

⁴This messenger was John the Baptist. He was in the wilderness and preached that people should be baptized to show that they had repented of their sins and turned to God to be forgiven. ⁵All of Judea, including all the people of Jerusalem, went out to see and hear John. And when they confessed their sins, he baptized them in the Jordan River. ⁶His clothes were woven from coarse camel hair, and he wore a leather belt around his waist. For food he ate locusts and wild honey.

⁷John announced: "Someone is coming soon who is greater than I am—so much greater that I'm not even worthy to stoop down like a slave and untie the straps of his sandals. ⁸I baptize you with water, but he will baptize you with the Holy Spirit!"

⁹One day Jesus came from Nazareth in Galilee, and John baptized him in the Jordan River. ¹⁰As Jesus came up out of the water, he saw the heavens splitting apart and the Holy Spirit descending on him like a dove. ¹¹And a voice from heaven said, "You are my dearly loved Son, and you bring me great joy."

~ Mark 1:1-11

Follow Me

Levi learned that there is only one calling for every believer – the call to discipleship. We are all called to follow Jesus full-time. It doesn't matter what our occupation is, we are permanently in Jesus' service, 24/7. Along with Levi, we are lifelong disciples of Jesus.

¹³Then Jesus went out to the lakeshore again and taught the crowds that were coming to him. ¹⁴As he walked along, he saw Levi son of Alphaeus sitting at his tax collector's booth. "Follow me and be my disciple," Jesus said to him. So Levi got up and followed him.

¹⁵Later, Levi invited Jesus and his disciples to his home as dinner guests, along with many tax collectors and other disreputable sinners. (There were many people of this kind among Jesus' followers.) ¹⁶But when the teachers of religious law who were Pharisees saw him eating with tax collectors and other sinners, they asked his disciples, "Why does he eat with such scum?"

¹⁷When Jesus heard this, he told them, "Healthy people don't need a doctor—sick people do. I have come to call not those who think they are righteous, but those who know they are sinners."

~ Mark 2:13-17

The unforgivable sin

The religious leaders said that Jesus was possessed by Satan and that Satan gave Him power to drive out evil spirits. Jesus proved them wrong. The only Spirit that Jesus was concerned with was the Holy Spirit. He said that any blasphemy against the Spirit was unforgivable.

²⁰One time Jesus entered a house, and the crowds began to gather again. Soon he and his disciples couldn't even find time to eat. ²¹When his family heard what was happening, they tried to take him away. "He's out of his mind," they said.

²²But the teachers of religious law who had arrived from Jerusalem said, "He's possessed by Satan, the prince of demons. That's where he gets the power to cast out demons."

²³Jesus called them over and responded with an illustration. "How can Satan cast out Satan?" he asked. ²⁴"A kingdom divided by civil war will collapse. ²⁵Similarly, a family splintered by feuding will fall apart. ²⁶And if Satan is divided and fights against himself, how can he stand? He would never survive. ²⁷Let me illustrate this further. Who is powerful enough to enter the house of a strong man like Satan and plunder his goods? Only someone even stronger—someone who could tie him up and then plunder his house.

²⁸"I tell you the truth, all sin and blasphemy can be forgiven, ²⁹but anyone who blasphemes the Holy Spirit will never be forgiven. This is a sin with eternal consequences."

³⁰He told them this because they were saying, "He's possessed by an evil spirit."

~ Mark 3:20-30

The Kingdom is independent

Jesus told many parables about God's new world. One such parable was when He compared the Kingdom to seed that grew by itself. The Kingdom is not dependent on human effort or hard work. God maintains His Kingdom and makes it grow.

[26]Jesus also said, "The Kingdom of God is like a farmer who scatters seed on the ground. [27]Night and day, while he's asleep or awake, the seed sprouts and grows, but he does not understand how it happens. [28]The earth produces the crops on its own. First a leaf blade pushes through, then the heads of wheat are formed, and finally the grain ripens. [29]And as soon as the grain is ready, the farmer comes and harvests it with a sickle, for the harvest time has come."

[30]Jesus said, "How can I describe the Kingdom of God? What story should I use to illustrate it? [31]It is like a mustard seed planted in the ground. It is the smallest of all seeds, [32]but it becomes the largest of all garden plants; it grows long branches, and birds can make nests in its shade."

[33]Jesus used many similar stories and illustrations to teach the people as much as they could understand. [34]In fact, in his public ministry he never taught without using parables; but afterward, when he was alone with his disciples, he explained everything to them.

~ Mark 4:26-34

What is in your hand?

Jesus fed thousands with the five loaves of bread and two fish in the disciples' hands. God can perform miracles with the little we have in our hands, if only we trust Him with it. Then the kingdom of God floods over all human boundaries.

35Late in the afternoon his disciples came to him and said, "This is a remote place, and it's already getting late. 36Send the crowds away so they can go to the nearby farms and villages and buy something to eat."

37But Jesus said, "You feed them."

"With what?" they asked. "We'd have to work for months to earn enough money to buy food for all these people!"

38"How much bread do you have?" he asked. "Go and find out."

They came back and reported, "We have five loaves of bread and two fish."

39Then Jesus told the disciples to have the people sit down in groups on the green grass. 40So they sat down in groups of fifty or a hundred.

41Jesus took the five loaves and two fish, looked up toward heaven, and blessed them. Then, breaking the loaves into pieces, he kept giving the bread to the disciples so they could distribute it to the people. He also divided the fish for everyone to share. 42They all ate as much as they wanted, 43and afterward, the disciples picked up twelve baskets of leftover bread and fish. 44A total of 5,000 men and their families were fed from those loaves!

~ Mark 6:35-44

Do you wonder about Jesus?

The question about who Jesus really is, is not a new question. Jesus asked the disciples, "Who do people say I am?" Peter gave the only correct answer, "You are the Messiah." This is the answer of all answers. This answer is equal to eternal life.

²²When they arrived at Bethsaida, some people brought a blind man to Jesus, and they begged him to touch the man and heal him. ²³Jesus took the blind man by the hand and led him out of the village. Then, spitting on the man's eyes, he laid his hands on him and asked, "Can you see anything now?"

²⁴The man looked around. "Yes," he said, "I see people, but I can't see them very clearly. They look like trees walking around."

²⁵Then Jesus placed his hands on the man's eyes again, and his eyes were opened. His sight was completely restored, and he could see everything clearly. ²⁶Jesus sent him away, saying, "Don't go back into the village on your way home."

²⁷Jesus and his disciples left Galilee and went up to the villages near Caesarea Philippi. As they were walking along, he asked them, "Who do people say I am?"

²⁸"Well," they replied, "some say John the Baptist, some say Elijah, and others say you are one of the other prophets."

²⁹Then he asked them, "But who do you say I am?"

Peter replied, "You are the Messiah."

³⁰But Jesus warned them not to tell anyone about him.

~ Mark 8:22-30

Holy marriages

Jesus restores broken marriages. That's why He takes marriage back to paradise in Mark 10. One man and one woman in lifelong harmony before God is the original heavenly plan.

¹Then Jesus left Capernaum and went down to the region of Judea and into the area east of the Jordan River. Once again crowds gathered around him, and as usual he was teaching them.

²Some Pharisees came and tried to trap him with this question: "Should a man be allowed to divorce his wife?"

³Jesus answered them with a question: "What did Moses say in the law about divorce?"

⁴"Well, he permitted it," they replied. "He said a man can give his wife a written notice of divorce and send her away."

⁵But Jesus responded, "He wrote this commandment only as a concession to your hard hearts. ⁶But 'God made them male and female' from the beginning of creation. ⁷This explains why a man leaves his father and mother and is joined to his wife, ⁸and the two are united into one.' Since they are no longer two but one, ⁹let no one split apart what God has joined together."

¹⁰Later, when he was alone with his disciples in the house, they brought up the subject again. ¹¹He told them, "Whoever divorces his wife and marries someone else commits adultery against her. ¹²And if a woman divorces her husband and marries someone else, she commits adultery."

~ Mark 10:1-12

Give God your service

Give to Caesar what belongs to Caesar. And what might that be? Money! Jesus says that we must pay our taxes. But we must also give to God what belongs to Him. He has the right to our entire lives. Therefore we need to be living sacrifices in His service.

¹³Later the leaders sent some Pharisees and supporters of Herod to trap Jesus into saying something for which he could be arrested. ¹⁴"Teacher," they said, "we know how honest you are. You are impartial and don't play favorites. You teach the way of God truthfully. Now tell us—is it right to pay taxes to Caesar or not? ¹⁵Should we pay them, or shouldn't we?"

Jesus saw through their hypocrisy and said, "Why are you trying to trap me? Show me a Roman coin, and I'll tell you." ¹⁶When they handed it to him, he asked, "Whose picture and title are stamped on it?"

"Caesar's," they replied.

¹⁷"Well, then," Jesus said, "give to Caesar what belongs to Caesar, and give to God what belongs to God."

His reply completely amazed them.

~ Mark 12:13-17

Extravagant living

It's good to be thrifty. But please be extravagant when it comes to Jesus. Learn from the woman in Bethany who spent more than a year's income on a jar of expensive perfume which she poured on Jesus' feet. Spend your life on God in His service, it will pay eternal dividends.

¹It was now two days before Passover and the Festival of Unleavened Bread. The leading priests and the teachers of religious law were still looking for an opportunity to capture Jesus secretly and kill him. ²"But not during the Passover celebration," they agreed, "or the people may riot."

³Meanwhile, Jesus was in Bethany at the home of Simon, a man who had previously had leprosy. While he was eating, a woman came in with a beautiful alabaster jar of expensive perfume made from essence of nard. She broke open the jar and poured the perfume over his head.

⁴Some of those at the table were indignant. "Why waste such expensive perfume?" they asked. ⁵"It could have been sold for a year's wages and the money given to the poor!" So they scolded her harshly.

⁶But Jesus replied, "Leave her alone. Why criticize her for doing such a good thing to me? ⁷You will always have the poor among you, and you can help them whenever you want to. But you will not always have me. ⁸She has done what she could and has anointed my body for burial ahead of time. ⁹I tell you the truth, wherever the Good News is preached throughout the world, this woman's deed will be remembered and discussed."

~ Mark 14:1-9

To deny Jesus

We all remember Peter's shame when he denied Jesus three times. But we often tend to put our own safety and comfort first. Fortunately, Jesus still shows grace to those who deny Him.

[66]Meanwhile, Peter was in the courtyard below. One of the servant girls who worked for the high priest came by [67]and noticed Peter warming himself at the fire. She looked at him closely and said, "You were one of those with Jesus of Nazareth."

[68]But Peter denied it. "I don't know what you're talking about," he said, and he went out into the entryway. Just then, a rooster crowed.

[69]When the servant girl saw him standing there, she began telling the others, "This man is definitely one of them!" [70]But Peter denied it again.

A little later some of the other bystanders confronted Peter and said, "You must be one of them, because you are a Galilean."

[71]Peter swore, "A curse on me if I'm lying—I don't know this man you're talking about!" [72]And immediately the rooster crowed the second time.

Suddenly, Jesus' words flashed through Peter's mind: "Before the rooster crows twice, you will deny three times that you even know me." And he broke down and wept.

~ Mark 14:66-72

Life through His death

As Jesus breathed His last on the cross, a miracle took place. The Roman officer on duty testified there and then that Jesus was truly the Son of God. In Jesus' death there is life. Through His death other people suddenly arise from their spiritual death.

³³At noon, darkness fell across the whole land until three o'clock. ³⁴Then at three o'clock Jesus called out with a loud voice, *"Eloi, Eloi, lema sabachthani?"* which means "My God, my God, why have you abandoned me?"

³⁵Some of the bystanders misunderstood and thought he was calling for the prophet Elijah. ³⁶One of them ran and filled a sponge with sour wine, holding it up to him on a reed stick so he could drink. "Wait!" he said. "Let's see whether Elijah comes to take him down!"

³⁷Then Jesus uttered another loud cry and breathed his last. ³⁸And the curtain in the sanctuary of the Temple was torn in two, from top to bottom.

³⁹When the Roman officer who stood facing him saw how he had died, he exclaimed, "This man truly was the Son of God!"

⁴⁰Some women were there, watching from a distance, including Mary Magdalene, Mary (the mother of James the younger and of Joseph), and Salome. ⁴¹They had been followers of Jesus and had cared for him while he was in Galilee. Many other women who had come with him to Jerusalem were also there.

~ Mark 15:33-41

"He isn't here"

Good news resounds from the angel's mouth when the women arrive at Jesus' empty tomb. They hear that He is not there anymore. He has risen from the dead. He has overcome all counter-forces. He lives. Death has died. Eternal life is now forever here.

¹Saturday evening, when the Sabbath ended, Mary Magdalene, Mary the mother of James, and Salome went out and purchased burial spices so they could anoint Jesus' body. ²Very early on Sunday morning, just at sunrise, they went to the tomb. ³On the way they were asking each other, "Who will roll away the stone for us from the entrance to the tomb?" ⁴But as they arrived, they looked up and saw that the stone, which was very large, had already been rolled aside.

⁵When they entered the tomb, they saw a young man clothed in a white robe sitting on the right side. The women were shocked, ⁶but the angel said, "Don't be alarmed. You are looking for Jesus of Nazareth, who was crucified. He isn't here! He is risen from the dead! Look, this is where they laid his body. ⁷Now go and tell his disciples, including Peter, that Jesus is going ahead of you to Galilee. You will see him there, just as he told you before he died."

⁸The women fled from the tomb, trembling and bewildered, and they said nothing to anyone because they were too frightened.

Then they briefly reported all this to Peter and his companions. Afterward Jesus himself sent them out from east to west with the sacred and unfailing message of salvation that gives eternal life. Amen.

~ Mark 16:1-8

Sing when the Savior comes

Mary cannot but sing when she hears that she is going to bring the Son of God into the world. Then it is time to make music. Jesus' coming is cause for celebration because roles are reversed – now the insignificant are seen as important in God's eyes.

46Mary responded, "Oh, how my soul praises the Lord. 47How my spirit rejoices in God my Savior! 48For he took notice of his lowly servant girl, and from now on all generations will call me blessed. 49For the Mighty One is holy, and he has done great things for me. 50He shows mercy from generation to generation to all who fear him. 51His mighty arm has done tremendous things! He has scattered the proud and haughty ones. 52He has brought down princes from their thrones and exalted the humble. 53He has filled the hungry with good things and sent the rich away with empty hands. 54He has helped his servant Israel and remembered to be merciful. 55For he made this promise to our ancestors, to Abraham and his children forever."

~ Luke 1:46-55

A new day has dawned

When the angel tells the shepherds that Jesus is coming, he also teaches them about a new day that has dawned. God's new day introduces the absence of fear. Now it's time to be joyful, even for outcasts like the shepherds. Peace reigns as Jesus arrives.

⁸That night there were shepherds staying in the fields nearby, guarding their flocks of sheep. ⁹Suddenly, an angel of the Lord appeared among them, and the radiance of the Lord's glory surrounded them. They were terrified, ¹⁰but the angel reassured them. "Don't be afraid!" he said. "I bring you good news that will bring great joy to all people. ¹¹The Savior—yes, the Messiah, the Lord—has been born today in Bethlehem, the city of David! ¹²And you will recognize him by this sign: You will find a baby wrapped snugly in strips of cloth, lying in a manger."

¹³Suddenly, the angel was joined by a vast host of others—the armies of heaven—praising God and saying,

¹⁴"Glory to God in highest heaven, and peace on earth to those with whom God is pleased."

¹⁵When the angels had returned to heaven, the shepherds said to each other, "Let's go to Bethlehem! Let's see this thing that has happened, which the Lord has told us about."

¹⁶They hurried to the village and found Mary and Joseph. And there was the baby, lying in the manger. ¹⁷After seeing him, the shepherds told everyone what had happened and what the angel had said to them about this child.

¹⁸All who heard the shepherds' story were astonished.

~ Luke 2:8-18

God's Year of Jubilee

When Jesus delivered His induction sermon in Nazareth, God's Year of Jubilee began. It was time for God's bonus year of forgiveness and pardon. It was time for the poor to hear the Good News and the blind to see. Now the year of grace from the Lord is finally in our midst.

¹⁴Then Jesus returned to Galilee, filled with the Holy Spirit's power. Reports about him spread quickly through the whole region. ¹⁵He taught regularly in their synagogues and was praised by everyone.

¹⁶When he came to the village of Nazareth, his boyhood home, he went as usual to the synagogue on the Sabbath and stood up to read the Scriptures. ¹⁷The scroll of Isaiah the prophet was handed to him. He unrolled the scroll and found the place where this was written:

¹⁸"The Spirit of the Lord is upon me, for he has anointed me to bring Good News to the poor. He has sent me to proclaim that captives will be released, that the blind will see, that the oppressed will be set free, ¹⁹and that the time of the Lord's favor has come."

²⁰He rolled up the scroll, handed it back to the attendant, and sat down. All eyes in the synagogue looked at him intently. ²¹Then he began to speak to them. "The Scripture you've just heard has been fulfilled this very day!"

²²Everyone spoke well of him and was amazed by the gracious words that came from his lips. "How can this be?" they asked. "Isn't this Joseph's son?"

~ Luke 4:14-22

Unprecedented faith

Jesus had not seen faith like that of the Roman officer from Capernaum. He takes Jesus at His word and believes that his slave will be healed without Jesus coming to his house. And it did happen exactly like this. Unflinching faith moves heaven and earth. Why don't you try it?

¹When Jesus had finished saying all this to the people, he returned to Capernaum. ²At that time the highly valued slave of a Roman officer was sick and near death. ³When the officer heard about Jesus, he sent some respected Jewish elders to ask him to come and heal his slave. ⁴So they earnestly begged Jesus to help the man. "If anyone deserves your help, he does," they said, ⁵"for he loves the Jewish people and even built a synagogue for us."

⁶So Jesus went with them. But just before they arrived at the house, the officer sent some friends to say, "Lord, don't trouble yourself by coming to my home, for I am not worthy of such an honor. ⁷I am not even worthy to come and meet you. Just say the word from where you are, and my servant will be healed. ⁸I know this because I am under the authority of my superior officers, and I have authority over my soldiers. I only need to say, 'Go,' and they go, or 'Come,' and they come. And if I say to my slaves, 'Do this,' they do it."

⁹When Jesus heard this, he was amazed. Turning to the crowd that was following him, he said, "I tell you, I haven't seen faith like this in all Israel!" ¹⁰And when the officer's friends returned to his house, they found the slave completely healed.

~ Luke 7:1-10

No revenge

When the residents of a Samaritan village chase Jesus away, a few of His disciples expect a heavenly firework display. They want to take revenge. But Jesus puts a damper on their plans. He displays grace rather than heaping coals on the fire of judgment.

⁵¹As the time drew near for him to ascend to heaven, Jesus resolutely set out for Jerusalem. ⁵²He sent messengers ahead to a Samaritan village to prepare for his arrival. ⁵³But the people of the village did not welcome Jesus because he was on his way to Jerusalem.

⁵⁴When James and John saw this, they said to Jesus, "Lord, should we call down fire from heaven to burn them up?"

⁵⁵But Jesus turned and rebuked them. ⁵⁶So they went on to another village.

~ Luke 9:51-56

Mary and Martha

The hustling and bustling Martha learns that she must settle down and be calm. Mary, her sister, has got it right. She comes and sits at Jesus' feet in order to learn from Him. Mary discovers the one thing worth being concerned about, and it can't be taken away from her.

³⁸As Jesus and the disciples continued on their way to Jerusalem, they came to a certain village where a woman named Martha welcomed him into her home. ³⁹Her sister, Mary, sat at the Lord's feet, listening to what he taught. ⁴⁰But Martha was distracted by the big dinner she was preparing. She came to Jesus and said, "Lord, doesn't it seem unfair to you that my sister just sits here while I do all the work? Tell her to come and help me."

⁴¹But the Lord said to her, "My dear Martha, you are worried and upset over all these details! ⁴²There is only one thing worth being concerned about. Mary has discovered it, and it will not be taken away from her."

~ Luke 10:38-42

Jesus is not an earthly broker

Jesus refused to sort out a dispute between two brothers about their father's estate. It was not His job. This is because He is not the answer to every possible problem. He is the One who came to reconcile people with God – that is His job. Understand and serve Him correctly.

¹³Then someone called from the crowd, "Teacher, please tell my brother to divide our father's estate with me."

¹⁴Jesus replied, "Friend, who made me a judge over you to decide such things as that?" ¹⁵Then he said, "Beware! Guard against every kind of greed. Life is not measured by how much you own."

¹⁶Then he told them a story: "A rich man had a fertile farm that produced fine crops. ¹⁷He said to himself, 'What should I do? I don't have room for all my crops.' ¹⁸Then he said, 'I know! I'll tear down my barns and build bigger ones. Then I'll have room enough to store all my wheat and other goods. ¹⁹And I'll sit back and say to myself, "My friend, you have enough stored away for years to come. Now take it easy! Eat, drink, and be merry!"'

²⁰"But God said to him, 'You fool! You will die this very night. Then who will get everything you worked for?'

²¹"Yes, a person is a fool to store up earthly wealth but not have a rich relationship with God."

~ Luke 12:13-21

Heavenly grace

Heavenly grace doesn't only concern giving people one more chance. It is much more than that. Heavenly grace is when Jesus gives the chance. When He guarantees that heavenly fertilizer will be given to every unfruitful tree, and that He will bear the risk of fruit-bearing on His own shoulders, then things start to happen.

¹About this time Jesus was informed that Pilate had murdered some people from Galilee as they were offering sacrifices at the Temple. ²"Do you think those Galileans were worse sinners than all the other people from Galilee?" Jesus asked. "Is that why they suffered? ³Not at all! And you will perish, too, unless you repent of your sins and turn to God. ⁴And what about the eighteen people who died when the tower in Siloam fell on them? Were they the worst sinners in Jerusalem? ⁵No, and I tell you again that unless you repent, you will perish, too."

⁶Then Jesus told this story: "A man planted a fig tree in his garden and came again and again to see if there was any fruit on it, but he was always disappointed. ⁷Finally, he said to his gardener, 'I've waited three years, and there hasn't been a single fig! Cut it down. It's just taking up space in the garden.'

⁸"The gardener answered, 'Sir, give it one more chance. Leave it another year, and I'll give it special attention and plenty of fertilizer. ⁹If we get figs next year, fine. If not, then you can cut it down.'"

~ Luke 13:1-9

AUGUST

Calculate the cost

It will cost you to follow Jesus, and it requires a carefully thought-through decision. You must decide whether you think you can do it. The path is steep and the route is difficult. Your destiny is to carry a cross – this is the only path to life.

²⁵A large crowd was following Jesus. He turned around and said to them, ²⁶"If you want to be my disciple, you must hate everyone else by comparison—your father and mother, wife and children, brothers and sisters—yes, even your own life. Otherwise, you cannot be my disciple. ²⁷And if you do not carry your own cross and follow me, you cannot be my disciple.

²⁸"But don't begin until you count the cost. For who would begin construction of a building without first calculating the cost to see if there is enough money to finish it? ²⁹Otherwise, you might complete only the foundation before running out of money, and then everyone would laugh at you. ³⁰They would say, 'There's the person who started that building and couldn't afford to finish it!'

³¹"Or what king would go to war against another king without first sitting down with his counselors to discuss whether his army of 10,000 could defeat the 20,000 soldiers marching against him? ³²And if he can't, he will send a delegation to discuss terms of peace while the enemy is still far away. ³³So you cannot become my disciple without giving up everything you own.

³⁴"Salt is good for seasoning. But if it loses its flavor, how do you make it salty again? ³⁵Flavorless salt is good neither for the soil nor for the manure pile. It is thrown away. Anyone with ears to hear should listen and understand!"

~ Luke 14:25-35

Ninety-nine to one

Jesus' ratio is 99:1. This means that He will leave ninety-nine sheep safely in the pen to go and search for the one missing sheep. The outcasts, the lonely, the broken and the lost are always first on His heavenly radar screen. He will follow them until He finds and saves them.

¹Tax collectors and other notorious sinners often came to listen to Jesus teach. ²This made the Pharisees and teachers of religious law complain that he was associating with such sinful people—even eating with them!

³So Jesus told them this story: ⁴"If a man has a hundred sheep and one of them gets lost, what will he do? Won't he leave the ninety-nine others in the wilderness and go to search for the one that is lost until he finds it? ⁵And when he has found it, he will joyfully carry it home on his shoulders. ⁶When he arrives, he will call together his friends and neighbors, saying, 'Rejoice with me because I have found my lost sheep.' ⁷In the same way, there is more joy in heaven over one lost sinner who repents and returns to God than over ninety-nine others who are righteous and haven't strayed away!

⁸"Or suppose a woman has ten silver coins and loses one. Won't she light a lamp and sweep the entire house and search carefully until she finds it? ⁹And when she finds it, she will call in her friends and neighbors and say, 'Rejoice with me because I have found my lost coin.' ¹⁰In the same way, there is joy in the presence of God's angels when even one sinner repents."

~ Luke 15:1-10

Only one out of ten noticed God

Of the ten lepers that were healed, only one recognized Jesus as God's Son. The other nine saw Him as an ordinary healer whom they would probably need again later. The leper from Samaria returned to glorify and thank God. Let us learn to see God daily.

¹¹As Jesus continued on toward Jerusalem, he reached the border between Galilee and Samaria. ¹²As he entered a village there, ten lepers stood at a distance, ¹³crying out, "Jesus, Master, have mercy on us!"

¹⁴He looked at them and said, "Go show yourselves to the priests." And as they went, they were cleansed of their leprosy.

¹⁵One of them, when he saw that he was healed, came back to Jesus, shouting, "Praise God!" ¹⁶He fell to the ground at Jesus' feet, thanking him for what he had done. This man was a Samaritan.

¹⁷Jesus asked, "Didn't I heal ten men? Where are the other nine? ¹⁸Has no one returned to give glory to God except this foreigner?" ¹⁹And Jesus said to the man, "Stand up and go. Your faith has healed you."

~ Luke 17:11-19

Immediate mercy

When the tax collector sums up his entire life in one sentence, mercy is freely poured upon him. One sentence is more than enough when you appear before God as a beggar for mercy, with sin as your only "achievement." Then God will shower mercy upon you and save you at once.

[9]Then Jesus told this story to some who had great confidence in their own righteousness and scorned everyone else: [10]"Two men went to the Temple to pray. One was a Pharisee, and the other was a despised tax collector.

[11]The Pharisee stood by himself and prayed this prayer: 'I thank you, God, that I am not a sinner like everyone else. For I don't cheat, I don't sin, and I don't commit adultery. I'm certainly not like that tax collector! [12]I fast twice a week, and I give you a tenth of my income.'

[13]"But the tax collector stood at a distance and dared not even lift his eyes to heaven as he prayed. Instead, he beat his chest in sorrow, saying, 'O God, be merciful to me, for I am a sinner.'

[14]"I tell you, this sinner, not the Pharisee, returned home justified before God. For those who exalt themselves will be humbled, and those who humble themselves will be exalted."

~ Luke 18:9-14

The sign of betrayal

The most infamous kiss in history is surely that of Judas Iscariot. With this kiss he betrayed Jesus and handed Him over to the authorities. That which was supposed to be the symbol of love suddenly became a sign of betrayal. It is sad that the people closest to you often turn out to be the greatest betrayers.

⁴⁷But even as Jesus said this, a crowd approached, led by Judas, one of the twelve disciples. Judas walked over to Jesus to greet him with a kiss.

⁴⁸But Jesus said, "Judas, would you betray the Son of Man with a kiss?"

⁴⁹When the other disciples saw what was about to happen, they exclaimed, "Lord, should we fight? We brought the swords!" ⁵⁰And one of them struck at the high priest's slave, slashing off his right ear.

⁵¹But Jesus said, "No more of this." And he touched the man's ear and healed him.

⁵²Then Jesus spoke to the leading priests, the captains of the Temple guard, and the elders who had come for him. "Am I some dangerous revolutionary," he asked, "that you come with swords and clubs to arrest me? ⁵³Why didn't you arrest me in the Temple? I was there every day. But this is your moment, the time when the power of darkness reigns."

~ Luke 22:47-53

To see Jesus

On the day of His resurrection, Jesus traveled to Emmaus with two disillusioned men. The resurrected Jesus' comfort is His presence, the Word and a piece of bread that He later broke with them. Then their eyes were opened. Even today, He walks beside doubters such as these.

²⁵Then Jesus said to them, "You foolish people! You find it so hard to believe all that the prophets wrote in the Scriptures. ²⁶Wasn't it clearly predicted that the Messiah would have to suffer all these things before entering his glory?" ²⁷Then Jesus took them through the writings of Moses and all the prophets, explaining from all the Scriptures the things concerning himself.

²⁸By this time they were nearing Emmaus and the end of their journey. Jesus acted as if he were going on, ²⁹but they begged him, "Stay the night with us, since it is getting late." So he went home with them. ³⁰As they sat down to eat, he took the bread and blessed it. Then he broke it and gave it to them. ³¹Suddenly, their eyes were opened, and they recognized him. And at that moment he disappeared!

³²They said to each other, "Didn't our hearts burn within us as he talked with us on the road and explained the Scriptures to us?" ³³And within the hour they were on their way back to Jerusalem. There they found the eleven disciples and the others who had gathered with them, ³⁴who said, "The Lord has really risen! He appeared to Peter."

~ Luke 24:25-34

From joy to joy

The gospel of Luke is encircled with joy. It begins with Zechariah, Mary and Elizabeth's joy, and ends with the disciples' joyous celebration after seeing Jesus ascend to heaven. The Lord of the crib and the cross is also the One who ascends to heaven to prepare a place for us. This is cause for celebration!

⁴¹Still they stood there in disbelief, filled with joy and wonder. Then he asked them, "Do you have anything here to eat?" ⁴²They gave him a piece of broiled fish, ⁴³and he ate it as they watched.

⁴⁴Then he said, "When I was with you before, I told you that everything written about me in the law of Moses and the prophets and in the Psalms must be fulfilled." ⁴⁵Then he opened their minds to understand the Scriptures. ⁴⁶And he said, "Yes, it was written long ago that the Messiah would suffer and die and rise from the dead on the third day. ⁴⁷It was also written that this message would be proclaimed in the authority of his name to all the nations, beginning in Jerusalem: 'There is forgiveness of sins for all who repent.' ⁴⁸You are witnesses of all these things.

⁴⁹"And now I will send the Holy Spirit, just as my Father promised. But stay here in the city until the Holy Spirit comes and fills you with power from heaven."

⁵⁰Then Jesus led them to Bethany, and lifting his hands to heaven, he blessed them. ⁵¹While he was blessing them, he left them and was taken up to heaven.

⁵²So they worshiped him and then returned to Jerusalem filled with great joy. ⁵³And they spent all of their time in the Temple, praising God.

~ Luke 24:41-53

The eternal Word

John's beginning is an eternity before the beginning in Genesis 1. John tells about the Word that has always existed. This Word became flesh when Jesus came to earth. Then we saw His glory as He reflected God's brilliance and majesty.

⁹The one who is the true light, who gives light to everyone, was coming into the world. ¹⁰He came into the very world he created, but the world didn't recognize him. ¹¹He came to his own people, and even they rejected him. ¹²But to all who believed him and accepted him, he gave the right to become children of God. ¹³They are reborn—not with a physical birth resulting from human passion or plan, but a birth that comes from God.

¹⁴So the Word became human and made his home among us. He was full of unfailing love and faithfulness. And we have seen his glory, the glory of the Father's one and only Son.

¹⁵John testified about him when he shouted to the crowds, "This is the one I was talking about when I said, 'Someone is coming after me who is far greater than I am, for he existed long before me.'"

¹⁶From his abundance we have all received one gracious blessing after another. ¹⁷For the law was given through Moses, but God's unfailing love and faithfulness came through Jesus Christ.

¹⁸No one has ever seen God. But the unique One, who is himself God, is near to the Father's heart. He has revealed God to us.

~ John 1:9-18

A wedding celebration

The famous wedding in Cana is the first of eight miracles in John's gospel. These miracles reveal Jesus' divine glory. Weddings are a time of celebration. Jesus turned water into wine so that everyone would know that the heavenly Groom had arrived.

¹The next day there was a wedding celebration in the village of Cana in Galilee. Jesus' mother was there, ²and Jesus and his disciples were also invited to the celebration.

³The wine supply ran out during the festivities, so Jesus' mother told him, "They have no more wine."

⁴"Dear woman, that's not our problem," Jesus replied. "My time has not yet come."

⁵But his mother told the servants, "Do whatever he tells you."

⁶Standing nearby were six stone water jars, used for Jewish ceremonial washing. Each could hold twenty to thirty gallons. ⁷Jesus told the servants, "Fill the jars with water." When the jars had been filled, ⁸he said, "Now dip some out, and take it to the master of ceremonies." So the servants followed his instructions.

⁹When the master of ceremonies tasted the water that was now wine, not knowing where it had come from (though, of course, the servants knew), he called the bridegroom over. ¹⁰"A host always serves the best wine first," he said. "Then, when everyone has had a lot to drink, he brings out the less expensive wine. But you have kept the best until now!"

¹¹This miraculous sign at Cana in Galilee was the first time Jesus revealed his glory. And his disciples believed in him.

~ John 2:1-11

Night visitor

Nicodemus's night visit to Jesus is an eye-opener for him. He hears that he must be born again if he wants to understand God. Jesus is different. He is the One sent by God who you must serve and follow on His terms, otherwise faith in Him remains an unachievable dream.

¹There was a man named Nicodemus, a Jewish religious leader who was a Pharisee. ²After dark one evening, he came to speak with Jesus. "Rabbi," he said, "we all know that God has sent you to teach us. Your miraculous signs are evidence that God is with you."

³Jesus replied, "I tell you the truth, unless you are born again, you cannot see the Kingdom of God."

⁴"What do you mean?" exclaimed Nicodemus. "How can an old man go back into his mother's womb and be born again?"

⁵Jesus replied, "I assure you, no one can enter the Kingdom of God without being born of water and the Spirit. ⁶Humans can reproduce only human life, but the Holy Spirit gives birth to spiritual life. ⁷So don't be surprised when I say, 'You must be born again.' ⁸The wind blows wherever it wants. Just as you can hear the wind but can't tell where it comes from or where it is going, so you can't explain how people are born of the Spirit."

⁹"How are these things possible?" Nicodemus asked.

¹⁰Jesus replied, "You are a respected Jewish teacher, and yet you don't understand these things?"

~ John 3:1-10

A woman is saved

Women were not allowed to speak to men in public; especially women from other nationalities. Jesus, however, spoke to the Samaritan woman. And what a conversation it was – one that led to salvation. Jesus revealed Himself as the Messiah to her and her townsfolk.

¹⁹"Sir," the woman said, "you must be a prophet. ²⁰So tell me, why is it that you Jews insist that Jerusalem is the only place of worship, while we Samaritans claim it is here at Mount Gerizim, where our ancestors worshiped?"

²¹Jesus replied, "Believe me, dear woman, the time is coming when it will no longer matter whether you worship the Father on this mountain or in Jerusalem. ²²You Samaritans know very little about the one you worship, while we Jews know all about him, for salvation comes through the Jews. ²³But the time is coming—indeed it's here now—when true worshipers will worship the Father in spirit and in truth. The Father is looking for those who will worship him that way. ²⁴For God is Spirit, so those who worship him must worship in spirit and in truth."

²⁵The woman said, "I know the Messiah is coming—the one who is called Christ. When he comes, he will explain everything to us."

²⁶Then Jesus told her, "I Am the Messiah!"

²⁷Just then his disciples came back. They were shocked to find him talking to a woman, but none of them had the nerve to ask, "What do you want with her?" or "Why are you talking to her?" ²⁸The woman left her water jar beside the well and ran back to the village, telling everyone, ²⁹"Come and see a man who told me everything I ever did! Could he possibly be the Messiah?" ³⁰So the people came streaming from the village to see him.

~ John 4:19-30

The best Witness possible

When you are charged with one or other transgression, it is important to have the most trustworthy witnesses on your side. Jesus had no less than God as His witness. When the religious leaders questioned His integrity, God Himself stood in for the truthfulness of His preaching.

[31]"If I were to testify on my own behalf, my testimony would not be valid. [32]But someone else is also testifying about me, and I assure you that everything he says about me is true. [33]In fact, you sent investigators to listen to John the Baptist, and his testimony about me was true. [34]Of course, I have no need of human witnesses, but I say these things so you might be saved.

[35]"John was like a burning and shining lamp, and you were excited for a while about his message. [36]But I have a greater witness than John—my teachings and my miracles. The Father gave me these works to accomplish, and they prove that he sent me. [37]And the Father who sent me has testified about me himself. You have never heard his voice or seen him face to face, [38]and you do not have his message in your hearts, because you do not believe me—the one he sent to you.

[39]"You search the Scriptures because you think they give you eternal life. But the Scriptures point to me! [40]Yet you refuse to come to me to receive this life."

~ John 5:31-40

The words of eternal life

When Jesus' pronouncements became too much for a lot of people, they deserted Him. The twelve disciples, however, decided not to leave. The reason was that, through Jesus' words, they had found eternal life. They realized that Jesus was the Messiah. Therefore they could not leave Him.

⁶⁰Many of his disciples said, "This is very hard to understand. How can anyone accept it?"

⁶¹Jesus was aware that his disciples were complaining, so he said to them, "Does this offend you? ⁶²Then what will you think if you see the Son of Man ascend to heaven again? ⁶³The Spirit alone gives eternal life. Human effort accomplishes nothing. And the very words I have spoken to you are spirit and life. ⁶⁴But some of you do not believe me." (For Jesus knew from the beginning which ones didn't believe, and he knew who would betray him.) ⁶⁵Then he said, "That is why I said that people can't come to me unless the Father gives them to me."

⁶⁶At this point many of his disciples turned away and deserted him. ⁶⁷Then Jesus turned to the Twelve and asked, "Are you also going to leave?"

⁶⁸Simon Peter replied, "Lord, to whom would we go? You have the words that give eternal life. ⁶⁹We believe, and we know you are the Holy One of God."

~ John 6:60-69

The devil always gets the blame

The devil is always implicated when things go wrong. Jesus was even accused of being demon-possessed by His opponents. How awful! Yet He undauntedly continued to perform His Father's true works. Obedience has a high price. Learn this from Jesus.

⁴²Jesus told them, "If God were your Father, you would love me, because I have come to you from God. I am not here on my own, but he sent me. ⁴³Why can't you understand what I am saying? It's because you can't even hear me! ⁴⁴For you are the children of your father the devil, and you love to do the evil things he does. He was a murderer from the beginning. He has always hated the truth, because there is no truth in him. When he lies, it is consistent with his character; for he is a liar and the father of lies. ⁴⁵So when I tell the truth, you just naturally don't believe me! ⁴⁶Which of you can truthfully accuse me of sin? And since I am telling you the truth, why don't you believe me? ⁴⁷Anyone who belongs to God listens gladly to the words of God. But you don't listen because you don't belong to God."

⁴⁸The people retorted, "You Samaritan devil! Didn't we say all along that you were possessed by a demon?"

⁴⁹"No," Jesus said, "I have no demon in me. For I honor my Father—and you dishonor me. ⁵⁰And though I have no wish to glorify myself, God is going to glorify me. He is the true judge. ⁵¹I tell you the truth, anyone who obeys my teaching will never die!"

⁵²The people said, "Now we know you are possessed by a demon. Even Abraham and the prophets died, but you say, 'Anyone who obeys my teaching will never die!'"

~ John 8:42-52

Good Shepherd, safe sheep

Jesus calls Himself the Good Shepherd and this is good news for His sheep. He defends them to the death. He lays down His life for them. He holds them in His hand forever. No one can snatch them out of His almighty hand. This is divine protection.

22It was now winter, and Jesus was in Jerusalem at the time of Hanukkah, the Festival of Dedication. 23He was in the Temple, walking through the section known as Solomon's Colonnade. 24The people surrounded him and asked, "How long are you going to keep us in suspense? If you are the Messiah, tell us plainly."

25Jesus replied, "I have already told you, and you don't believe me. The proof is the work I do in my Father's name. 26But you don't believe me because you are not my sheep. 27My sheep listen to my voice; I know them, and they follow me. 28I give them eternal life, and they will never perish. No one can snatch them away from me, 29for my Father has given them to me, and he is more powerful than anyone else. No one can snatch them from the Father's hand. 30The Father and I are one."

31Once again the people picked up stones to kill him. 32Jesus said, "At my Father's direction I have done many good works. For which one are you going to stone me?"

~ John 10:22-32

The hour has come

John speaks often about the hour – Jesus' final hour on earth. This is the time in which Jesus would die on the cross as the world's only hope. Therefore John also describes it as an hour of glory, even though it is surrounded by death.

[20]Some Greeks who had come to Jerusalem for the Passover celebration [21]paid a visit to Philip, who was from Bethsaida in Galilee. They said, "Sir, we want to meet Jesus."

[22]Philip told Andrew about it, and they went together to ask Jesus.

[23]Jesus replied, "Now the time has come for the Son of Man to enter into his glory. [24]I tell you the truth, unless a kernel of wheat is planted in the soil and dies, it remains alone. But its death will produce many new kernels—a plentiful harvest of new lives. [25]Those who love their life in this world will lose it. Those who care nothing for their life in this world will keep it for eternity. [26]Anyone who wants to be my disciple must follow me, because my servants must be where I am. And the Father will honor anyone who serves me.

[27]"Now my soul is deeply troubled. Should I pray, 'Father, save me from this hour'? But this is the very reason I came! [28]Father, bring glory to your name."

Then a voice spoke from heaven, saying, "I have already brought glory to my name, and I will do so again."

~ John 12:20-28

The Comforter is coming

Jesus called the Holy Spirit the Comforter and heavenly Advocate. He came in Jesus' place once His earthly mission was completed. He came to guide us in the Lord's truth. He also came to confirm the unity of the Triune God among Christ's followers.

[16]"And I will ask the Father, and he will give you another Advocate, who will never leave you. [17]He is the Holy Spirit, who leads into all truth. The world cannot receive him, because it isn't looking for him and doesn't recognize him. But you know him, because he lives with you now and later will be in you.

[18]No, I will not abandon you as orphans—I will come to you. [19]Soon the world will no longer see me, but you will see me. Since I live, you also will live. [20]When I am raised to life again, you will know that I am in my Father, and you are in me, and I am in you. [21]Those who accept my commandments and obey them are the ones who love me. And because they love me, my Father will love them. And I will love them and reveal myself to each of them."

[22]Judas (not Judas Iscariot, but the other disciple with that name) said to him, "Lord, why are you going to reveal yourself only to us and not to the world at large?"

[23]Jesus replied, "All who love me will do what I say. My Father will love them, and we will come and make our home with each of them. [24]Anyone who doesn't love me will not obey me. And remember, my words are not my own. What I am telling you is from the Father who sent me. [25]I am telling you these things now while I am still with you. [26]But when the Father sends the Advocate as my representative—that is, the Holy Spirit—he will teach you everything and will remind you of everything I have told you."

~ John 14:16-26

Pruning leads to growth

To undergo pruning is painful but necessary. Without pruning healthy growth is impossible. We are branches that are connected to the heavenly grapevine, and without pruning we will not bear fruit. Then the fate that awaits us is being removed from the vine. To be cut off and thrown away is not an option.

[1]"I am the true grapevine, and my Father is the gardener. [2]He cuts off every branch of mine that doesn't produce fruit, and he prunes the branches that do bear fruit so they will produce even more. [3]You have already been pruned and purified by the message I have given you. [4]Remain in me, and I will remain in you. For a branch cannot produce fruit if it is severed from the vine, and you cannot be fruitful unless you remain in me.

[5]"Yes, I am the vine; you are the branches. Those who remain in me, and I in them, will produce much fruit. For apart from me you can do nothing. [6]Anyone who does not remain in me is thrown away like a useless branch and withers. Such branches are gathered into a pile to be burned. [7]But if you remain in me and my words remain in you, you may ask for anything you want, and it will be granted! [8]When you produce much fruit, you are my true disciples. This brings great glory to my Father.

[9]"I have loved you even as the Father has loved me. Remain in my love. [10]When you obey my commandments, you remain in my love, just as I obey my Father's commandments and remain in his love. [11]I have told you these things so that you will be filled with my joy. Yes, your joy will overflow!"

~ John 15:1-11

When departure is good

Jesus said that His going away was to our advantage because the Holy Spirit would come to us in His absence. During Jesus' time on earth He could only be in one place at a time. The spirit can be everywhere at the same time. Therefore, the Spirit's coming is to our benefit. He leads us in the truth everywhere and at all times.

⁵"But now I am going away to the one who sent me, and not one of you is asking where I am going. ⁶Instead, you grieve because of what I've told you. ⁷But in fact, it is best for you that I go away, because if I don't, the Advocate won't come. If I do go away, then I will send him to you. ⁸And when he comes, he will convict the world of its sin, and of God's righteousness, and of the coming judgment. ⁹The world's sin is that it refuses to believe in me. ¹⁰Righteousness is available because I go to the Father, and you will see me no more. ¹¹Judgment will come because the ruler of this world has already been judged.

¹²"There is so much more I want to tell you, but you can't bear it now. ¹³When the Spirit of truth comes, he will guide you into all truth. He will not speak on his own but will tell you what he has heard. He will tell you about the future. ¹⁴He will bring me glory by telling you whatever he receives from me. ¹⁵All that belongs to the Father is mine; this is why I said, 'The Spirit will tell you whatever he receives from me.'"

~ John 16:5-15

Keep them safe

The church isn't a spiritual airport where everyone diligently waits for the next flight to heaven. We are not busy emigrating from this world. Jesus specifically wants us in the world. This is where we, as His witnesses, must be. For this reason He prays for our protection in the world.

¹³"Now I am coming to you. I told them many things while I was with them in this world so they would be filled with my joy. ¹⁴I have given them your word. And the world hates them because they do not belong to the world, just as I do not belong to the world. ¹⁵I'm not asking you to take them out of the world, but to keep them safe from the evil one. ¹⁶They do not belong to this world any more than I do. ¹⁷Make them holy by your truth; teach them your word, which is truth. ¹⁸Just as you sent me into the world, I am sending them into the world. ¹⁹And I give myself as a holy sacrifice for them so they can be made holy by your truth.

²⁰"I am praying not only for these disciples but also for all who will ever believe in me through their message. ²¹I pray that they will all be one, just as you and I are one—as you are in me, Father, and I am in you. And may they be in us so that the world will believe you sent me."

~ John 17:13-21

Not of this world

Jesus is a King, but His Kingdom looks different. It doesn't come with force and violence. We don't need swords and guns to force people into it. This is what Jesus taught Pilate when He stood before him. Jesus came to bring truth and life that will last forever.

[33]But when they came to Jesus, they saw that he was already dead, so they didn't break his legs. [34]One of the soldiers, however, pierced his side with a spear, and immediately blood and water flowed out. [35](This report is from an eyewitness giving an accurate account. He speaks the truth so that you also can believe.) [36]These things happened in fulfillment of the Scriptures that say, "Not one of his bones will be broken," [37]and "They will look on the one they pierced."

[38]Afterward Joseph of Arimathea, who had been a secret disciple of Jesus (because he feared the Jewish leaders), asked Pilate for permission to take down Jesus' body. When Pilate gave permission, Joseph came and took the body away. [39]With him came Nicodemus, the man who had come to Jesus at night. He brought about seventy-five pounds of perfumed ointment made from myrrh and aloes. [40]Following Jewish burial custom, they wrapped Jesus' body with the spices in long sheets of linen cloth.

~ John 19:33-40

Women first

Mary Magdalene was the first to witness Jesus' resurrection. Jesus then delegated her to go and share the news with the disciples. She was also the first to announce Jesus' resurrection. She was an apostle to the apostles.

11Mary was standing outside the tomb crying, and as she wept, she stooped and looked in. 12She saw two white-robed angels, one sitting at the head and the other at the foot of the place where the body of Jesus had been lying. 13"Dear woman, why are you crying?" the angels asked her.

"Because they have taken away my Lord," she replied, "and I don't know where they have put him."

14She turned to leave and saw someone standing there. It was Jesus, but she didn't recognize him. 15"Dear woman, why are you crying?" Jesus asked her. "Who are you looking for?"

She thought he was the gardener. "Sir," she said, "if you have taken him away, tell me where you have put him, and I will go and get him."

16"Mary!" Jesus said.

She turned to him and cried out, "Rabboni!" (which is Hebrew for "Teacher").

17"Don't cling to me," Jesus said, "for I haven't yet ascended to the Father. But go find my brothers and tell them, 'I am ascending to my Father and your Father, to my God and your God.'"

18Mary Magdalene found the disciples and told them, "I have seen the Lord!" Then she gave them his message.

~ John 20:11-18

Believe without seeing

Thomas is known for his unbelief. He reckoned that seeing is believing. Finally he also saw Jesus. But Jesus made it clear to him that the true heroes of the faith are those who believe, even though they don't see. This is the kind of faith that changes the world. This is earth-shattering faith.

[24]One of the twelve disciples, Thomas (nicknamed the Twin), was not with the others when Jesus came. [25]They told him, "We have seen the Lord!"

But he replied, "I won't believe it unless I see the nail wounds in his hands, put my fingers into them, and place my hand into the wound in his side."

[26]Eight days later the disciples were together again, and this time Thomas was with them. The doors were locked; but suddenly, as before, Jesus was standing among them. "Peace be with you," he said. [27]Then he said to Thomas, "Put your finger here, and look at my hands. Put your hand into the wound in my side. Don't be faithless any longer. Believe!"

[28]"My Lord and my God!" Thomas exclaimed.

[29]Then Jesus told him, "You believe because you have seen me. Blessed are those who believe without seeing me."

[30]The disciples saw Jesus do many other miraculous signs in addition to the ones recorded in this book. [31]But these are written so that you may continue to believe that Jesus is the Messiah, the Son of God, and that by believing in him you will have life by the power of his name.

~ John 20:24-31

The Spirit is coming

Acts 1 begins the second part of Luke's great writing on Jesus and the Holy Spirit. We hear that Jesus' ascension meant the coming of the Holy Spirit to the church. He came to baptize with the Spirit and to drench people with His heavenly power.

¹In my first book I told you, Theophilus, about everything Jesus began to do and teach ²until the day he was taken up to heaven after giving his chosen apostles further instructions through the Holy Spirit. ³During the forty days after his crucifixion, he appeared to the apostles from time to time, and he proved to them in many ways that he was actually alive. And he talked to them about the Kingdom of God.

⁴Once when he was eating with them, he commanded them, "Do not leave Jerusalem until the Father sends you the gift he promised, as I told you before. ⁵John baptized with water, but in just a few days you will be baptized with the Holy Spirit."

⁶So when the apostles were with Jesus, they kept asking him, "Lord, has the time come for you to free Israel and restore our kingdom?"

⁷He replied, "The Father alone has the authority to set those dates and times, and they are not for you to know. ⁸But you will receive power when the Holy Spirit comes upon you. And you will be my witnesses, telling people about me everywhere—in Jerusalem, throughout Judea, in Samaria, and to the ends of the earth."

~ Acts 1:1-8

Young and old stand in line for renewal

When the Spirit descended at Pentecost, Peter used the book of Joel to explain the events that took place. Joel prophesied that young men would have visions and old men would dream dreams. Therefore the young are not too young and the old are not too old to sign up for service in God's team.

[14]Then Peter stepped forward with the eleven other apostles and shouted to the crowd, "Listen carefully, all of you, fellow Jews and residents of Jerusalem! Make no mistake about this. [15]These people are not drunk, as some of you are assuming. Nine o'clock in the morning is much too early for that. [16]No, what you see was predicted long ago by the prophet Joel:

[17]'In the last days,' God says, 'I will pour out my Spirit upon all people. Your sons and daughters will prophesy. Your young men will see visions, and your old men will dream dreams.

[18]'In those days I will pour out my Spirit even on my servants—men and women alike—and they will prophesy.

[19]'And I will cause wonders in the heavens above and signs on the earth below—blood and fire and clouds of smoke.

[20]'The sun will become dark, and the moon will turn blood red before that great and glorious day of the LORD arrives.

[21]But everyone who calls on the name of the LORD will be saved.'

~ Acts 2:14-21

More than money

Peter didn't have any money to give the lame beggar when he stood and spoke to him outside the temple. But he could graciously offer healing in the name of Jesus. The beggar got far more than he asked for that day. Healing instead of money – for the first time in his life he could walk!

¹Peter and John went to the Temple one afternoon to take part in the three o'clock prayer service. ²As they approached the Temple, a man lame from birth was being carried in. Each day he was put beside the Temple gate, the one called the Beautiful Gate, so he could beg from the people going into the Temple. ³When he saw Peter and John about to enter, he asked them for some money.

⁴Peter and John looked at him intently, and Peter said, "Look at us!" ⁵The lame man looked at them eagerly, expecting some money. ⁶But Peter said, "I don't have any silver or gold for you. But I'll give you what I have. In the name of Jesus Christ the Nazarene, get up and walk!"

⁷Then Peter took the lame man by the right hand and helped him up. And as he did, the man's feet and ankles were instantly healed and strengthened. ⁸He jumped up, stood on his feet, and began to walk! Then, walking, leaping, and praising God, he went into the Temple with them.

⁹All the people saw him walking and heard him praising God. ¹⁰When they realized he was the lame beggar they had seen so often at the Beautiful Gate, they were absolutely astounded! ¹¹They all rushed out in amazement to Solomon's Colonnade, where the man was holding tightly to Peter and John.

~ Acts 3:1-11

Share everything

The first congregation in Jerusalem was exceptional. They truly cared about one another and shared their possessions. Their hearts were open to each other. The first church started off filled with care, faith and concern for each other. We should be the same.

[32]All the believers were united in heart and mind. And they felt that what they owned was not their own, so they shared everything they had. [33]The apostles testified powerfully to the resurrection of the Lord Jesus, and God's great blessing was upon them all. [34]There were no needy people among them, because those who owned land or houses would sell them [35]and bring the money to the apostles to give to those in need.

[36]For instance, there was Joseph, the one the apostles nicknamed Barnabas (which means "Son of Encouragement"). He was from the tribe of Levi and came from the island of Cyprus. [37]He sold a field he owned and brought the money to the apostles.

~ Acts 4:32-37

How to handle problems

**It wasn't just moonshine and roses for the first con-
gregation in Jerusalem. But when problems arose
they were handled correctly. Immediately and openly the apostles took the lead and handled the matter
transparently. The wonderful result of this was
reconciliation between the aggravated parties and
yet further church growth!**

¹But as the believers rapidly multiplied, there were rumblings
of discontent. The Greek-speaking believers complained about
the Hebrew-speaking believers, saying that their widows were
being discriminated against in the daily distribution of food.

²So the Twelve called a meeting of all the believers. They
said, "We apostles should spend our time teaching the word
of God, not running a food program. ³And so, brothers, select
seven men who are well respected and are full of the Spirit and
wisdom. We will give them this responsibility. ⁴Then we apostles
can spend our time in prayer and teaching the word."

⁵Everyone liked this idea, and they chose the following:
Stephen (a man full of faith and the Holy Spirit), Philip, Procorus,
Nicanor, Timon, Parmenas, and Nicolas of Antioch (an earlier
convert to the Jewish faith). ⁶These seven were presented to
the apostles, who prayed for them as they laid their hands on
them.

⁷So God's message continued to spread. The number of believers greatly increased in Jerusalem, and many of the Jewish
priests were converted, too.

~ Acts 6:1-7

No earthly dwelling for God

Stephen, the first martyr, signed his own death sentence when he declared the temple redundant. He explained that Christ was the new Sanctuary of God. In and through Christ, God is now dynamically on the move. He changes us into living temples of the Holy Spirit.

⁴⁶"David found favor with God and asked for the privilege of building a permanent Temple for the God of Jacob. ⁴⁷But it was Solomon who actually built it. ⁴⁸However, the Most High doesn't live in temples made by human hands. As the prophet says,

⁴⁹'Heaven is my throne, and the earth is my footstool. Could you build me a temple as good as that?' asks the Lord. 'Could you build me such a resting place? ⁵⁰Didn't my hands make both heaven and earth?'

⁵¹"You stubborn people! You are heathen at heart and deaf to the truth. Must you forever resist the Holy Spirit? That's what your ancestors did, and so do you! ⁵²Name one prophet your ancestors didn't persecute! They even killed the ones who predicted the coming of the Righteous One—the Messiah whom you betrayed and murdered. ⁵³You deliberately disobeyed God's law, even though you received it from the hands of angels."

⁵⁴The Jewish leaders were infuriated by Stephen's accusation, and they shook their fists at him in rage. ⁵⁵But Stephen, full of the Holy Spirit, gazed steadily into heaven and saw the glory of God, and he saw Jesus standing in the place of honor at God's right hand. ⁵⁶And he told them, "Look, I see the heavens opened and the Son of Man standing in the place of honor at God's right hand!"

~ Acts 7:46-56

From persecutor to follower

Paul was initially an enemy of the first Christians. He tried to eradicate this sect with all his might. But then he came face to face with the resurrected Christ on his way to Damascus. Everything changed from that day. From then on he served his new Lord with all his might for the rest of his life.

[1]Meanwhile, Saul was uttering threats with every breath and was eager to kill the Lord's followers. So he went to the high priest. [2]He requested letters addressed to the synagogues in Damascus, asking for their cooperation in the arrest of any followers of the Way he found there. He wanted to bring them—both men and women—back to Jerusalem in chains.

[3]As he was approaching Damascus on this mission, a light from heaven suddenly shone down around him. [4]He fell to the ground and heard a voice saying to him, "Saul! Saul! Why are you persecuting me?"

[5]"Who are you, lord?" Saul asked.

And the voice replied, "I am Jesus, the one you are persecuting! [6]Now get up and go into the city, and you will be told what you must do."

[7]The men with Saul stood speechless, for they heard the sound of someone's voice but saw no one! [8]Saul picked himself up off the ground, but when he opened his eyes he was blind. So his companions led him by the hand to Damascus. [9]He remained there blind for three days and did not eat or drink.

[10]Now there was a believer in Damascus named Ananias. The Lord spoke to him in a vision, calling, "Ananias!"

"Yes, Lord!" he replied.

[11]The Lord said, "Go over to Straight Street, to the house of Judas. When you get there, ask for a man from Tarsus named Saul. He is praying to me right now."

~ Acts 9:1-11

Signs and wonders

The time of the Spirit is also the time of signs and wonders. Peter, a once-timid disciple of Christ, was empowered by the Spirit. Through his ministry the sick were healed and the dead were raised to life. Today, the resurrected Lord still makes His power known through His followers.

³⁶There was a believer in Joppa named Tabitha (which in Greek is Dorcas). She was always doing kind things for others and helping the poor. ³⁷About this time she became ill and died. Her body was washed for burial and laid in an upstairs room. ³⁸But the believers had heard that Peter was nearby at Lydda, so they sent two men to beg him, "Please come as soon as possible!"

³⁹So Peter returned with them; and as soon as he arrived, they took him to the upstairs room. The room was filled with widows who were weeping and showing him the coats and other clothes Dorcas had made for them. ⁴⁰But Peter asked them all to leave the room; then he knelt and prayed. Turning to the body he said, "Get up, Tabitha." And she opened her eyes! When she saw Peter, she sat up! ⁴¹He gave her his hand and helped her up. Then he called in the widows and all the believers, and he presented her to them alive.

⁴²The news spread through the whole town, and many believed in the Lord. ⁴³And Peter stayed a long time in Joppa, living with Simon, a tanner of hides.

~ Acts 9:36-43

SEPTEMBER

Understanding revelations

Visions are sometimes difficult to understand. God instructed Peter three times to eat unclean food, but his own tradition prohibited him. Peter refused because he didn't understand the vision. From Peter we can learn that humility and discernment are necessary when one is on God's terrain.

[9]The next day as Cornelius's messengers were nearing the town, Peter went up on the flat roof to pray. It was about noon, [10]and he was hungry. But while a meal was being prepared, he fell into a trance. [11]He saw the sky open, and something like a large sheet was let down by its four corners. [12]In the sheet were all sorts of animals, reptiles, and birds. [13]Then a voice said to him, "Get up, Peter; kill and eat them."

[14]"No, Lord," Peter declared. "I have never eaten anything that our Jewish laws have declared impure and unclean."

[15]But the voice spoke again: "Do not call something unclean if God has made it clean." [16]The same vision was repeated three times. Then the sheet was suddenly pulled up to heaven.

[17]Peter was very perplexed. What could the vision mean? Just then the men sent by Cornelius found Simon's house. Standing outside the gate, [18]they asked if a man named Simon Peter was staying there.

[19]Meanwhile, as Peter was puzzling over the vision, the Holy Spirit said to him, "Three men have come looking for you. [20]Get up, go downstairs, and go with them without hesitation. Don't worry, for I have sent them."

~ Acts 10:9-20

The days of tradition are numbered

Peter got into trouble with the leaders in Jerusalem after he led Cornelius, a Gentile, to Christ. They were uncomfortable with the fact that Peter went into Gentiles' homes. When the Spirit appears, such manmade traditions are unimportant. They only stand in God's way.

¹Soon the news reached the apostles and other believers in Judea that the Gentiles had received the word of God. ²But when Peter arrived back in Jerusalem, the Jewish believers criticized him. ³"You entered the home of Gentiles and even ate with them!" they said.

⁴Then Peter told them exactly what had happened. ⁵"I was in the town of Joppa," he said, "and while I was praying, I went into a trance and saw a vision. Something like a large sheet was let down by its four corners from the sky. And it came right down to me. ⁶When I looked inside the sheet, I saw all sorts of tame and wild animals, reptiles, and birds. ⁷And I heard a voice say, 'Get up, Peter; kill and eat them.'

⁸"'No, Lord,' I replied. 'I have never eaten anything that our Jewish laws have declared impure or unclean.'

⁹"But the voice from heaven spoke again: 'Do not call something unclean if God has made it clean.' ¹⁰This happened three times before the sheet and all it contained was pulled back up to heaven.

¹¹"Just then three men who had been sent from Caesarea arrived at the house where we were staying. ¹²The Holy Spirit told me to go with them and not to worry that they were Gentiles. These six brothers here accompanied me, and we soon entered the home of the man who had sent for us."

~ Acts 11:1-12

Faith brings rest

Peter slept peacefully while he was chained between the soldiers. Even with a death sentence on his head he was able to sleep, knowing that God was in control. Later, the angel even had to wake him up to get him out of prison. Are you able to sleep peacefully because of your faith?

⁶The night before Peter was to be placed on trial, he was asleep, fastened with two chains between two soldiers. Others stood guard at the prison gate. ⁷Suddenly, there was a bright light in the cell, and an angel of the Lord stood before Peter. The angel struck him on the side to awaken him and said, "Quick! Get up!" And the chains fell off his wrists. ⁸Then the angel told him, "Get dressed and put on your sandals." And he did. "Now put on your coat and follow me," the angel ordered.

⁹So Peter left the cell, following the angel. But all the time he thought it was a vision. He didn't realize it was actually happening. ¹⁰They passed the first and second guard posts and came to the iron gate leading to the city, and this opened for them all by itself. So they passed through and started walking down the street, and then the angel suddenly left him.

¹¹Peter finally came to his senses. "It's really true!" he said. "The Lord has sent his angel and saved me from Herod and from what the Jewish leaders had planned to do to me!"

~ Acts 12:6-11

The Good News must be spread

Paul acted as the leader of the congregation of the church in Antioch for a short time. During this time the Holy Spirit called him and the other leaders to be missionaries to the world. Without wavering, Paul and Barnabas set out to be at the forefront of God's mission to spread the gospel. There is Good News and it has to be shared with all!

¹Among the prophets and teachers of the church at Antioch of Syria were Barnabas, Simeon (called "the black man"), Lucius (from Cyrene), Manaen (the childhood companion of King Herod Antipas), and Saul. ²One day as these men were worshiping the Lord and fasting, the Holy Spirit said, "Dedicate Barnabas and Saul for the special work to which I have called them." ³So after more fasting and prayer, the men laid their hands on them and sent them on their way.

⁴So Barnabas and Saul were sent out by the Holy Spirit. They went down to the seaport of Seleucia and then sailed for the island of Cyprus. ⁵There, in the town of Salamis, they went to the Jewish synagogues and preached the word of God. John Mark went with them as their assistant.

⁶Afterward they traveled from town to town across the entire island until finally they reached Paphos, where they met a Jewish sorcerer, a false prophet named Bar-Jesus. ⁷He had attached himself to the governor, Sergius Paulus, who was an intelligent man. The governor invited Barnabas and Saul to visit him, for he wanted to hear the word of God. ⁸But Elymas, the sorcerer (as his name means in Greek), interfered and urged the governor to pay no attention to what Barnabas and Saul said. He was trying to keep the governor from believing.

~ Acts 13:1-8

From heroes to anti-heroes
in the blink of an eye

When Paul and Barnabas arrived in Lystra the people regarded them as Roman gods. When the two missionaries tried to deny this claim the crowds turned against them. They stoned Paul, but God saved Paul's life and enabled him and Barnabas to go elsewhere and spread the news about Jesus.

[12]They decided that Barnabas was the Greek god Zeus and that Paul was Hermes, since he was the chief speaker. [13]Now the temple of Zeus was located just outside the town. So the priest of the temple and the crowd brought bulls and wreaths of flowers to the town gates, and they prepared to offer sacrifices to the apostles.

[14]But when the apostles Barnabas and Paul heard what was happening, they tore their clothing in dismay and ran out among the people, shouting, [15]"Friends, why are you doing this? We are merely human beings—just like you! We have come to bring you the Good News that you should turn from these worthless things and turn to the living God, who made heaven and earth, the sea, and everything in them. [16]In the past he permitted all the nations to go their own ways, [17]but he never left them without evidence of himself and his goodness. For instance, he sends you rain and good crops and gives you food and joyful hearts." [18]But even with these words, Paul and Barnabas could scarcely restrain the people from sacrificing to them.

[19]Then some Jews arrived from Antioch and Iconium and won the crowds to their side. They stoned Paul and dragged him out of town, thinking he was dead. [20]But as the believers gathered around him, he got up and went back into the town. The next day he left with Barnabas for Derbe.

~ Acts 14:12-20

Nothing is to be added to the gospel message

Early on people tried to water down the gospel through adding all kinds of things to it, such as circumcision. Paul protested against this. He refused to degrade the gospel and maintain human traditions.

¹While Paul and Barnabas were at Antioch of Syria, some men from Judea arrived and began to teach the believers: "Unless you are circumcised as required by the law of Moses, you cannot be saved." ²Paul and Barnabas disagreed with them, arguing vehemently. Finally, the church decided to send Paul and Barnabas to Jerusalem, accompanied by some local believers, to talk to the apostles and elders about this question. ³The church sent the delegates to Jerusalem, and they stopped along the way in Phoenicia and Samaria to visit the believers. They told them—much to everyone's joy—that the Gentiles, too, were being converted.

⁴When they arrived in Jerusalem, Barnabas and Paul were welcomed by the whole church, including the apostles and elders. They reported everything God had done through them. ⁵But then some of the believers who belonged to the sect of the Pharisees stood up and insisted, "The Gentile converts must be circumcised and required to follow the law of Moses."

⁶So the apostles and elders met together to resolve this issue. ⁷At the meeting, after a long discussion, Peter stood and addressed them as follows: "Brothers, you all know that God chose me from among you some time ago to preach to the Gentiles so that they could hear the Good News and believe. ⁸God knows people's hearts, and he confirmed that he accepts Gentiles by giving them the Holy Spirit, just as he did to us."

~ Acts 15:1-8

Yet will I sing

Paul and Silas were severely beaten in Philippi and were then placed in prison. Yet this did not get them down. That night they sang until the prison shook. Heaven and earth noticed their singing.

²²A mob quickly formed against Paul and Silas, and the city officials ordered them stripped and beaten with wooden rods. ²³They were severely beaten, and then they were thrown into prison. The jailer was ordered to make sure they didn't escape. ²⁴So the jailer put them into the inner dungeon and clamped their feet in the stocks.

²⁵Around midnight Paul and Silas were praying and singing hymns to God, and the other prisoners were listening. ²⁶Suddenly, there was a massive earthquake, and the prison was shaken to its foundations. All the doors immediately flew open, and the chains of every prisoner fell off! ²⁷The jailer woke up to see the prison doors wide open. He assumed the prisoners had escaped, so he drew his sword to kill himself. ²⁸But Paul shouted to him, "Stop! Don't kill yourself! We are all here!"

²⁹The jailer called for lights and ran to the dungeon and fell down trembling before Paul and Silas. ³⁰Then he brought them out and asked, "Sirs, what must I do to be saved?"

³¹They replied, "Believe in the Lord Jesus and you will be saved, along with everyone in your household." ³²And they shared the word of the Lord with him and with all who lived in his household.

~ Acts 16:22-32

The world is upside-down

The crowd in Thessalonica accused Paul and Silas of causing trouble all over the world. This is the best accusation imaginable if you take it to mean that they were successful in spreading the Good News! Let us also turn the world upside-down with the life-changing message of the gospel.

¹Paul and Silas then traveled through the towns of Amphipolis and Apollonia and came to Thessalonica, where there was a Jewish synagogue. ²As was Paul's custom, he went to the synagogue service, and for three Sabbaths in a row he used the Scriptures to reason with the people. ³He explained the prophecies and proved that the Messiah must suffer and rise from the dead. He said, "This Jesus I'm telling you about is the Messiah." ⁴Some of the Jews who listened were persuaded and joined Paul and Silas, along with many God-fearing Greek men and quite a few prominent women.

⁵But some of the Jews were jealous, so they gathered some troublemakers from the marketplace to form a mob and start a riot. They attacked the home of Jason, searching for Paul and Silas so they could drag them out to the crowd. ⁶Not finding them there, they dragged out Jason and some of the other believers instead and took them before the city council. "Paul and Silas have caused trouble all over the world," they shouted, "and now they are here disturbing our city, too. ⁷And Jason has welcomed them into his home. They are all guilty of treason against Caesar, for they profess allegiance to another king, named Jesus."

⁸The people of the city, as well as the city council, were thrown into turmoil by these reports. ⁹So the officials forced Jason and the other believers to post bond, and then they released them.

~ Acts 17:1-9

When the gospel causes businesses to close!

Approximately three years after Paul preached in Ephesus, one of the seven wonders of the ancient world, the temple of the goddess Diana-Artemis, hit financial trouble. For this reason the silversmiths who sold small statues of her arranged a huge protest. Paul's preaching of the gospel indeed changes the world!

²³About that time, serious trouble developed in Ephesus concerning the Way. ²⁴It began with Demetrius, a silversmith who had a large business manufacturing silver shrines of the Greek goddess Artemis. He kept many craftsmen busy. ²⁵He called them together, along with others employed in similar trades, and addressed them as follows:

"Gentlemen, you know that our wealth comes from this business. ²⁶But as you have seen and heard, this man Paul has persuaded many people that handmade gods aren't really gods at all. And he's done this not only here in Ephesus but throughout the entire province! ²⁷Of course, I'm not just talking about the loss of public respect for our business. I'm also concerned that the temple of the great goddess Artemis will lose its influence and that Artemis—this magnificent goddess worshiped throughout the province of Asia and all around the world—will be robbed of her great prestige!"

²⁸At this their anger boiled, and they began shouting, "Great is Artemis of the Ephesians!" ²⁹Soon the whole city was filled with confusion. Everyone rushed to the amphitheater, dragging along Gaius and Aristarchus, who were Paul's traveling companions from Macedonia. ³⁰Paul wanted to go in, too, but the believers wouldn't let him.

~ Acts 19:23-30

Hard work enables others to live

When Paul departed from Ephesus for the last time he made the importance of integrity and hard work clear to the elders. He explained that hard work is an important way for God's people to feed the poor. We don't live and work for ourselves only, but for others too.

30"Even some men from your own group will rise up and distort the truth in order to draw a following. 31Watch out! Remember the three years I was with you—my constant watch and care over you night and day, and my many tears for you.

32"And now I entrust you to God and the message of his grace that is able to build you up and give you an inheritance with all those he has set apart for himself.

33"I have never coveted anyone's silver or gold or fine clothes. 34You know that these hands of mine have worked to supply my own needs and even the needs of those who were with me. 35And I have been a constant example of how you can help those in need by working hard. You should remember the words of the Lord Jesus: 'It is more blessed to give than to receive.'"

36When he had finished speaking, he knelt and prayed with them. 37They all cried as they embraced and kissed him good-bye. 38They were sad most of all because he had said that they would never see him again. Then they escorted him down to the ship.

~ Acts 20:30-38

The cost of following Jesus

Paul paid a high price for following Jesus. He was arrested in the temple and was finally imprisoned. His witness before the crowds almost cost him his life. Being Jesus' disciple is not an easy task.

²²"Don't let anyone know you told me this," the commander warned the young man.

²³Then the commander called two of his officers and ordered, "Get 200 soldiers ready to leave for Caesarea at nine o'clock tonight. Also take 200 spearmen and 70 mounted troops. ²⁴Provide horses for Paul to ride, and get him safely to Governor Felix."

²⁵Then he wrote this letter to the governor: ²⁶"From Claudius Lysias, to his Excellency, Governor Felix: Greetings!

²⁷"This man was seized by some Jews, and they were about to kill him when I arrived with the troops. When I learned that he was a Roman citizen, I removed him to safety. ²⁸Then I took him to their high council to try to learn the basis of the accusations against him. ²⁹I soon discovered the charge was something regarding their religious law—certainly nothing worthy of imprisonment or death. ³⁰But when I was informed of a plot to kill him, I immediately sent him on to you. I have told his accusers to bring their charges before you."

~ Acts 23:22-30

Before kings and princes

Jesus said that His followers would testify before the authorities for His sake. This is exactly what Paul did before the Roman governor Felix, and later before Agrippa and Festus, when he testified about his living faith in God. In these types of situations the Holy Spirit places the right words in our mouths.

¹⁰The governor then motioned for Paul to speak. Paul said, "I know, sir, that you have been a judge of Jewish affairs for many years, so I gladly present my defense before you. ¹¹You can quickly discover that I arrived in Jerusalem no more than twelve days ago to worship at the Temple. ¹²My accusers never found me arguing with anyone in the Temple, nor stirring up a riot in any synagogue or on the streets of the city. ¹³These men cannot prove the things they accuse me of doing.

¹⁴"But I admit that I follow the Way, which they call a cult. I worship the God of our ancestors, and I firmly believe the Jewish law and everything written in the prophets. ¹⁵I have the same hope in God that these men have, that he will raise both the righteous and the unrighteous. ¹⁶Because of this, I always try to maintain a clear conscience before God and all people.

¹⁷"After several years away, I returned to Jerusalem with money to aid my people and to offer sacrifices to God. ¹⁸My accusers saw me in the Temple as I was completing a purification ceremony. There was no crowd around me and no rioting."

~ Acts 24:10-18

Safe in the storm

It was Paul's presence on the ship to Rome that caused everyone's lives to be spared. In Jonah's case God first had to get him off the boat, but with Paul it was very different. He was a living witness for the Lord; for this reason everyone around him was saved.

[21]No one had eaten for a long time. Finally, Paul called the crew together and said, "Men, you should have listened to me in the first place and not left Crete. You would have avoided all this damage and loss. [22]But take courage! None of you will lose your lives, even though the ship will go down. [23]For last night an angel of the God to whom I belong and whom I serve stood beside me, [24]and he said, 'Don't be afraid, Paul, for you will surely stand trial before Caesar! What's more, God in his goodness has granted safety to everyone sailing with you.' [25]So take courage! For I believe God. It will be just as he said. [26]But we will be shipwrecked on an island."

[27]About midnight on the fourteenth night of the storm, as we were being driven across the Sea of Adria, the sailors sensed land was near. [28]They dropped a weighted line and found that the water was 120 feet deep. But a little later they measured again and found it was only 90 feet deep. [29]At this rate they were afraid we would soon be driven against the rocks along the shore, so they threw out four anchors from the back of the ship and prayed for daylight. [30]Then the sailors tried to abandon the ship; they lowered the lifeboat as though they were going to put out anchors from the front of the ship.

[31]But Paul said to the commanding officer and the soldiers, "You will all die unless the sailors stay aboard."

~ Acts 27:21-31

To the ends of the earth

Acts 1:8 says that the Holy Spirit would take the gospel to the ends of the earth. According to Luke this has already been accomplished, because in that day Rome was on the other side of the world. From Jerusalem to Rome the Holy Spirit's mighty wind carried the Good News.

16When we arrived in Rome, Paul was permitted to have his own private lodging, though he was guarded by a soldier.

17Three days after Paul's arrival, he called together the local Jewish leaders. He said to them, "Brothers, I was arrested in Jerusalem and handed over to the Roman government, even though I had done nothing against our people or the customs of our ancestors. 18The Romans tried me and wanted to release me, because they found no cause for the death sentence.

19But when the Jewish leaders protested the decision, I felt it necessary to appeal to Caesar, even though I had no desire to press charges against my own people. 20I asked you to come here today so we could get acquainted and so I could explain to you that I am bound with this chain because I believe that the hope of Israel—the Messiah—has already come."

21They replied, "We have had no letters from Judea or reports against you from anyone who has come here. 22But we want to hear what you believe, for the only thing we know about this movement is that it is denounced everywhere."

23So a time was set, and on that day a large number of people came to Paul's lodging. He explained and testified about the Kingdom of God and tried to persuade them about Jesus from the Scriptures. Using the law of Moses and the books of the prophets, he spoke to them from morning until evening.

~ Acts 28:16-23

A power that doesn't destroy, but saves

In Romans 1:16-17 Paul sums up the message of this letter in a nutshell. He says that the power of God is at work, saving everyone who believes. This salvation comes through faith when we are set free from our sins. God's power is a power that saves, not destroys.

¹⁰One of the things I always pray for is the opportunity, God willing, to come at last to see you. ¹¹For I long to visit you so I can bring you some spiritual gift that will help you grow strong in the Lord. ¹²When we get together, I want to encourage you in your faith, but I also want to be encouraged by yours.

¹³I want you to know, dear brothers and sisters, that I planned many times to visit you, but I was prevented until now. I want to work among you and see spiritual fruit, just as I have seen among other Gentiles. ¹⁴For I have a great sense of obligation to people in both the civilized world and the rest of the world, to the educated and uneducated alike. ¹⁵So I am eager to come to you in Rome, too, to preach the Good News.

¹⁶For I am not ashamed of this Good News about Christ. It is the power of God at work, saving everyone who believes—the Jew first and also the Gentile. ¹⁷This Good News tells us how God makes us right in his sight. This is accomplished from start to finish by faith. As the Scriptures say, "It is through faith that a righteous person has life."

~ Romans 1:10-17

Being religious does not make you a child of God

Paul was disenchanted with Judaism because the Jews' religiosity made them blind to God. They possessed all the holy items – the law, the temple, circumcision – yet they were still not in a living relationship with God. Religion is often a stumbling block for true faith.

[17]You who call yourselves Jews are relying on God's law, and you boast about your special relationship with him. [18]You know what he wants; you know what is right because you have been taught his law.

[19]You are convinced that you are a guide for the blind and a light for people who are lost in darkness. [20]You think you can instruct the ignorant and teach children the ways of God. For you are certain that God's law gives you complete knowledge and truth.

[21]Well then, if you teach others, why don't you teach yourself? You tell others not to steal, but do you steal? [22]You say it is wrong to commit adultery, but do you commit adultery? You condemn idolatry, but do you use items stolen from pagan temples? [23]You are so proud of knowing the law, but you dishonor God by breaking it. [24]No wonder the Scriptures say, "The Gentiles blaspheme the name of God because of you."

~ Romans 2:17-24

Salvation is here

Salvation without good works. Redemption without quid pro quo. The pure gospel is that Christ became the sacrificial Lamb in our place and took the sins of the world on His shoulders. This is God's Good News. Christ shares it with every undeserving believer.

21But now God has shown us a way to be made right with him without keeping the requirements of the law, as was promised in the writings of Moses and the prophets long ago. 22We are made right with God by placing our faith in Jesus Christ. And this is true for everyone who believes, no matter who we are.

23For everyone has sinned; we all fall short of God's glorious standard. 24Yet God, with undeserved kindness, declares that we are righteous. He did this through Christ Jesus when he freed us from the penalty for our sins. 25For God presented Jesus as the sacrifice for sin. People are made right with God when they believe that Jesus sacrificed his life, shedding his blood. This sacrifice shows that God was being fair when he held back and did not punish those who sinned in times past, 26for he was looking ahead and including them in what he would do in this present time. God did this to demonstrate his righteousness, for he himself is fair and just, and he declares sinners to be right in his sight when they believe in Jesus.

27Can we boast, then, that we have done anything to be accepted by God? No, because our acquittal is not based on obeying the law. It is based on faith. 28So we are made right with God through faith and not by obeying the law.

~ Romans 3:21-28

Christ died

Romans 5:1-11 tells us that Christ died for us when we were still helpless (v. 6); sinners (v. 6), and His enemies (v. 10). When we were at our furthest from God, He did everything He could to draw us close to Himself.

¹Therefore, since we have been made right in God's sight by faith, we have peace with God because of what Jesus Christ our Lord has done for us. ²Because of our faith, Christ has brought us into this place of undeserved privilege where we now stand, and we confidently and joyfully look forward to sharing God's glory.

³We can rejoice, too, when we run into problems and trials, for we know that they help us develop endurance. ⁴And endurance develops strength of character, and character strengthens our confident hope of salvation. ⁵And this hope will not lead to disappointment. For we know how dearly God loves us, because he has given us the Holy Spirit to fill our hearts with his love.

⁶When we were utterly helpless, Christ came at just the right time and died for us sinners. ⁷Now, most people would not be willing to die for an upright person, though someone might perhaps be willing to die for a person who is especially good. ⁸But God showed his great love for us by sending Christ to die for us while we were still sinners. ⁹And since we have been made right in God's sight by the blood of Christ, he will certainly save us from God's condemnation. ¹⁰For since our friendship with God was restored by the death of his Son while we were still his enemies, we will certainly be saved through the life of his Son. ¹¹So now we can rejoice in our wonderful new relationship with God because our Lord Jesus Christ has made us friends of God.

~ Romans 5:1-11

You dare not continue in sin

Must we keep on sinning so that God can show us more grace? Paul asks this question in Romans 6. Of course not! We are dead to sin. We have been crucified along with Christ. Our old selves have died and been buried a long time ago. We now live a new life.

¹Well then, should we keep on sinning so that God can show us more and more of his wonderful grace? ²Of course not! Since we have died to sin, how can we continue to live in it?

³Or have you forgotten that when we were joined with Christ Jesus in baptism, we joined him in his death? ⁴For we died and were buried with Christ by baptism. And just as Christ was raised from the dead by the glorious power of the Father, now we also may live new lives.

⁵Since we have been united with him in his death, we will also be raised to life as he was. ⁶We know that our old sinful selves were crucified with Christ so that sin might lose its power in our lives. We are no longer slaves to sin. ⁷For when we died with Christ we were set free from the power of sin. ⁸And since we died with Christ, we know we will also live with him. ⁹We are sure of this because Christ was raised from the dead, and he will never die again. Death no longer has any power over him. ¹⁰When he died, he died once to break the power of sin. But now that he lives, he lives for the glory of God. ¹¹So you also should consider yourselves to be dead to the power of sin and alive to God through Christ Jesus.

~ Romans 6:1-11

Punishment has been canceled for all eternity

The good news is that God's punishment has been canceled for followers of Christ. He took the pain and punishment fully on Himself. We are now free. We can now live a new life in the power of the Holy Spirit. Now we can be who we are meant to be: children of God.

[1]So now there is no condemnation for those who belong to Christ Jesus. [2]And because you belong to him, the power of the life-giving Spirit has freed you from the power of sin that leads to death. [3]The law of Moses was unable to save us because of the weakness of our sinful nature. So God did what the law could not do. He sent his own Son in a body like the bodies we sinners have. And in that body God declared an end to sin's control over us by giving his Son as a sacrifice for our sins. [4]He did this so that the just requirement of the law would be fully satisfied for us, who no longer follow our sinful nature but instead follow the Spirit.

[5]Those who are dominated by the sinful nature think about sinful things, but those who are controlled by the Holy Spirit think about things that please the Spirit. [6]So letting your sinful nature control your mind leads to death. But letting the Spirit control your mind leads to life and peace.

~ Romans 8:1-6

Israel – the problem!

In Romans 9-11 Paul reflects on the position of Israel after Christ's coming, and knows that not every Israelite is a true Israelite. In other words, not all who are born into the nation of Israel are truly members of God's people. Faith has always weaved through history like a golden thread. Some believe and some don't. Therefore embrace God's grace.

¹With Christ as my witness, I speak with utter truthfulness. My conscience and the Holy Spirit confirm it. ²My heart is filled with bitter sorrow and unending grief ³for my people, my Jewish brothers and sisters. I would be willing to be forever cursed—cut off from Christ!—if that would save them. ⁴They are the people of Israel, chosen to be God's adopted children. God revealed his glory to them. He made covenants with them and gave them his law. He gave them the privilege of worshiping him and receiving his wonderful promises. ⁵Abraham, Isaac, and Jacob are their ancestors, and Christ himself was an Israelite as far as his human nature is concerned. And he is God, the one who rules over everything and is worthy of eternal praise! Amen.

⁶Well then, has God failed to fulfill his promise to Israel? No, for not all who are born into the nation of Israel are truly members of God's people! ⁷Being descendants of Abraham doesn't make them truly Abraham's children. For the Scriptures say, "Isaac is the son through whom your descendants will be counted," though Abraham had other children, too. ⁸This means that Abraham's physical descendants are not necessarily children of God. Only the children of the promise are considered to be Abraham's children. ⁹For God had promised, "I will return about this time next year, and Sarah will have a son."

~ Romans 9:1-9

Faith involves hearing and speaking

Good News begins by God's people telling others. Others then hear the Good News and it changes their hearts. For this reason the steps of those who bring the Good News sound like music. We must confess with our mouths and take the Good News to others.

[8]In fact, it says, "The message is very close at hand; it is on your lips and in your heart."

And that message is the very message about faith that we preach: [9]If you confess with your mouth that Jesus is Lord and believe in your heart that God raised him from the dead, you will be saved. [10]For it is by believing in your heart that you are made right with God, and it is by confessing with your mouth that you are saved. [11]As the Scriptures tell us, "Anyone who trusts in him will never be disgraced." [12]Jew and Gentile are the same in this respect. They have the same Lord, who gives generously to all who call on him. [13]For "Everyone who calls on the name of the LORD will be saved."

[14]But how can they call on him to save them unless they believe in him? And how can they believe in him if they have never heard about him? And how can they hear about him unless someone tells them? [15]And how will anyone go and tell them without being sent? That is why the Scriptures say, "How beautiful are the feet of messengers who bring good news!"

[16]But not everyone welcomes the Good News, for Isaiah the prophet said, "LORD, who has believed our message?" [17]So faith comes from hearing, that is, hearing the Good News about Christ.

~ Romans 10:8-17

Living sacrifices

The days of sacrificing dead animals are over – it is now time for living sacrifices. God asks for living people who will dedicate their whole lives to Him. When He renews their thoughts they will know His will, and what is good and right in His sight.

[1]And so, dear brothers and sisters, I plead with you to give your bodies to God because of all he has done for you. Let them be a living and holy sacrifice—the kind he will find acceptable. This is truly the way to worship him. [2]Don't copy the behavior and customs of this world, but let God transform you into a new person by changing the way you think. Then you will learn to know God's will for you, which is good and pleasing and perfect.

[3]Because of the privilege and authority God has given me, I give each of you this warning: Don't think you are better than you really are. Be honest in your evaluation of yourselves, measuring yourselves by the faith God has given us.

[6]In his grace, God has given us different gifts for doing certain things well. So if God has given you the ability to prophesy, speak out with as much faith as God has given you. [7]If your gift is serving others, serve them well. If you are a teacher, teach well. [8]If your gift is to encourage others, be encouraging. If it is giving, give generously. If God has given you leadership ability, take the responsibility seriously. And if you have a gift for showing kindness to others, do it gladly.

~ Romans 12:1-3, 6-8

You are not on your own spiritual planet

Faith is not a self-centered affair. Take others into account. Even if you are right, you sometimes choose to be the least in the Kingdom. The essence of the kingdom of God is obedience to God and peace and joy in the Holy Spirit. In this there can be no compromise.

[13]So let's stop condemning each other. Decide instead to live in such a way that you will not cause another believer to stumble and fall.

[14]I know and am convinced on the authority of the Lord Jesus that no food, in and of itself, is wrong to eat. But if someone believes it is wrong, then for that person it is wrong. [15]And if another believer is distressed by what you eat, you are not acting in love if you eat it. Don't let your eating ruin someone for whom Christ died. [16]Then you will not be criticized for doing something you believe is good.

[17]For the Kingdom of God is not a matter of what we eat or drink, but of living a life of goodness and peace and joy in the Holy Spirit.

[20]Don't tear apart the work of God over what you eat. Remember, all foods are acceptable, but it is wrong to eat something if it makes another person stumble. [21]It is better not to eat meat or drink wine or do anything else if it might cause another believer to stumble. [22]You may believe there's nothing wrong with what you are doing, but keep it between yourself and God. Blessed are those who don't feel guilty for doing something they have decided is right.

~ Romans 14:13-17, 20-22

Care for each other

Romans 16 is a remarkable chapter. Here Paul intimately greets a group of fellow believers in service of the gospel. He makes it clear that faith is a band that ties us together every day until the end. Therefore it results in compassion and goodwill between believers.

[6]Give my greetings to Mary, who has worked so hard for your benefit. [7]Greet Andronicus and Junia, my fellow Jews, who were in prison with me. They are highly respected among the apostles and became followers of Christ before I did. [8]Greet Ampliatus, my dear friend in the Lord. [9]Greet Urbanus, our co-worker in Christ, and my dear friend Stachys.

[10]Greet Apelles, a good man whom Christ approves. And give my greetings to the believers from the household of Aristobulus. [11]Greet Herodion, my fellow Jew. Greet the Lord's people from the household of Narcissus. [12]Give my greetings to Tryphena and Tryphosa, the Lord's workers, and to dear Persis, who has worked so hard for the Lord. [13]Greet Rufus, whom the Lord picked out to be his very own; and also his dear mother, who has been a mother to me.

[14]Give my greetings to Asyncritus, Phlegon, Hermes, Patrobas, Hermas, and the brothers and sisters who meet with them. [15]Give my greetings to Philologus, Julia, Nereus and his sister, and to Olympas and all the believers who meet with them. [16]Greet each other in Christian love. All the churches of Christ send you their greetings.

~ Romans 16:6-16

Set your priorities straight

One of the most underrated verses in the New Testament is 1 Corinthians 1:17. Here Paul explains that the gospel doesn't concern the practice of baptism as much as it does Christ's preaching. Sacraments are secondary to the Word of God. Too often baptism is an issue that causes division in the church because verse 17 is overlooked.

10I appeal to you, dear brothers and sisters, by the authority of our Lord Jesus Christ, to live in harmony with each other. Let there be no divisions in the church. Rather, be of one mind, united in thought and purpose. 11For some members of Chloe's household have told me about your quarrels, my dear brothers and sisters. 12Some of you are saying, "I am a follower of Paul." Others are saying, "I follow Apollos," or "I follow Peter," or "I follow only Christ."

13Has Christ been divided into factions? Was I, Paul, crucified for you? Were any of you baptized in the name of Paul? Of course not! 14I thank God that I did not baptize any of you except Crispus and Gaius, 15for now no one can say they were baptized in my name. 16(Oh yes, I also baptized the household of Stephanas, but I don't remember baptizing anyone else.) 17For Christ didn't send me to baptize, but to preach the Good News—and not with clever speech, for fear that the cross of Christ would lose its power.

18The message of the cross is foolish to those who are headed for destruction! But we who are being saved know it is the very power of God.

~ 1 Corinthians 1:10-18

The crucified Christ is the heartbeat of the gospel

When Paul highlights the essence of the gospel, he cannot but discover it in the crucified Christ. The gospel stands on this. You either believe in the story of the cross and the empty tomb or you lose the heartbeat of the gospel. It's as simple as that.

[1]When I first came to you, dear brothers and sisters, I didn't use lofty words and impressive wisdom to tell you God's secret plan. [2]For I decided that while I was with you I would forget everything except Jesus Christ, the one who was crucified. [3]I came to you in weakness—timid and trembling. [4]And my message and my preaching were very plain. Rather than using clever and persuasive speeches, I relied only on the power of the Holy Spirit. [5]I did this so you would trust not in human wisdom but in the power of God.

[6]Yet when I am among mature believers, I do speak with words of wisdom, but not the kind of wisdom that belongs to this world or to the rulers of this world, who are soon forgotten. [7]No, the wisdom we speak of is the mystery of God—his plan that was previously hidden, even though he made it for our ultimate glory before the world began. [8]But the rulers of this world have not understood it; if they had, they would not have crucified our glorious Lord.

~ 1 Corinthians 2:1-8

Build with fireproof material

Leaders in the church must make sure that they build with the correct building material. It must be fireproof material, not wood, hay or straw. This means that only the pure and genuine gospel of Christ is the building material with which to build up believers.

[10]Because of God's grace to me, I have laid the foundation like an expert builder. Now others are building on it. But whoever is building on this foundation must be very careful. [11]For no one can lay any foundation other than the one we already have—Jesus Christ.

[12]Anyone who builds on that foundation may use a variety of materials—gold, silver, jewels, wood, hay, or straw. [13]But on the judgment day, fire will reveal what kind of work each builder has done. The fire will show if a person's work has any value. [14]If the work survives, that builder will receive a reward. [15]But if the work is burned up, the builder will suffer great loss. The builder will be saved, but like someone barely escaping through a wall of flames.

[16]Don't you realize that all of you together are the temple of God and that the Spirit of God lives in you? [17]God will destroy anyone who destroys this temple. For God's temple is holy, and you are that temple.

[18]Stop deceiving yourselves. If you think you are wise by this world's standards, you need to become a fool to be truly wise.

~ 1 Corinthians 3:10-18

Holy living

In verse 9 Paul refers to one of his previous letters which the Corinthians misunderstood. They thought Paul meant that they must withdraw from the world completely. He then explained that what he meant was that they must live holy lives, set apart for God.

⁹When I wrote to you before, I told you not to associate with people who indulge in sexual sin. ¹⁰But I wasn't talking about unbelievers who indulge in sexual sin, or are greedy, or cheat people, or worship idols. You would have to leave this world to avoid people like that. ¹¹I meant that you are not to associate with anyone who claims to be a believer yet indulges in sexual sin, or is greedy, or worships idols, or is abusive, or is a drunkard, or cheats people. Don't even eat with such people.

¹²It isn't my responsibility to judge outsiders, but it certainly is your responsibility to judge those inside the church who are sinning. ¹³God will judge those on the outside; but as the Scriptures say, "You must remove the evil person from among you."

~ 1 Corinthians 5:9-13

Living temples of God

As Christians we are God's living, earthly dwelling places. Our bodies are His property and we can't just do with them as we please. Our lives are under completely new management. We stand as life-long constructions of the Holy Spirit. We have been bought at a high price through Christ's sacrificial death.

[12]You say, "I am allowed to do anything"—but not everything is good for you. And even though "I am allowed to do anything," I must not become a slave to anything. [13]You say, "Food was made for the stomach, and the stomach for food." (This is true, though someday God will do away with both of them.) But you can't say that our bodies were made for sexual immorality. They were made for the Lord, and the Lord cares about our bodies. [14]And God will raise us from the dead by his power, just as he raised our Lord from the dead.

[15]Don't you realize that your bodies are actually parts of Christ? Should a man take his body, which is part of Christ, and join it to a prostitute? Never! [16]And don't you realize that if a man joins himself to a prostitute, he becomes one body with her? For the Scriptures say, "The two are united into one." [17]But the person who is joined to the Lord is one spirit with him.

[18]Run from sexual sin! No other sin so clearly affects the body as this one does. For sexual immorality is a sin against your own body. [19]Don't you realize that your body is the temple of the Holy Spirit, who lives in you and was given to you by God? You do not belong to yourself, [20]for God bought you with a high price. So you must honor God with your body.

~ 1 Corinthians 6:12-20

OCTOBER

Run to win!

Paul was probably a spectator at the great Isthmian Games in Corinth. He then applied some of these images to our faith. He said we must be boxers who knock our opponents out. We must run to win the heavenly prize that Christ will give us.

¹⁹Even though I am a free man with no master, I have become a slave to all people to bring many to Christ. ²⁰When I was with the Jews, I lived like a Jew to bring the Jews to Christ. When I was with those who follow the Jewish law, I too lived under that law. Even though I am not subject to the law, I did this so I could bring to Christ those who are under the law. ²¹When I am with the Gentiles who do not follow the Jewish law, I too live apart from that law so I can bring them to Christ. But I do not ignore the law of God; I obey the law of Christ.

²²When I am with those who are weak, I share their weakness, for I want to bring the weak to Christ. Yes, I try to find common ground with everyone, doing everything I can to save some. ²³I do everything to spread the Good News and share in its blessings.

²⁴Don't you realize that in a race everyone runs, but only one person gets the prize? So run to win! ²⁵All athletes are disciplined in their training. They do it to win a prize that will fade away, but we do it for an eternal prize. ²⁶So I run with purpose in every step. I am not just shadowboxing.

~ 1 Corinthians 9:19-26

One for all and all for one

One Corinthians 12-14 discusses the correct use of the spiritual gifts that God has granted us according to His will. Most importantly, we must use these gifts to glorify God, but also to benefit and uplift others. If we don't use them in this way we should rather not use them at all.

[12] The human body has many parts, but the many parts make up one whole body. So it is with the body of Christ. [13] Some of us are Jews, some are Gentiles, some are slaves, and some are free. But we have all been baptized into one body by one Spirit, and we all share the same Spirit.

[14] Yes, the body has many different parts, not just one part. [15] If the foot says, "I am not a part of the body because I am not a hand," that does not make it any less a part of the body. [16] And if the ear says, "I am not part of the body because I am not an eye," would that make it any less a part of the body? [17] If the whole body were an eye, how would you hear? Or if your whole body were an ear, how would you smell anything?

[18] But our bodies have many parts, and God has put each part just where he wants it. [19] How strange a body would be if it had only one part! [20] Yes, there are many parts, but only one body. [21] The eye can never say to the hand, "I don't need you." The head can't say to the feet, "I don't need you."

[22] In fact, some parts of the body that seem weakest and least important are actually the most necessary.

~ 1 Corinthians 12:12-22

The gospel in a nutshell

In verses 3-8 of 1 Corinthians Paul shares the heart of the Good News as it grew in stature in the early church. These verses explain who Jesus is and why the church cannot continue to exist without confessing that Jesus died and rose from the dead.

[1]Let me now remind you, dear brothers and sisters, of the Good News I preached to you before. You welcomed it then, and you still stand firm in it. [2]It is this Good News that saves you if you continue to believe the message I told you—unless, of course, you believed something that was never true in the first place.

[3]I passed on to you what was most important and what also been passed on to me. Christ died for our sins, just as the Scriptures said. [4]He was buried, and he was raised from the dead on the third day, just as the Scriptures said. [5]He was seen by Peter and then by the Twelve. [6]After that, he was seen by more than 500 of his followers at one time, most of whom are still alive, though some have died. [7]Then he was seen by James and later by all the apostles. [8]Last of all, as though I had been born at the wrong time, I also saw him.

~ 1 Corinthians 15:1-8

Comforted to comfort others

In 2 Corinthians 1 Paul explains that you and I are never the final receptors of God's heavenly comfort. Paul learned to encourage other believers through the comfort he received in the midst of trials. God's comfort to us must be passed on to others.

³All praise to God, the Father of our Lord Jesus Christ. God is our merciful Father and the source of all comfort. ⁴He comforts us in all our troubles so that we can comfort others. When they are troubled, we will be able to give them the same comfort God has given us. ⁵For the more we suffer for Christ, the more God will shower us with his comfort through Christ.

⁶Even when we are weighed down with troubles, it is for your comfort and salvation! For when we ourselves are comforted, we will certainly comfort you. Then you can patiently endure the same things we suffer. ⁷We are confident that as you share in our sufferings, you will also share in the comfort God gives us.

⁸We think you ought to know, dear brothers and sisters, about the trouble we went through in the province of Asia. We were crushed and overwhelmed beyond our ability to endure, and we thought we would never live through it. ⁹In fact, we expected to die. But as a result, we stopped relying on ourselves and learned to rely only on God, who raises the dead. ¹⁰And he did rescue us from mortal danger, and he will rescue us again. We have placed our confidence in him, and he will continue to rescue us.

~ 2 Corinthians 1:3-10

A sweet fragrance

Our lives are a fragrance that rises up to God. We spread a life-giving perfume because Christ is in us. Our fragrance brings life and death. To those who are being saved, we are a life-giving perfume. To those who are perishing, we are a smell of death. All we can do is continue to be a sweet fragrance to God.

¹²When I came to the city of Troas to preach the Good News of Christ, the Lord opened a door of opportunity for me. ¹³But I had no peace of mind because my dear brother Titus hadn't yet arrived with a report from you. So I said good-bye and went on to Macedonia to find him.

¹⁴But thank God! He has made us his captives and continues to lead us along in Christ's triumphal procession. Now he uses us to spread the knowledge of Christ everywhere, like a sweet perfume. ¹⁵Our lives are a Christ-like fragrance rising up to God. But this fragrance is perceived differently by those who are being saved and by those who are perishing. ¹⁶To those who are perishing, we are a dreadful smell of death and doom. But to those who are being saved, we are a life-giving perfume. And who is adequate for such a task as this?

¹⁷You see, we are not like the many hucksters who preach for personal profit. We preach the word of God with sincerity and with Christ's authority, knowing that God is watching us.

~ 2 Corinthians 2:12-17

New creations

Anyone who is in Christ is a new creation because of God's grace. He sent Christ to pay the price for our sins. He brought heaven and earth together. Faith is the manner in which we cross the bridge from earth to heaven.

[11]Because we understand our fearful responsibility to the Lord, we work hard to persuade others. God knows we are sincere, and I hope you know this, too.

[12]Are we commending ourselves to you again? No, we are giving you a reason to be proud of us, so you can answer those who brag about having a spectacular ministry rather than having a sincere heart. [13]If it seems we are crazy, it is to bring glory to God. And if we are in our right minds, it is for your benefit. [14]Either way, Christ's love controls us. Since we believe that Christ died for all, we also believe that we have all died to our old life. [15]He died for everyone so that those who receive his new life will no longer live for themselves. Instead, they will live for Christ, who died and was raised for them.

[16]So we have stopped evaluating others from a human point of view. At one time we thought of Christ merely from a human point of view. How differently we know him now! [17]This means that anyone who belongs to Christ has become a new person. The old life is gone; a new life has begun!

[18]And all of this is a gift from God, who brought us back to himself through Christ. And God has given us this task of reconciling people to him. [19]For God was in Christ, reconciling the world to himself, no longer counting people's sins against them. And he gave us this wonderful message of reconciliation.

~ 2 Corinthians 5:11-19

The way to give

In 2 Corinthians 8-9 Paul encourages the congregation to raise money for Jerusalem. In this regard the Macedonian Christians serves as important examples. They gave in the right way: first they gave themselves to God and then to Paul's project. God first, money second.

¹Now I want you to know, dear brothers and sisters, what God in his kindness has done through the churches in Macedonia. ²They are being tested by many troubles, and they are very poor. But they are also filled with abundant joy, which has overflowed in rich generosity.

³For I can testify that they gave not only what they could afford, but far more. And they did it of their own free will. ⁴They begged us again and again for the privilege of sharing in the gift for the believers in Jerusalem. ⁵They even did more than we had hoped, for their first action was to give themselves to the Lord and to us, just as God wanted them to do.

⁶So we have urged Titus, who encouraged your giving in the first place, to return to you and encourage you to finish this ministry of giving. ⁷Since you excel in so many ways—in your faith, your gifted speakers, your knowledge, your enthusiasm, and your love from us—I want you to excel also in this gracious act of giving.

⁸I am not commanding you to do this. But I am testing how genuine your love is by comparing it with the eagerness of the other churches.

~ 2 Corinthians 8:1-8

Weakness is strength

Paul explains that his thorn in the flesh is his own weakness in his service to God. When he prayed that it be taken away, God told him that heavenly power only works in human weakness. We are strong when we are weak because then God's all-conquering power descends on us.

⁵That experience is worth boasting about, but I'm not going to do it. I will boast only about my weaknesses. ⁶If I wanted to boast, I would be no fool in doing so, because I would be telling the truth. But I won't do it, because I don't want anyone to give me credit beyond what they can see in my life or hear in my message, ⁷even though I have received such wonderful revelations from God. So to keep me from becoming proud, I was given a thorn in my flesh, a messenger from Satan to torment me and keep me from becoming proud.

⁸Three different times I begged the Lord to take it away. ⁹Each time he said, "My grace is all you need. My power works best in weakness." So now I am glad to boast about my weaknesses, so that the power of Christ can work through me. ¹⁰That's why I take pleasure in my weaknesses, and in the insults, hardships, persecutions, and troubles that I suffer for Christ. For when I am weak, then I am strong.

~ 2 Corinthians 12:5-10

Watch out for false teaching

Be on the lookout for those who twist the true gospel. Don't even unquestioningly trust an angel. Test all teaching against the truth of the gospel as revealed through the apostles. The enemy is continually trying to water down the Good News.

¹This letter is from Paul, an apostle. I was not appointed by any group of people or any human authority, but by Jesus Christ himself and by God the Father, who raised Jesus from the dead.

²All the brothers and sisters here join me in sending this letter to the churches of Galatia. ³May God our Father and the Lord Jesus Christ give you grace and peace. ⁴Jesus gave his life for our sins, just as God our Father planned, in order to rescue us from this evil world in which we live. ⁵All glory to God forever and ever! Amen.

⁶I am shocked that you are turning away so soon from God, who called you to himself through the loving mercy of Christ. You are following a different way that pretends to be the Good News ⁷but is not the Good News at all. You are being fooled by those who deliberately twist the truth concerning Christ.

⁸Let God's curse fall on anyone, including us or even an angel from heaven, who preaches a different kind of Good News than the one we preached to you. ⁹I say again what we have said before: If anyone preaches any other Good News than the one you welcomed, let that person be cursed.

~ Galatians 1:1-9

Be honest

It takes courage to confront the leaders of a church. But when Paul discovered that Peter, Barnabas and other church leaders had fallen back into outdated Jewish customs regarding food, he publically confronted them. Tradition must never interfere with our freedom as Christians.

[11]But when Peter came to Antioch, I had to oppose him to his face, for what he did was very wrong. [12]When he first arrived, he ate with the Gentile Christians, who were not circumcised. But afterward, when some friends of James came, Peter wouldn't eat with the Gentiles anymore. He was afraid of criticism from these people who insisted on the necessity of circumcision. [13]As a result, other Jewish Christians followed Peter's hypocrisy, and even Barnabas was led astray by their hypocrisy.

[14]When I saw that they were not following the truth of the gospel message, I said to Peter in front of all the others, "Since you, a Jew by birth, have discarded the Jewish laws and are living like a Gentile, why are you now trying to make these Gentiles follow the Jewish traditions?

[15]"You and I are Jews by birth, not 'sinners' like the Gentiles. [16]Yet we know that a person is made right with God by faith in Jesus Christ, not by obeying the law. And we have believed in Christ Jesus, so that we might be made right with God because of our faith in Christ, not because we have obeyed the law. For no one will ever be made right with God by obeying the law."

[17]But suppose we seek to be made right with God through faith in Christ and then we are found guilty because we have abandoned the law. Would that mean Christ has led us into sin? Absolutely not! [18]Rather, I am a sinner if I rebuild the old system of law I already tore down.

~ Galatians 2:11-18

The price of our sin

For a few hours Christ took the most humiliating position in the entire universe. He took upon Himself the curse for our sins and endured God's punishment. He took our punishment and bore it upon Himself for our sakes.

⁷The real children of Abraham, then, are those who put their faith in God.

⁸What's more, the Scriptures looked forward to this time when God would declare the Gentiles to be righteous because of their faith. God proclaimed this good news to Abraham long ago when he said, "All nations will be blessed through you." ⁹So all who put their faith in Christ share the same blessing Abraham received because of his faith.

¹⁰But those who depend on the law to make them right with God are under his curse, for the Scriptures say, "Cursed is everyone who does not observe and obey all the commands that are written in God's Book of the Law." ¹¹So it is clear that no one can be made right with God by trying to keep the law. For the Scriptures say, "It is through faith that a righteous person has life." ¹²This way of faith is very different from the way of law, which says, "It is through obeying the law that a person has life."

¹³But Christ has rescued us from the curse pronounced by the law. When he was hung on the cross, he took upon himself the curse for our wrongdoing. For it is written in the Scriptures, "Cursed is everyone who is hung on a tree." ¹⁴Through Christ Jesus, God has blessed the Gentiles with the same blessing he promised to Abraham, so that we who are believers might receive the promised Holy Spirit through faith.

~ Galatians 3:7-14

Abba, Father in our hearts

In our hearts the Holy Spirit calls out: Abba, Father. It is the Spirit's echo. He brings us very close to God and makes Him tangible, real. That is why we no longer feel like slaves who live in fear of God. We are now heirs of eternal life.

26For you are all children of God through faith in Christ Jesus. 27And all who have been united with Christ in baptism have put on Christ, like putting on new clothes. 28There is no longer Jew or Gentile, slave or free, male and female. For you are all one in Christ Jesus. 29And now that you belong to Christ, you are the true children of Abraham. You are his heirs, and God's promise to Abraham belongs to you.

4 1Think of it this way. If a father dies and leaves an inheritance for his young children, those children are not much better off than slaves until they grow up, even though they actually own everything their father had. 2They have to obey their guardians until they reach whatever age their father set.

3And that's the way it was with us before Christ came. We were like children; we were slaves to the basic spiritual principles of this world. 4But when the right time came, God sent his Son, born of a woman, subject to the law. 5God sent him to buy freedom for us who were slaves to the law, so that he could adopt us as his very own children. 6And because we are his children, God has sent the Spirit of his Son into our hearts, prompting us to call out, "Abba, Father." 7Now you are no longer a slave but God's own child. And since you are his child, God has made you his heir.

~ Galatians 3:26-4:7

Tradition can hamper the gospel

Paul is upset when some Galatian Christians fall back into outdated customs such as circumcision. This is not only a straying, but also falling away from the gospel. This breaks the believers' bond with Christ. Don't give up your freedom in Christ like they did.

[1]So Christ has truly set us free. Now make sure that you stay free, and don't get tied up again in slavery to the law. [2]Listen! I, Paul, tell you this: If you are counting on circumcision to make you right with God, then Christ will be of no benefit to you. [3]I'll say it again. If you are trying to find favor with God by being circumcised, you must obey every regulation in the whole law of Moses. [4]For if you are trying to make yourselves right with God by keeping the law, you have been cut off from Christ! You have fallen away from God's grace.

[5]But we who live by the Spirit eagerly wait to receive by faith the righteousness God has promised to us. [6]For when we place our faith in Christ Jesus, there is no benefit in being circumcised or being uncircumcised. What is important is faith expressing itself in love.

[7]You were running the race so well. Who has held you back from following the truth? [8]It certainly isn't God, for he is the one who called you to freedom. [9]This false teaching is like a little yeast that spreads through the whole batch of dough! [10]I am trusting the Lord to keep you from believing false teachings. God will judge that person, whoever he is, who has been confusing you.

[11]Dear brothers and sisters, if I were still preaching that you must be circumcised—as some say I do—why am I still being persecuted? If I were no longer preaching salvation through the cross of Christ, no one would be offended.

~ Galatians 5:1-11

Sow wisely

Carefully consider where you sow your life. If you sow on sin's terrain you will reap disaster. But if you pour your life out on God's field, you will reap a heavenly harvest. Sow correctly by using every opportunity you can to do good.

[1]Dear brothers and sisters, if another believer is overcome by some sin, you who are godly should gently and humbly help that person back onto the right path. And be careful not to fall into the same temptation yourself. [2]Share each other's burdens, and in this way obey the law of Christ.

[3]If you think you are too important to help someone, you are only fooling yourself. You are not that important. [4]Pay careful attention to your own work, for then you will get the satisfaction of a job well done, and you won't need to compare yourself to anyone else. [5]For we are each responsible for our own conduct.

[6]Those who are taught the word of God should provide for their teachers, sharing all good things with them.

[7]Don't be misled—you cannot mock the justice of God. You will always harvest what you plant. [8]Those who live only to satisfy their own sinful nature will harvest decay and death from that sinful nature. But those who live to please the Spirit will harvest everlasting life from the Spirit. [9]So let's not get tired of doing what is good. At just the right time we will reap a harvest of blessing if we don't give up. [10]Therefore, whenever we have the opportunity, we should do good to everyone—especially to those in the family of faith.

~ Galatians 6:1-10

Sing about grace

Ephesians 1:3-14 is a song of praise about God's overflowing grace. It tells that God decided to save us long before we were able to choose. This saving grace became ours when we started to believe in Christ. Then the floodgates of heaven opened up.

³All praise to God, the Father of our Lord Jesus Christ, who has blessed us with every spiritual blessing in the heavenly realms because we are united with Christ. ⁴Even before he made the world, God loved us and chose us in Christ to be holy and without fault in his eyes. ⁵God decided in advance to adopt us into his own family by bringing us to himself through Jesus Christ. This is what he wanted to do, and it gave him great pleasure.

⁶So we praise God for the glorious grace he has poured out on us who belong to his dear Son. ⁷He is so rich in kindness and grace that he purchased our freedom with the blood of his Son and forgave our sins. ⁸He has showered his kindness on us, along with all wisdom and understanding.

⁹God has now revealed to us his mysterious plan regarding Christ, a plan to fulfill his own good pleasure. ¹⁰And this is the plan: At the right time he will bring everything together under the authority of Christ—everything in heaven and on earth. ¹¹Furthermore, because we are united with Christ, we have received an inheritance from God, for he chose us in advance, and he makes everything work out according to his plan.

~ Ephesians 1:3-11

Rich in mercy

God is rich in mercy and He offers salvation to His enemies. His grace and goodness are abundant and He saved us when we were in bondage to sin. He bestows limitless mercy on sinners and it is through His mercy that we can now be called His children.

[1]Once you were dead because of your disobedience and your many sins. [2]You used to live in sin, just like the rest of the world, obeying the devil—the commander of the powers in the unseen world. He is the spirit at work in the hearts of those who refuse to obey God. [3]All of us used to live that way, following the passionate desires and inclinations of our sinful nature. By our very nature we were subject to God's anger, just like everyone else.

[4]But God is so rich in mercy, and he loved us so much, [5]that even though we were dead because of our sins, he gave us life when he raised Christ from the dead. (It is only by God's grace that you have been saved!) [6]For he raised us from the dead along with Christ and seated us with him in the heavenly realms because we are united with Christ Jesus. [7]So God can point to us in all future ages as examples of the incredible wealth of his grace and kindness toward us, as shown in all he has done for us who are united with Christ Jesus.

[8]God saved you by his grace when you believed. And you can't take credit for this; it is a gift from God. [9]Salvation is not a reward for the good things we have done, so none of us can boast about it. [10]For we are God's masterpiece. He has created us anew in Christ Jesus, so we can do the good things he planned for us long ago.

~ Ephesians 2:1-10

More than we can ask or think

God is greater and infinitely more than we can ever ask or think. He is the Lord. Paul prayed that the Lord would open His children's eyes to see the full extent of God's goodness. He prayed that they would be made complete with all the fullness of God.

[12]Because of Christ and our faith in him, we can now come boldly and confidently into God's presence. [13]So please don't lose heart because of my trials here. I am suffering for you, so you should feel honored.

[14]When I think of all this, I fall to my knees and pray to the Father, [15]the Creator of everything in heaven and on earth. [16]I pray that from his glorious, unlimited resources he will empower you with inner strength through his Spirit. [17]Then Christ will make his home in your hearts as you trust in him. Your roots will grow down into God's love and keep you strong. [18]And may you have the power to understand, as all God's people should, how wide, how long, how high, and how deep his love is. [19]May you experience the love of Christ, though it is too great to understand fully. Then you will be made complete with all the fullness of life and power that comes from God.

[20]Now all glory to God, who is able, through his mighty power at work within us, to accomplish infinitely more than we might ask or think. [21]Glory to him in the church and in Christ Jesus through all generations forever and ever! Amen

~ Ephesians 3:12-21

God's living gifts

When Christ returned to heaven it was a time of triumph and a time of giving gifts. The gifts He gave were living people: apostles, prophets, evangelists, pastors and teachers. These gifts function to keep Christ's earthly church on track and to build believers up in the faith.

⁴For there is one body and one Spirit, just as you have been called to one glorious hope for the future. ⁵There is one Lord, one faith, one baptism, ⁶and one God and Father, who is over all and in all and living through all.

⁷However, he has given each one of us a special gift through the generosity of Christ. ⁸That is why the Scriptures say,

"When he ascended to the heights, he led a crowd of captives and gave gifts to his people."

⁹Notice that it says "he ascended." This clearly means that Christ also descended to our lowly world. ¹⁰And the same one who descended is the one who ascended higher than all the heavens, so that he might fill the entire universe with himself.

¹¹Now these are the gifts Christ gave to the church: the apostles, the prophets, the evangelists, and the pastors and teachers. ¹²Their responsibility is to equip God's people to do his work and build up the church, the body of Christ. ¹³This will continue until we all come to such unity in our faith and knowledge of God's Son that we will be mature in the Lord, measuring up to the full and complete standard of Christ. ¹⁴Then we will no longer be immature like children. We won't be tossed and blown about by every wind of new teaching. We will not be influenced when people try to trick us with lies so clever they sound like the truth.

~ Ephesians 4:4-14

Use your time wisely

Paul urges us to use our time wisely. Time is loaded with possibilities; both positive and negative. We have to decide what we will do with all the seconds, minutes, hours and days at our disposal. We must use our time wisely by allowing the Holy Spirit to fill us with His power every day.

⁸For once you were full of darkness, but now you have light from the Lord. So live as people of light! ⁹For this light within you produces only what is good and right and true.

¹⁰Carefully determine what pleases the Lord. ¹¹Take no part in the worthless deeds of evil and darkness; instead, expose them. ¹²It is shameful even to talk about the things that ungodly people do in secret. ¹³But their evil intentions will be exposed when the light shines on them, ¹⁴for the light makes everything visible. This is why it is said,

"Awake, O sleeper, rise up from the dead, and Christ will give you light."

¹⁵So be careful how you live. Don't live like fools, but like those who are wise. ¹⁶Make the most of every opportunity in these evil days. ¹⁷Don't act thoughtlessly, but understand what the Lord wants you to do. ¹⁸Don't be drunk with wine, because that will ruin your life. Instead, be filled with the Holy Spirit, ¹⁹singing psalms and hymns and spiritual songs among yourselves, and making music to the Lord in your hearts. ²⁰And give thanks for everything to God the Father in the name of our Lord Jesus Christ.

~ Ephesians 5:8-20

Put on the full armor of God

Paul tells us to put on the full armor of God. Put on the helmet of salvation. Gird yourself with the belt of truth. Put on the body armor of God's righteousness and hold up the shield of faith. On your feet wear the peace that comes from the Good News. Let the Word of God be your sword.

[10]A final word: Be strong in the Lord and in his mighty power. [11]Put on all of God's armor so that you will be able to stand firm against all strategies of the devil. [12]For we are not fighting against flesh-and-blood enemies, but against evil rulers and authorities of the unseen world, against mighty powers in this dark world, and against evil spirits in the heavenly places.

[13]Therefore, put on every piece of God's armor so you will be able to resist the enemy in the time of evil. Then after the battle you will still be standing firm. [14]Stand your ground, putting on the belt of truth and the body armor of God's righteousness. [15]For shoes, put on the peace that comes from the Good News so that you will be fully prepared. [16]In addition to all of these, hold up the shield of faith to stop the fiery arrows of the devil. [17]Put on salvation as your helmet, and take the sword of the Spirit, which is the word of God.

[18]Pray in the Spirit at all times and on every occasion. Stay alert and be persistent in your prayers for all believers everywhere.

[19]And pray for me, too. Ask God to give me the right words so I can boldly explain God's mysterious plan that the Good News is for Jews and Gentiles alike. [20]I am in chains now, still preaching this message as God's ambassador. So pray that I will keep on speaking boldly for him, as I should.

~ Ephesians 6:10-20

Everything works for good

Sometimes we don't understand why we must go through difficulties. But then we discover that the Lord has used our time of suffering to His glory. Paul experienced how his time of suffering led to a great number of soldiers coming to hear about Christ. God alone can change pain and hurt into something good.

¹²And I want you to know, my dear brothers and sisters, that everything that has happened to me here has helped to spread the Good News. ¹³For everyone here, including the whole palace guard, knows that I am in chains because of Christ. ¹⁴And because of my imprisonment, most of the believers here have gained confidence and boldly speak God's message without fear.

¹⁵It's true that some are preaching out of jealousy and rivalry. But others preach about Christ with pure motives. ¹⁶They preach because they love me, for they know I have been appointed to defend the Good News. ¹⁷Those others do not have pure motives as they preach about Christ. They preach with selfish ambition, not sincerely, intending to make my chains more painful to me. ¹⁸But that doesn't matter. Whether their motives are false or genuine, the message about Christ is being preached either way, so I rejoice. And I will continue to rejoice.

~ Philippians 1:12-18

Living for Jesus

Paul made a wonderful confession of faith in verse 21. Christ is his only reason for living and only Christ means everything to him. Nothing and no one else meant as much to Paul as the living Christ. This is why Paul lived for Christ and was not afraid of death.

[18]But that doesn't matter. Whether their motives are false or genuine, the message about Christ is being preached either way, so I rejoice. And I will continue to rejoice. [19]For I know that as you pray for me and the Spirit of Jesus Christ helps me, this will lead to my deliverance.

[20]For I fully expect and hope that I will never be ashamed, but that I will continue to be bold for Christ, as I have been in the past. And I trust that my life will bring honor to Christ, whether I live or die. [21]For to me, living means living for Christ, and dying is even better. [22]But if I live, I can do more fruitful work for Christ. So I really don't know which is better. [23]I'm torn between two desires: I long to go and be with Christ, which would be far better for me. [24]But for your sakes, it is better that I continue to live.

[25]Knowing this, I am convinced that I will remain alive so I can continue to help all of you grow and experience the joy of your faith. [26]And when I come to you again, you will have even more reason to take pride in Christ Jesus because of what he is doing through me.

~ Philippians 1:18-26

Jesus Christ is Lord

Philippians 2:6-11 presents deep theological issues in the form of a song. Paul sings about Jesus. He tells how Jesus gave up His divine position and became a slave. He then humbled Himself even further and went to the cross. Then God elevated Him to the place of highest honor so that every knee will bow before Him.

¹Is there any encouragement from belonging to Christ? Any comfort from his love? Any fellowship together in the Spirit? Are your hearts tender and compassionate? ²Then make me truly happy by agreeing wholeheartedly with each other, loving one another, and working together with one mind and purpose.

³Don't be selfish; don't try to impress others. Be humble, thinking of others as better than yourselves. ⁴Don't look out only for your own interests, but take an interest in others, too.

⁵You must have the same attitude that Christ Jesus had.

⁶Though he was God, he did not think of equality with God as something to cling to.

⁷Instead, he gave up his divine privileges; he took the humble position of a slave and was born as a human being. When he appeared in human form,

⁸he humbled himself in obedience to God and died a criminal's death on a cross.

⁹Therefore, God elevated him to the place of highest honor and gave him the name above all other names,

¹⁰that at the name of Jesus every knee should bow, in heaven and on earth and under the earth,

¹¹and every tongue confess that Jesus Christ is Lord, to the glory of God the Father.

~ Philippians 2:1-11

Of infinite value

What Paul once considered valuable he now counts as worthless. The only thing that matters to him is knowing Christ Jesus his Lord. Jesus is the only and true reason for living.

²Watch out for those dogs, those people who do evil, those mutilators who say you must be circumcised to be saved. ³For we who worship by the Spirit of God are the ones who are truly circumcised. We rely on what Christ Jesus has done for us. We put no confidence in human effort, ⁴though I could have confidence in my own effort if anyone could. Indeed, if others have reason for confidence in their own efforts, I have even more!

⁵I was circumcised when I was eight days old. I am a pure-blooded citizen of Israel and a member of the tribe of Benjamin— a real Hebrew if there ever was one! I was a member of the Pharisees, who demand the strictest obedience to the Jewish law. ⁶I was so zealous that I harshly persecuted the church. And as for righteousness, I obeyed the law without fault.

⁷I once thought these things were valuable, but now I consider them worthless because of what Christ has done. ⁸Yes, everything else is worthless when compared with the infinite value of knowing Christ Jesus my Lord. For his sake I have discarded everything else, counting it all as garbage, so that I could gain Christ ⁹and become one with him. I no longer count on my own righteousness through obeying the law; rather, I become righteous through faith in Christ. For God's way of making us right with himself depends on faith. ¹⁰I want to know Christ and experience the mighty power that raised him from the dead. I want to suffer with him, sharing in his death, ¹¹so that one way or another I will experience the resurrection from the dead!

~ Philippians 3:2-11

Citizens of heaven

This world is not our home and our final address is somewhere else. Actually, we are already living as citizens of our new address. Paul makes it clear that we are citizens of heaven. We have eternal citizenship in our hearts. And for this reason we can live with hope in this life.

¹²I don't mean to say that I have already achieved these things or that I have already reached perfection. But I press on to possess that perfection for which Christ Jesus first possessed me.

¹³No, dear brothers and sisters, I have not achieved it, but I focus on this one thing: Forgetting the past and looking forward to what lies ahead, ¹⁴I press on to reach the end of the race and receive the heavenly prize for which God, through Christ Jesus, is calling us.

¹⁵Let all who are spiritually mature agree on these things. If you disagree on some point, I believe God will make it plain to you. ¹⁶But we must hold on to the progress we have already made.

¹⁷Dear brothers and sisters, pattern your lives after mine, and learn from those who follow our example. ¹⁸For I have told you often before, and I say it again with tears in my eyes, that there are many whose conduct shows they are really enemies of the cross of Christ. ¹⁹They are headed for destruction. Their god is their appetite, they brag about shameful things, and they think only about this life here on earth.

²⁰But we are citizens of heaven, where the Lord Jesus Christ lives. And we are eagerly waiting for him to return as our Savior. ²¹He will take our weak mortal bodies and change them into glorious bodies like his own, using the same power with which he will bring everything under his control.

~ Philippians 3:12-21

Stop worrying

We are natural worry-warts. We do it spontaneously and no one even has to teach us how to do it. Paul, however, warns that worry has no place in a believer's life. We must rather take all our needs to God in prayer and supplication.

¹Therefore, my dear brothers and sisters, stay true to the Lord. I love you and long to see you, dear friends, for you are my joy and the crown I receive for my work.

²Now I appeal to Euodia and Syntyche. Please, because you belong to the Lord, settle your disagreement. ³And I ask you, my true partner, to help these two women, for they worked hard with me in telling others the Good News. They worked along with Clement and the rest of my co-workers, whose names are written in the Book of Life.

⁴Always be full of joy in the Lord. I say it again—rejoice! ⁵Let everyone see that you are considerate in all you do. Remember, the Lord is coming soon.

⁶Don't worry about anything; instead, pray about everything. Tell God what you need, and thank him for all he has done. ⁷Then you will experience God's peace, which exceeds anything we can understand. His peace will guard your hearts and minds as you live in Christ Jesus.

⁸And now, dear brothers and sisters, one final thing. Fix your thoughts on what is true, and honorable, and right, and pure, and lovely, and admirable. Think about things that are excellent and worthy of praise. ⁹Keep putting into practice all you learned and received from me—everything you heard from me and saw me doing. Then the God of peace will be with you.

~ Philippians 4:1-9

I can do everything

In Philippians 4:12 Paul is not saying that faith will change you into a superhuman. What he is saying is that faith enables us to handle everything that life sends our way. Faith brings endurance and endurance brings hope.

[10]How I praise the Lord that you are concerned about me again. I know you have always been concerned for me, but you didn't have the chance to help me. [11]Not that I was ever in need, for I have learned how to be content with whatever I have. [12]I know how to live on almost nothing or with everything. I have learned the secret of living in every situation, whether it is with a full stomach or empty, with plenty or little. [13]For I can do everything through Christ, who gives me strength. [14]Even so, you have done well to share with me in my present difficulty.

[15]As you know, you Philippians were the only ones who gave me financial help when I first brought you the Good News and then traveled on from Macedonia. No other church did this. [16]Even when I was in Thessalonica you sent help more than once. [17]I don't say this because I want a gift from you. Rather, I want you to receive a reward for your kindness.

[18]At the moment I have all I need—and more! I am generously supplied with the gifts you sent me with Epaphroditus. They are a sweet-smelling sacrifice that is acceptable and pleasing to God. [19]And this same God who takes care of me will supply all your needs from his glorious riches, which have been given to us in Christ Jesus. [20]Now all glory to God our Father forever and ever! Amen.

~ Philippians 4:10-20

Look at Jesus, see God!

In Colossians 1:15-20 Paul sings about Christ's greatness and supremacy as the One who reigns over the entire universe. He is the everlasting Lord who existed before anything else and who holds everything together, both things visible and invisible. And by His grace, Christ also holds our lives in His powerful hand.

¹⁵Christ is the visible image of the invisible God. He existed before anything was created and is supreme over all creation, ¹⁶for through him God created everything in the heavenly realms and on earth. He made the things we can see and the things we can't see—such as thrones, kingdoms, rulers, and authorities in the unseen world. Everything was created through him and for him. ¹⁷He existed before anything else, and he holds all creation together. ¹⁸Christ is also the head of the church, which is his body. He is the beginning, supreme over all who rise from the dead. So he is first in everything. ¹⁹For God in all his fullness was pleased to live in Christ, ²⁰and through him God reconciled everything to himself. He made peace with everything in heaven and on earth by means of Christ's blood on the cross.

²¹This includes you who were once far away from God. You were his enemies, separated from him by your evil thoughts and actions. ²²Yet now he has reconciled you to himself through the death of Christ in his physical body. As a result, he has brought you into his own presence, and you are holy and blameless as you stand before him without a single fault. ²³But you must continue to believe this truth and stand firmly in it. Don't drift away from the assurance you received when you heard the Good News. The Good News has been preached all over the world, and I, Paul, have been appointed as God's servant to proclaim it.

~ Colossians 1:15-23

Forget outdated rituals

It is ridiculously easy to exchange the true gospel for a handful of outdated religious traditions. To keep Sabbaths, festivals and other rituals looks pious, even impressive. But Paul doubts whether this helps in conquering man's sinful nature. All that matters is to sincerely follow Jesus.

[16]So don't let anyone condemn you for what you eat or drink, or for not celebrating certain holy days or new moon ceremonies or Sabbaths. [17]For these rules are only shadows of the reality yet to come. And Christ himself is that reality. [18]Don't let anyone condemn you by insisting on pious self-denial or the worship of angels, saying they have had visions about these things. Their sinful minds have made them proud, [19]and they are not connected to Christ, the head of the body. For he holds the whole body together with its joints and ligaments, and it grows as God nourishes it.

[20]You have died with Christ, and he has set you free from the spiritual powers of this world. So why do you keep on following the rules of the world, such as, [21]"Don't handle! Don't taste! Don't touch!"? [22]Such rules are mere human teachings about things that deteriorate as we use them. [23]These rules may seem wise because they require strong devotion, pious self-denial, and severe bodily discipline. But they provide no help in conquering a person's evil desires.

~ Colossians 2:16-23

Wear the right clothes

The right clothes to wear for the gospel are not church clothes, but work clothes. It is to clothe yourself with tenderhearted mercy, kindness, humility, gentleness and patience. If we put on Christ's clothes we will treat others with respect and forgive those who have offended us.

¹²Since God chose you to be the holy people he loves, you must clothe yourselves with tenderhearted mercy, kindness, humility, gentleness, and patience. ¹³Make allowance for each other's faults, and forgive anyone who offends you. Remember, the Lord forgave you, so you must forgive others. ¹⁴Above all, clothe yourselves with love, which binds us all together in perfect harmony. ¹⁵And let the peace that comes from Christ rule in your hearts. For as members of one body you are called to live in peace. And always be thankful.

¹⁶Let the message about Christ, in all its richness, fill your lives. Teach and counsel each other with all the wisdom he gives. Sing psalms and hymns and spiritual songs to God with thankful hearts. ¹⁷And whatever you do or say, do it as a representative of the Lord Jesus, giving thanks through him to God the Father.

~ Colossians 3:12-17

Keep on praying

Pray without ceasing, but pray wisely. Prayer is not a spiritual lever with which we can manipulate God. Prayer is to stand up for other believers. It is to lift up their names to God's throne of grace and to plead that God will touch their lives.

¹Masters, be just and fair to your slaves. Remember that you also have a Master—in heaven.

²Devote yourselves to prayer with an alert mind and a thankful heart. ³Pray for us, too, that God will give us many opportunities to speak about his mysterious plan concerning Christ. That is why I am here in chains. ⁴Pray that I will proclaim this message as clearly as I should.

⁵Live wisely among those who are not believers, and make the most of every opportunity. ⁶Let your conversation be gracious and attractive so that you will have the right response for everyone.

⁷Tychicus will give you a full report about how I am getting along. He is a beloved brother and faithful helper who serves with me in the Lord's work. ⁸I have sent him to you for this very purpose—to let you know how we are doing and to encourage you. ⁹I am also sending Onesimus, a faithful and beloved brother, one of your own people. He and Tychicus will tell you everything that's happening here.

¹⁰Aristarchus, who is in prison with me, sends you his greetings, and so does Mark, Barnabas's cousin. As you were instructed before, make Mark welcome if he comes your way. ¹¹Jesus (the one we call Justus) also sends his greetings. These are the only Jewish believers among my co-workers; they are working with me here for the Kingdom of God. And what a comfort they have been!

~ Colossians 4:1-11

NOVEMBER

Faith, hope and love

In verse 3 Paul captures the heartbeat of the gospel when he speaks about how the Thessalonian congregation's faith is expressed through their deeds. He also tells how they are acting out their love and how strong their expectations are that Christ will return. Faith, hope and love are a winning combination.

²We always thank God for all of you and pray for you constantly. ³As we pray to our God and Father about you, we think of your faithful work, your loving deeds, and the enduring hope you have because of our Lord Jesus Christ.

⁴We know, dear brothers and sisters, that God loves you and has chosen you to be his own people. ⁵For when we brought you the Good News, it was not only with words but also with power, for the Holy Spirit gave you full assurance that what we said was true. And you know of our concern for you from the way we lived when we were with you. ⁶So you received the message with joy from the Holy Spirit in spite of the severe suffering it brought you. In this way, you imitated both us and the Lord. ⁷As a result, you have become an example to all the believers in Greece—throughout both Macedonia and Achaia.

⁸And now the word of the Lord is ringing out from you to people everywhere, even beyond Macedonia and Achaia, for wherever we go we find people telling us about your faith in God. We don't need to tell them about it, ⁹for they keep talking about the wonderful welcome you gave us and how you turned away from idols to serve the living and true God. ¹⁰And they speak of how you are looking forward to the coming of God's Son from heaven—Jesus, whom God raised from the dead. He is the one who has rescued us from the terrors of the coming judgment.

~ 1 Thessalonians 1:2-10

Like a mother

Paul's great compassion for his congregation is demonstrated in verses 7-8. He lovingly cares for his congregation, like a mother cares for and nurtures her newborn baby. Love concerns relationships full of gentleness and this makes believers magnetic.

¹You yourselves know, dear brothers and sisters, that our visit to you was not a failure. ²You know how badly we had been treated at Philippi just before we came to you and how much we suffered there. Yet our God gave us the courage to declare his Good News to you boldly, in spite of great opposition. ³So you can see we were not preaching with any deceit or impure motives or trickery.

⁴For we speak as messengers approved by God to be entrusted with the Good News. Our purpose is to please God, not people. He alone examines the motives of our hearts. ⁵Never once did we try to win you with flattery, as you well know. And God is our witness that we were not pretending to be your friends just to get your money! ⁶As for human praise, we have never sought it from you or anyone else. ⁷As apostles of Christ we certainly had a right to make some demands of you, but instead we were like children among you. Or we were like a mother feeding and caring for her own children. ⁸We loved you so much that we shared with you not only God's Good News but our own lives, too.

¹⁰You yourselves are our witnesses—and so is God—that we were devout and honest and faultless toward all of you believers. ¹¹And you know that we treated each of you as a father treats his own children. ¹²We pleaded with you, encouraged you, and urged you to live your lives in a way that God would consider worthy. For he called you to share in his Kingdom and glory.

~ 1 Thessalonians 2:1-8, 10-12

Integrity in a nutshell

Faith does not simply consist of theories and nice-sounding words. It is rather a way of living in the presence of the Triune God and in the company of other people. Faith affects our marriage, our relationships with other people and our day-to-day living. Faith can be touched, seen and experienced.

¹Finally, dear brothers and sisters, we urge you in the name of the Lord Jesus to live in a way that pleases God, as we have taught you. You live this way already, and we encourage you to do so even more. ²For you remember what we taught you by the authority of the Lord Jesus. ³God's will is for you to be holy, so stay away from all sexual sin. ⁴Then each of you will control his own body and live in holiness and honor—⁵not in lustful passion like the pagans who do not know God and his ways.

⁶Never harm or cheat a Christian brother in this matter by violating his wife, for the Lord avenges all such sins, as we have solemnly warned you before. ⁷God has called us to live holy lives, not impure lives. ⁸Therefore, anyone who refuses to live by these rules is not disobeying human teaching but is rejecting God, who gives his Holy Spirit to you.

⁹But we don't need to write to you about the importance of loving each other, for God himself has taught you to love one another. ¹⁰Indeed, you already show your love for all the believers throughout Macedonia. Even so, dear brothers and sisters, we urge you to love them even more.

~ 1 Thessalonians 4:1-10

Don't be lazy

Paul warns against laziness. He tells the congregation in Thessalonica to work hard and mind their own business. We should not constantly interfere in other people's lives and make our opinions about them known.

12Dear brothers and sisters, honor those who are your leaders in the Lord's work. They work hard among you and give you spiritual guidance. 13Show them great respect and wholehearted love because of their work. And live peacefully with each other.

14Brothers and sisters, we urge you to warn those who are lazy. Encourage those who are timid. Take tender care of those who are weak. Be patient with everyone.

15See that no one pays back evil for evil, but always try to do good to each other and to all people.

16Always be joyful. 17Never stop praying. 18Be thankful in all circumstances, for this is God's will for you who belong to Christ Jesus. 19Do not stifle the Holy Spirit. 20Do not scoff at prophecies, 21but test everything that is said. Hold on to what is good. 22Stay away from every kind of evil.

23Now may the God of peace make you holy in every way, and may your whole spirit and soul and body be kept blameless until our Lord Jesus Christ comes again. 24God will make this happen, for he who calls you is faithful.

25Dear brothers and sisters, pray for us.

26Greet all the brothers and sisters with Christian love.

28May the grace of our Lord Jesus Christ be with you.

~ 1 Thessalonians 5:12-26, 28

Judgment awaits

God makes Himself known as the God of love, but this doesn't cancel out His judgment. The day of reckoning is on the horizon. He warns us about it ahead of time so that we can't hide behind all kinds of excuses on that last day.

[3]Dear brothers and sisters, we can't help but thank God for you, because your faith is flourishing and your love for one another is growing. [4]We proudly tell God's other churches about your endurance and faithfulness in all the persecutions and hardships you are suffering. [5]And God will use this persecution to show his justice and to make you worthy of his Kingdom, for which you are suffering.

[6]In his justice he will pay back those who persecute you. [7]And God will provide rest for you who are being persecuted and also for us when the Lord Jesus appears from heaven. He will come with his mighty angels, [8]in flaming fire, bringing judgment on those who don't know God and on those who refuse to obey the Good News of our Lord Jesus. [9]They will be punished with eternal destruction, forever separated from the Lord and from his glorious power. [10]When he comes on that day, he will receive glory from his holy people—praise from all who believe. And this includes you, for you believed what we told you about him.

[11]So we keep on praying for you, asking our God to enable you to live a life worthy of his call. May he give you the power to accomplish all the good things your faith prompts you to do.

~ 2 Thessalonians 1:3-11

Stand firm

Paul tells us to live lives dedicated to God in light of the approaching end of the world. God is our fortress. We endure till the end so that we can inherit the divine glory of Christ. The way to do this is to be obedient to the truth of our faith.

[3]Don't be fooled by what they say. For that day will not come until there is a great rebellion against God and the man of lawlessness is revealed—the one who brings destruction. [4]He will exalt himself and defy everything that people call god and every object of worship. He will even sit in the temple of God, claiming that he himself is God.

[5]Don't you remember that I told you about all this when I was with you? [6]And you know what is holding him back, for he can be revealed only when his time comes. [7]For this lawlessness is already at work secretly, and it will remain secret until the one who is holding it back steps out of the way. [8]Then the man of lawlessness will be revealed, but the Lord Jesus will kill him with the breath of his mouth and destroy him by the splendor of his coming. [9]This man will come to do the work of Satan with counterfeit power and signs and miracles. [10]He will use every kind of evil deception to fool those on their way to destruction, because they refuse to love and accept the truth that would save them. [11]So God will cause them to be greatly deceived, and they will believe these lies. [12]Then they will be condemned for enjoying evil rather than believing the truth.

~ 2 Thessalonians 2:3-12

No work, no food

In Thessalonica a few believers stopped working and expected fellow believers to provide for them while they piously waited for the Second Coming. Paul admonished them for this and told them to start working immediately. Those who don't work don't get to eat.

[6]And now, dear brothers and sisters, we give you this command in the name of our Lord Jesus Christ: Stay away from all believers who live idle lives and don't follow the tradition they received from us. [7]For you know that you ought to imitate us. We were not idle when we were with you. [8]We never accepted food from anyone without paying for it. We worked hard day and night so we would not be a burden to any of you. [9]We certainly had the right to ask you to feed us, but we wanted to give you an example to follow. [10]Even while we were with you, we gave you this command: "Those unwilling to work will not get to eat."

[11]Yet we hear that some of you are living idle lives, refusing to work and meddling in other people's business. [12]We command such people and urge them in the name of the Lord Jesus Christ to settle down and work to earn their own living. [13]As for the rest of you, dear brothers and sisters, never get tired of doing good.

[14]Take note of those who refuse to obey what we say in this letter. Stay away from them so they will be ashamed. [15]Don't think of them as enemies, but warn them as you would a brother or sister.

~ 2 Thessalonians 3:6-15

Deemed trustworthy

It is an honor when Christ deems you trustworthy enough to live and work for Him. It is an indescribable privilege to be called to serve Him in full-time ministry. Then, along with Paul, you silently bow before the Lord who appointed you in His great mercy.

[12]I thank Christ Jesus our Lord, who has given me strength to do his work. He considered me trustworthy and appointed me to serve him, [13]even though I used to blaspheme the name of Christ. In my insolence, I persecuted his people. But God had mercy on me because I did it in ignorance and unbelief. [14]Oh, how generous and gracious our Lord was! He filled me with the faith and love that come from Christ Jesus.

[15]This is a trustworthy saying, and everyone should accept it: "Christ Jesus came into the world to save sinners"—and I am the worst of them all. [16]But God had mercy on me so that Christ Jesus could use me as a prime example of his great patience with even the worst sinners. Then others will realize that they, too, can believe in him and receive eternal life. [17]All honor and glory to God forever and ever! He is the eternal King, the unseen one who never dies; he alone is God. Amen.

[18]Timothy, my son, here are my instructions for you, based on the prophetic words spoken about you earlier. May they help you fight well in the Lord's battles. [19]Cling to your faith in Christ, and keep your conscience clear. For some people have deliberately violated their consciences; as a result, their faith has been shipwrecked.

~ 1 Timothy 1:12-19

Intercede for leaders

We must continually pray for those in leadership positions in society so that we can live in peace and quiet every day. We must pray for an orderly and God-fearing society. Through our prayers we must take part in God's governance of the world.

[1]I urge you, first of all, to pray for all people. Ask God to help them; intercede on their behalf, and give thanks for them. [2]Pray this way for kings and all who are in authority so that we can live peaceful and quiet lives marked by godliness and dignity. [3]This is good and pleases God our Savior, [4]who wants everyone to be saved and to understand the truth. [5]For there is only one God and one Mediator who can reconcile God and humanity— the man Christ Jesus. [6]He gave his life to purchase freedom for everyone. This is the message God gave to the world at just the right time. [7]And I have been chosen as a preacher and apostle to teach the Gentiles this message about faith and truth. I'm not exaggerating—just telling the truth.

[8]In every place of worship, I want men to pray with holy hands lifted up to God, free from anger and controversy. [9]And I want women to be modest in their appearance. They should wear decent and appropriate clothing and not draw attention to themselves by the way they fix their hair or by wearing gold or pearls or expensive clothes. [10]For women who claim to be devoted to God should make themselves attractive by the good things they do.

~ 1 Timothy 2:1-10

The essence of Christ

In verse 16 Paul poignantly sums up Christ's work. He tells how Jesus came to earth as a human being, and His integrity was confirmed everywhere by the Holy Spirit. When Christ completed His earthly mission, He was taken to heaven in glory. He is Lord over all.

8In the same way, deacons must be well respected and have integrity. They must not be heavy drinkers or dishonest with money. 9They must be committed to the mystery of the faith now revealed and must live with a clear conscience. 10Before they are appointed as deacons, let them be closely examined. If they pass the test, then let them serve as deacons.

11In the same way, their wives must be respected and must not slander others. They must exercise self-control and be faithful in everything they do.

12A deacon must be faithful to his wife, and he must manage his children and household well. 13Those who do well as deacons will be rewarded with respect from others and will have increased confidence in their faith in Christ Jesus.

14I am writing these things to you now, even though I hope to be with you soon, 15so that if I am delayed, you will know how people must conduct themselves in the household of God. This is the church of the living God, which is the pillar and foundation of the truth.

16Without question, this is the great mystery of our faith: Christ was revealed in a human body and vindicated by the Spirit. He was seen by angels and announced to the nations. He was believed in throughout the world and taken to heaven in glory.

~ 1 Timothy 3:8-16

Flee towards God

Sometimes you have to flee very quickly. When temptation rears its ugly head, you must quickly get away. Make sure that you and sin are never in the same place at the same time. Flee to God. Let Him be your shelter. Then you will be safe and protected.

[11]But you, Timothy, are a man of God; so run from all these evil things. Pursue righteousness and a godly life, along with faith, love, perseverance, and gentleness. [12]Fight the good fight for the true faith. Hold tightly to the eternal life to which God has called you, which you have confessed so well before many witnesses. [13]And I charge you before God, who gives life to all, and before Christ Jesus, who gave a good testimony before Pontius Pilate, [14]that you obey this command without wavering. Then no one can find fault with you from now until our Lord Jesus Christ comes again. [15]For at just the right time Christ will be revealed from heaven by the blessed and only almighty God, the King of all kings and Lord of all lords. [16]He alone can never die, and he lives in light so brilliant that no human can approach him. No human eye has ever seen him, nor ever will. All honor and power to him forever! Amen.

[17]Teach those who are rich in this world not to be proud and not to trust in their money, which is so unreliable. Their trust should be in God, who richly gives us all we need for our enjoyment. [18]Tell them to use their money to do good. They should be rich in good works and generous to those in need, always being ready to share with others.

~ 1 Timothy 6:11-18

Clear conscience

A clear conscience is an exceptional blessing from God. How many people can say that they serve God with a clear conscience? How many people's private and public lives are in harmony with each other? Only genuine faith in the Triune God frees people from hypocrisy.

³Timothy, I thank God for you—the God I serve with a clear conscience, just as my ancestors did. Night and day I constantly remember you in my prayers. ⁴I long to see you again, for I remember your tears as we parted. And I will be filled with joy when we are together again.

⁵I remember your genuine faith, for you share the faith that first filled your grandmother Lois and your mother, Eunice. And I know that same faith continues strong in you. ⁶This is why I remind you to fan into flames the spiritual gift God gave you when I laid my hands on you. ⁷For God has not given us a spirit of fear and timidity, but of power, love, and self-discipline. ⁸So never be ashamed to tell others about our Lord. And don't be ashamed of me, either, even though I'm in prison for him. With the strength God gives you, be ready to suffer with me for the sake of the Good News.

⁹For God saved us and called us to live a holy life. He did this, not because we deserved it, but because that was his plan from before the beginning of time—to show us his grace through Christ Jesus. ¹⁰And now he has made all of this plain to us by the appearing of Christ Jesus, our Savior. He broke the power of death and illuminated the way to life and immortality through the Good News.

~ 2 Timothy 1:3-10

Die to live

To walk with Christ on His path of suffering is to walk towards life. To die with Him is to find life. To experience persecution is to be on your way to the place where Christ reigns. Christ is the only One we sacrifice all for and live for.

[1]Timothy, my dear son, be strong through the grace that God gives you in Christ Jesus. [2]You have heard me teach things that have been confirmed by many reliable witnesses. Now teach these truths to other trustworthy people who will be able to pass them on to others.

[3]Endure suffering along with me, as a good soldier of Christ Jesus. [4]Soldiers don't get tied up in the affairs of civilian life, for then they cannot please the officer who enlisted them. [5]And athletes cannot win the prize unless they follow the rules. [6]And hardworking farmers should be the first to enjoy the fruit of their labor. [7]Think about what I am saying. The Lord will help you understand all these things.

[8]Always remember that Jesus Christ, a descendant of King David, was raised from the dead. This is the Good News I preach. [9]And because I preach this Good News, I am suffering and have been chained like a criminal. But the word of God cannot be chained. [10]So I am willing to endure anything if it will bring salvation and eternal glory in Christ Jesus to those God has chosen. [11]This is a trustworthy saying:

If we die with him, we will also live with him.

~ 2 Timothy 2:1-11

God's breath is in the Word

The Word was called to life by God. The aim of this Word is to focus our lives on God. It serves as a guideline to keep our lives on the right course, on God's course. Through the Word God shapes our lives to do His will.

[6]They are the kind who work their way into people's homes and win the confidence of vulnerable women who are burdened with the guilt of sin and controlled by various desires. [7](Such women are forever following new teachings, but they are never able to understand the truth.) [8]These teachers oppose the truth just as Jannes and Jambres opposed Moses. They have depraved minds and a counterfeit faith. [9]But they won't get away with this for long. Someday everyone will recognize what fools they are, just as with Jannes and Jambres.

[10]But you, Timothy, certainly know what I teach, and how I live, and what my purpose in life is. You know my faith, my patience, my love, and my endurance. [11]You know how much persecution and suffering I have endured. You know all about how I was persecuted in Antioch, Iconium, and Lystra—but the Lord rescued me from all of it. [12]Yes, and everyone who wants to live a godly life in Christ Jesus will suffer persecution. [13]But evil people and impostors will flourish. They will deceive others and will themselves be deceived.

[14]But you must remain faithful to the things you have been taught. You know they are true, for you know you can trust those who taught you. [15]You have been taught the holy Scriptures from childhood, and they have given you the wisdom to receive the salvation that comes by trusting in Christ Jesus.

~ 2 Timothy 3:6-15

On course until the end

When the Lord is the sum total of your existence, you live for Him until the end. Paul lived full-speed for Christ until he crossed the winning line. His whole life was focused on Christ; therefore that he ran through death's finishing line short of breath. There Christ waited for him with the heavenly victor's crown.

³For a time is coming when people will no longer listen to sound and wholesome teaching. They will follow their own desires and will look for teachers who will tell them whatever their itching ears want to hear. ⁴They will reject the truth and chase after myths.

⁵But you should keep a clear mind in every situation. Don't be afraid of suffering for the Lord. Work at telling others the Good News, and fully carry out the ministry God has given you.

⁶As for me, my life has already been poured out as an offering to God. The time of my death is near. ⁷I have fought the good fight, I have finished the race, and I have remained faithful. ⁸And now the prize awaits me—the crown of righteousness, which the Lord, the righteous Judge, will give me on the day of his return. And the prize is not just for me but for all who eagerly look forward to his appearing.

⁹Timothy, please come as soon as you can. ¹⁰Demas has deserted me because he loves the things of this life and has gone to Thessalonica. Crescens has gone to Galatia, and Titus has gone to Dalmatia. ¹¹Only Luke is with me. Bring Mark with you when you come, for he will be helpful to me in my ministry. ¹²I sent Tychicus to Ephesus. ¹³When you come, be sure to bring the coat I left with Carpus at Troas. Also bring my books, and especially my papers.

~ 2 Timothy 4:3-13

First character and then talent

Character is what God seeks first in the lives of His earthly leaders. Not talent first, but character. Thus holy lives rather than effective ministries. Elders and other church leaders must have a holy way of life that surpasses their talents and learned abilities.

⁵I left you on the island of Crete so you could complete our work there and appoint elders in each town as I instructed you. ⁶An elder must live a blameless life. He must be faithful to his wife, and his children must be believers who don't have a reputation for being wild or rebellious. ⁷An elder is a manager of God's household, so he must live a blameless life. He must not be arrogant or quick-tempered; he must not be a heavy drinker, violent, or dishonest with money.

⁸Rather, he must enjoy having guests in his home, and he must love what is good. He must live wisely and be just. He must live a devout and disciplined life. ⁹He must have a strong belief in the trustworthy message he was taught; then he will be able to encourage others with wholesome teaching and show those who oppose it where they are wrong.

¹⁰For there are many rebellious people who engage in useless talk and deceive others. This is especially true of those who insist on circumcision for salvation. ¹¹They must be silenced, because they are turning whole families away from the truth by their false teaching. And they do it only for money.

~ Titus 1:5-11

Set free from slavery

Christ paid the price to free us from the grip of death, sin and the law. Christ gave His life for us so that we can live pure lives. We are now His and our lives are under His control. We are His people, His special people here on earth. For this reason we can live enthusiastically.

[6]In the same way, encourage the young men to live wisely. [7]And you yourself must be an example to them by doing good works of every kind. Let everything you do reflect the integrity and seriousness of your teaching. [8]Teach the truth so that your teaching can't be criticized. Then those who oppose us will be ashamed and have nothing bad to say about us.

[9]Slaves must always obey their masters and do their best to please them. They must not talk back [10]or steal, but must show themselves to be entirely trustworthy and good. Then they will make the teaching about God our Savior attractive in every way.

[11]For the grace of God has been revealed, bringing salvation to all people. [12]And we are instructed to turn from godless living and sinful pleasures. We should live in this evil world with wisdom, righteousness, and devotion to God, [13]while we look forward with hope to that wonderful day when the glory of our great God and Savior, Jesus Christ, will be revealed.

[14]He gave his life to free us from every kind of sin, to cleanse us, and to make us his very own people, totally committed to doing good deeds. [15]You must teach these things and encourage the believers to do them. You have the authority to correct them when necessary, so don't let anyone disregard what you say.

~ Titus 2:6-15

Tame your tongue

We must not slander, gossip or quarrel because such behavior is not fitting for followers of Christ. We are called to be gentle, loving and accommodating. We are the ones who must build bridges between people and also between God and people.

[1]Remind the believers to submit to the government and its officers. They should be obedient, always ready to do what is good. [2]They must not slander anyone and must avoid quarreling. Instead, they should be gentle and show true humility to everyone.

[3]Once we, too, were foolish and disobedient. We were misled and became slaves to many lusts and pleasures. Our lives were full of evil and envy, and we hated each other.

[4]But—"When God our Savior revealed his kindness and love, [5]he saved us, not because of the righteous things we had done, but because of his mercy. He washed away our sins, giving us a new birth and new life through the Holy Spirit. [6]He generously poured out the Spirit upon us through Jesus Christ our Savior. [7]Because of his grace he declared us righteous and gave us confidence that we will inherit eternal life."

[8]This is a trustworthy saying, and I want you to insist on these teachings so that all who trust in God will devote themselves to doing good. These teachings are good and beneficial for everyone.

~ Titus 3:1-8

Slave becomes brother

Onesimus was a slave and after he ran away from his master, Philemon, he landed in prison. Here he met Paul who led him to faith in Christ. Then Paul sent Onesimus back to Philemon as a brother. The slave became his master's brother and equal in Christ.

[8]That is why I am boldly asking a favor of you. I could demand it in the name of Christ because it is the right thing for you to do. [9]But because of our love, I prefer simply to ask you. Consider this as a request from me—Paul, an old man and now also a prisoner for the sake of Christ Jesus.

[10]I appeal to you to show kindness to my child, Onesimus. I became his father in the faith while here in prison. [11]Onesimus hasn't been of much use to you in the past, but now he is very useful to both of us. [12]I am sending him back to you, and with him comes my own heart. [13]I wanted to keep him here with me while I am in these chains for preaching the Good News, and he would have helped me on your behalf. [14]But I didn't want to do anything without your consent. I wanted you to help because you were willing, not because you were forced. [15]It seems you lost Onesimus for a little while so that you could have him back forever. [16]He is no longer like a slave to you. He is more than a slave, for he is a beloved brother, especially to me. Now he will mean much more to you, both as a man and as a brother in the Lord.

[17]So if you consider me your partner, welcome him as you would welcome me. [18]If he has wronged you in any way or owes you anything, charge it to me. [19]I, PAUL, WRITE THIS WITH MY OWN HAND: I WILL REPAY IT. AND I WON'T MENTION THAT YOU OWE ME YOUR VERY SOUL! [20]Yes, my brother, please do me this favor for the Lord's sake. Give me this encouragement in Christ.

~ Philemon v. 8-20

The end time is near

The writer of Hebrews says that we are in the final days. The dawn of the end times was when Christ came to earth. This is when God started to speak to us through Christ. He is God's official mouthpiece. He is the image of the invisible God. He is God in action.

[1] Long ago God spoke many times and in many ways to our ancestors through the prophets. [2] And now in these final days, he has spoken to us through his Son. God promised everything to the Son as an inheritance, and through the Son he created the universe. [3] The Son radiates God's own glory and expresses the very character of God, and he sustains everything by the mighty power of his command. When he had cleansed us from our sins, he sat down in the place of honor at the right hand of the majestic God in heaven.

[4] This shows that the Son is far greater than the angels, just as the name God gave him is greater than their names. [5] For God never said to any angel what he said to Jesus:

"You are my Son. Today I have become your Father." God also said,

"I will be his Father, and he will be my Son."

[6] And when he brought his supreme Son into the world, God said,

"Let all of God's angels worship him."

~ Hebrews 1:1-6

Defeated

Christ crushed Satan under His heel. Christ destroyed the one who has power over death and confiscated his weapons. Satan does not have the final say here on earth. Christ is the Victor over all powers.

[11]So now Jesus and the ones he makes holy have the same Father. That is why Jesus is not ashamed to call them his brothers and sisters. [12]For he said to God,

"I will proclaim your name to my brothers and sisters. I will praise you among your assembled people."

[13]He also said, "I will put my trust in him," that is, "I and the children God has given me."

[14]Because God's children are human beings—made of flesh and blood—the Son also became flesh and blood. For only as a human being could he die, and only by dying could he break the power of the devil, who had the power of death. [15]Only in this way could he set free all who have lived their lives as slaves to the fear of dying.

[16]We also know that the Son did not come to help angels; he came to help the descendants of Abraham. [17]Therefore, it was necessary for him to be made in every respect like us, his brothers and sisters, so that he could be our merciful and faithful High Priest before God. Then he could offer a sacrifice that would take away the sins of the people. [18]Since he himself has gone through suffering and testing, he is able to help us when we are being tested.

~ Hebrews 2:11-18

A High Priest who understands

We have a good and merciful High Priest in heaven. His name is Christ. He became human and therefore understands all our weaknesses. He knows exactly what battle we must fight every day. This is why we can approach Him freely and without inhibitions.

[8]Now if Joshua had succeeded in giving them this rest, God would not have spoken about another day of rest still to come. [9]So there is a special rest still waiting for the people of God. [10]For all who have entered into God's rest have rested from their labors, just as God did after creating the world. [11]So let us do our best to enter that rest. But if we disobey God, as the people of Israel did, we will fall.

[12]For the word of God is alive and powerful. It is sharper than the sharpest two-edged sword, cutting between soul and spirit, between joint and marrow. It exposes our innermost thoughts and desires. [13]Nothing in all creation is hidden from God. Everything is naked and exposed before his eyes, and he is the one to whom we are accountable.

[14]So then, since we have a great High Priest who has entered heaven, Jesus the Son of God, let us hold firmly to what we believe.

[15]This High Priest of ours understands our weaknesses, for he faced all of the same testings we do, yet he did not sin. [16]So let us come boldly to the throne of our gracious God. There we will receive his mercy, and we will find grace to help us when we need it most.

~ Hebrews 4:8-16

Growing spiritually

Spiritual growth is something everyone talks about. We all want to grow, but it happens to only a few people. The writer to the Hebrews says that spiritual growth goes hand in hand with new topics of discussion. We can't carry on speaking about basic teachings such as baptism, repentance and laying on of hands. We need to progress to further understanding in order to grow.

[1]So let us stop going over the basic teachings about Christ again and again. Let us go on instead and become mature in our understanding. Surely we don't need to start again with the fundamental importance of repenting from evil deeds and placing our faith in God. [2]You don't need further instruction about baptisms, the laying on of hands, the resurrection of the dead, and eternal judgment. [3]And so, God willing, we will move forward to further understanding.

[4]For it is impossible to bring back to repentance those who were once enlightened—those who have experienced the good things of heaven and shared in the Holy Spirit, [5]who have tasted the goodness of the word of God and the power of the age to come—[6]and who then turn away from God. It is impossible to bring such people back to repentance; by rejecting the Son of God, they themselves are nailing him to the cross once again and holding him up to public shame.

[7]When the ground soaks up the falling rain and bears a good crop for the farmer, it has God's blessing. [8]But if a field bears thorns and thistles, it is useless. The farmer will soon condemn that field and burn it.

~ Hebrews 6:1-8

A High Priest in heaven

Jesus is on our side. He is partial and looks after our interests all the time. He intercedes for us with the Father. He argues our case. His sacrifice on the cross was for us, and will always have saving power. As our only High Priest, Jesus can give us life.

¹Here is the main point: We have a High Priest who sat down in the place of honor beside the throne of the majestic God in heaven. ²There he ministers in the heavenly Tabernacle, the true place of worship that was built by the Lord and not by human hands.

³And since every high priest is required to offer gifts and sacrifices, our High Priest must make an offering, too. ⁴If he were here on earth, he would not even be a priest, since there already are priests who offer the gifts required by the law. ⁵They serve in a system of worship that is only a copy, a shadow of the real one in heaven. For when Moses was getting ready to build the Tabernacle, God gave him this warning: "Be sure that you make everything according to the pattern I have shown you here on the mountain."

⁶But now Jesus, our High Priest, has been given a ministry that is far superior to the old priesthood, for he is the one who mediates for us a far better covenant with God, based on better promises.

⁷If the first covenant had been faultless, there would have been no need for a second covenant to replace it. ⁸But when God found fault with the people, he said:

"The day is coming, says the Lord, when I will make a new covenant with the people of Israel and Judah."

~ Hebrews 8:1-8

Once and for all

Jesus' sacrifice on the cross was once and for all. No other sacrifice will ever be necessary because once was more than enough. Jesus' blood has paid the price. Christ's blood covers all our transgressions in God's presence.

[1]The old system under the law of Moses was only a shadow, a dim preview of the good things to come, not the good things themselves. The sacrifices under that system were repeated again and again, year after year, but they were never able to provide perfect cleansing for those who came to worship. [2]If they could have provided perfect cleansing, the sacrifices would have stopped, for the worshipers would have been purified once for all time, and their feelings of guilt would have disappeared.

[3]But instead, those sacrifices actually reminded them of their sins year after year. [4]For it is not possible for the blood of bulls and goats to take away sins. [5]That is why, when Christ came into the world, he said to God,

"You did not want animal sacrifices or sin offerings. But you have given me a body to offer. [6]You were not pleased with burnt offerings or other offerings for sin. [7]Then I said, 'Look, I have come to do your will, O God—as is written about me in the Scriptures.'"

~ Hebrews 10:1-7

Encouraged by the crowds

Surrounding us are the heavenly crowds who have already completed the race of faith. It is as if they encourage us to run with perseverance. We must listen to them and keep our eyes focused on Christ. Then we will run in the right Direction.

[1]Therefore, since we are surrounded by such a huge crowd of witnesses to the life of faith, let us strip off every weight that slows us down, especially the sin that so easily trips us up. And let us run with endurance the race God has set before us. [2]We do this by keeping our eyes on Jesus, the champion who initiates and perfects our faith. Because of the joy awaiting him, he endured the cross, disregarding its shame. Now he is seated in the place of honor beside God's throne. [3]Think of all the hostility he endured from sinful people; then you won't become weary and give up. [4]After all, you have not yet given your lives in your struggle against sin. [5]And have you forgotten the encouraging words God spoke to you as his children? He said,

"My child, don't make light of the LORD's discipline, and don't give up when he corrects you.

[6]For the LORD disciplines those he loves, and he punishes each one he accepts as his child."

~ Hebrews 12:1-6

Pass the test

James is clear that God does not test us through all life's difficulties. But He does watch to see what we do with the pain and suffering that life brings. He looks to see whether we remain faithful to Him.

¹²God blesses those who patiently endure testing and temptation. Afterward they will receive the crown of life that God has promised to those who love him.

¹³And remember, when you are being tempted, do not say, "God is tempting me." God is never tempted to do wrong, and he never tempts anyone else. ¹⁴Temptation comes from our own desires, which entice us and drag us away. ¹⁵These desires give birth to sinful actions. And when sin is allowed to grow, it gives birth to death.

¹⁶So don't be misled, my dear brothers and sisters. ¹⁷Whatever is good and perfect comes down to us from God our Father, who created all the lights in the heavens. He never changes or casts a shifting shadow. ¹⁸He chose to give birth to us by giving us his true word. And we, out of all creation, became his prized possession.

~ James 1:12-18

Be careful of money

Money often stands in the way of faith. James entreats us not to measure the value of our lives against money. Those who are rich must live as if they are poor before God, and those who are poor must live from the riches of God's goodness to them.

[5]Listen to me, dear brothers and sisters. Hasn't God chosen the poor in this world to be rich in faith? Aren't they the ones who will inherit the Kingdom he promised to those who love him? [6]But you dishonor the poor! Isn't it the rich who oppress you and drag you into court? [7]Aren't they the ones who slander Jesus Christ, whose noble name you bear?

[8]Yes indeed, it is good when you obey the royal law as found in the Scriptures: "Love your neighbor as yourself." [9]But if you favor some people over others, you are committing a sin. You are guilty of breaking the law.

[10]For the person who keeps all of the laws except one is as guilty as a person who has broken all of God's laws. [11]For the same God who said, "You must not commit adultery," also said, "You must not murder." So if you murder someone but do not commit adultery, you have still broken the law.

[12]So whatever you say or whatever you do, remember that you will be judged by the law that sets you free. [13]There will be no mercy for those who have not shown mercy to others. But if you have been merciful, God will be merciful when he judges you.

~ James 2:5-13

Wisdom shows

How do you know if someone is wise? Well, you see how they live. Wisdom shows. It's never just a theory. Wisdom is seen in humility and in a person's sincerity before God and others. Wisdom is also demonstrated in the way people control their tongue.

⁷People can tame all kinds of animals, birds, reptiles, and fish, ⁸but no one can tame the tongue. It is restless and evil, full of deadly poison. ⁹Sometimes it praises our Lord and Father, and sometimes it curses those who have been made in the image of God. ¹⁰And so blessing and cursing come pouring out of the same mouth. Surely, my brothers and sisters, this is not right! ¹¹Does a spring of water bubble out with both fresh water and bitter water? ¹²Does a fig tree produce olives, or a grapevine produce figs? No, and you can't draw fresh water from a salty spring.

¹³If you are wise and understand God's ways, prove it by living an honorable life, doing good works with the humility that comes from wisdom. ¹⁴But if you are bitterly jealous and there is selfish ambition in your heart, don't cover up the truth with boasting and lying. ¹⁵For jealousy and selfishness are not God's kind of wisdom. Such things are earthly, unspiritual, and demonic. ¹⁶For wherever there is jealousy and selfish ambition, there you will find disorder and evil of every kind.

¹⁷But the wisdom from above is first of all pure. It is also peace loving, gentle at all times, and willing to yield to others. It is full of mercy and good deeds. It shows no favoritism and is always sincere. ¹⁸And those who are peacemakers will plant seeds of peace and reap a harvest of righteousness.

~ James 3:7-18

Desire causes trouble

God is too quickly blamed for the difficulties and bad things that happen on earth. James makes it clear that war, crime and the like always have a human origin. The fire from hell that ignites these things is desire. Be careful of this!

[1]What is causing the quarrels and fights among you? Don't they come from the evil desires at war within you? [2]You want what you don't have, so you scheme and kill to get it. You are jealous of what others have, but you can't get it, so you fight and wage war to take it away from them. Yet you don't have what you want because you don't ask God for it. [3]And even when you ask, you don't get it because your motives are all wrong—you want only what will give you pleasure.

[4]You adulterers! Don't you realize that friendship with the world makes you an enemy of God? I say it again: If you want to be a friend of the world, you make yourself an enemy of God. [5]What do you think the Scriptures mean when they say that the spirit God has placed within us is filled with envy? [6]But he gives us even more grace to stand against such evil desires. As the Scriptures say,

"God opposes the proud but favors the humble."

[7]So humble yourselves before God. Resist the devil, and he will flee from you. [8]Come close to God, and God will come close to you. Wash your hands, you sinners; purify your hearts, for your loyalty is divided between God and the world.

~ James 4:1-8

DECEMBER

Don't expect God to bless everything you do

How easily we make God the One who must simply bless our plans. We do what we want during the week, but on Sundays we hastily ask Him to bless it all. Wrong! The right way is to bow before God's will.

11Don't speak evil against each other, dear brothers and sisters. If you criticize and judge each other, then you are criticizing and judging God's law. But your job is to obey the law, not to judge whether it applies to you. 12God alone, who gave the law, is the Judge. He alone has the power to save or to destroy. So what right do you have to judge your neighbor?

13Look here, you who say, "Today or tomorrow we are going to a certain town and will stay there a year. We will do business there and make a profit." 14How do you know what your life will be like tomorrow? Your life is like the morning fog—it's here a little while, then it's gone. 15What you ought to say is, "If the Lord wants us to, we will live and do this or that." 16Otherwise you are boasting about your own plans, and all such boasting is evil.

17Remember, it is sin to know what you ought to do and then not do it.

~ James 4:11-17

Pray, it works

We must pray when we are sick, but also when we are healthy. During times of hardship we must humble ourselves in prayer, but when we are well we must sing praises to His name. Above all, we must pray in faith. We must believe that God makes His Word come true.

[12]But most of all, my brothers and sisters, never take an oath, by heaven or earth or anything else. Just say a simple yes or no, so that you will not sin and be condemned.

[13]Are any of you suffering hardships? You should pray. Are any of you happy? You should sing praises.

[14]Are any of you sick? You should call for the elders of the church to come and pray over you, anointing you with oil in the name of the Lord. [15]Such a prayer offered in faith will heal the sick, and the Lord will make you well. And if you have committed any sins, you will be forgiven.

[16]Confess your sins to each other and pray for each other so that you may be healed. The earnest prayer of a righteous person has great power and produces wonderful results. [17]Elijah was as human as we are, and yet when he prayed earnestly that no rain would fall, none fell for three and a half years! [18]Then, when he prayed again, the sky sent down rain and the earth began to yield its crops.

~ James 5:12-18

Pure and impure

"Why do I have to go through difficulties?" Well, because troubles and trials purify your faith. Peter knows that hardship is like a fire that separates the pure from the impure. Trials and testing are none other than God's cleansing fire. Serve God even in times of difficulty. Then you will grow in the right direction.

³All praise to God, the Father of our Lord Jesus Christ. It is by his great mercy that we have been born again, because God raised Jesus Christ from the dead. Now we live with great expectation, ⁴and we have a priceless inheritance—an inheritance that is kept in heaven for you, pure and undefiled, beyond the reach of change and decay. ⁵And through your faith, God is protecting you by his power until you receive this salvation, which is ready to be revealed on the last day for all to see. ⁶So be truly glad. There is wonderful joy ahead, even though you have to endure many trials for a little while.

⁷These trials will show that your faith is genuine. It is being tested as fire tests and purifies gold—though your faith is far more precious than mere gold. So when your faith remains strong through many trials, it will bring you much praise and glory and honor on the day when Jesus Christ is revealed to the whole world.

⁸You love him even though you have never seen him. Though you do not see him now, you trust him; and you rejoice with a glorious, inexpressible joy. ⁹The reward for trusting him will be the salvation of your souls.

~ 1 Peter 1:3-9

Children of the King!

The Christians to whom Peter wrote suffered for their faith every day, but Peter reminded them that they were God's very own possessions. They were children of the King. They were God's new earthly priests. They are His chosen people.

⁴You are coming to Christ, who is the living cornerstone of God's temple. He was rejected by people, but he was chosen by God for great honor.

⁵And you are living stones that God is building into his spiritual temple. What's more, you are his holy priests. Through the mediation of Jesus Christ, you offer spiritual sacrifices that please God. ⁶As the Scriptures say,

"I am placing a cornerstone in Jerusalem, chosen for great honor, and anyone who trusts in him will never be disgraced."

⁷Yes, you who trust him recognize the honor God has given him. But for those who reject him,

"The stone that the builders rejected has now become the cornerstone."

⁸And, "He is the stone that makes people stumble, the rock that makes them fall."

They stumble because they do not obey God's word, and so they meet the fate that was planned for them.

⁹But you are not like that, for you are a chosen people. You are royal priests, a holy nation, God's very own possession. As a result, you can show others the goodness of God, for he called you out of the darkness into his wonderful light.

~ 1 Peter 2:4-9

Be humble

One of the most important spiritual lessons that Peter wants us to learn is that we must live humbly before God and other people. We must learn to accept the good and bad that life sends our way. If we must suffer, we must carry it worthily for Christ's sake.

18You who are slaves must accept the authority of your masters with all respect. Do what they tell you—not only if they are kind and reasonable, but even if they are cruel. 19For God is pleased with you when you do what you know is right and patiently endure unfair treatment. 20Of course, you get no credit for being patient if you are beaten for doing wrong. But if you suffer for doing good and endure it patiently, God is pleased with you.

21For God called you to do good, even if it means suffering, just as Christ suffered for you. He is your example, and you must follow in his steps.

22He never sinned, nor ever deceived anyone.

23He did not retaliate when he was insulted, nor threaten revenge when he suffered. He left his case in the hands of God, who always judges fairly.

24He personally carried our sins in his body on the cross so that we can be dead to sin and live for what is right. By his wounds you are healed.

25Once you were like sheep who wandered away. But now you have turned to your Shepherd, the Guardian of your souls.

~ 1 Peter 2:18-25

Go out of your way to do good

Peter teaches us to live wisely in a non-Christian world. We must continually do good and not unnecessarily cause trouble with other people. But if we undeservedly have to suffer for Christ, we must know that this is precisely the path that Jesus walked on this earth.

13Now, who will want to harm you if you are eager to do good? 14But even if you suffer for doing what is right, God will reward you for it. So don't worry or be afraid of their threats. 15Instead, you must worship Christ as Lord of your life. And if someone asks about your Christian hope, always be ready to explain it. 16But do this in a gentle and respectful way. Keep your conscience clear. Then if people speak against you, they will be ashamed when they see what a good life you live because you belong to Christ. 17Remember, it is better to suffer for doing good, if that is what God wants, than to suffer for doing wrong!

18Christ suffered for our sins once for all time. He never sinned, but he died for sinners to bring you safely home to God. He suffered physical death, but he was raised to life in the Spirit.

~ 1 Peter 3:13-18

Suffering with Christ

Suffering is part of the Christian life. Living religiously and piously won't lead to special treatment or prevent bad things from happening. Therefore we must learn to handle injustice as Christ did.

¹So then, since Christ suffered physical pain, you must arm yourselves with the same attitude he had, and be ready to suffer, too. For if you have suffered physically for Christ, you have finished with sin. ²You won't spend the rest of your lives chasing your own desires, but you will be anxious to do the will of God. ³You have had enough in the past of the evil things that godless people enjoy—their immorality and lust, their feasting and drunkenness and wild parties, and their terrible worship of idols.

⁴Of course, your former friends are surprised when you no longer plunge into the flood of wild and destructive things they do. So they slander you. ⁵But remember that they will have to face God, who will judge everyone, both the living and the dead. ⁶That is why the Good News was preached to those who are now dead—so although they were destined to die like all people, they now live forever with God in the Spirit.

⁷The end of the world is coming soon. Therefore, be earnest and disciplined in your prayers. ⁸Most important of all, continue to show deep love for each other, for love covers a multitude of sins.

~ 1 Peter 4:1-8

Humility is the key

The key to God's heart isn't obedience, long prayers, Bible studies and the like. The path to His heart is humility. We find true favor in His eyes when we humble and submit ourselves before Him.

⁵In the same way, you younger men must accept the authority of the elders. And all of you, serve each other in humility, for

"God opposes the proud but favors the humble."

⁶So humble yourselves under the mighty power of God, and at the right time he will lift you up in honor. ⁷Give all your worries and cares to God, for he cares about you.

⁸Stay alert! Watch out for your great enemy, the devil. He prowls around like a roaring lion, looking for someone to devour. ⁹Stand firm against him, and be strong in your faith. Remember that your Christian brothers and sisters all over the world are going through the same kind of suffering you are.

¹⁰In his kindness God called you to share in his eternal glory by means of Christ Jesus. So after you have suffered a little while, he will restore, support, and strengthen you, and he will place you on a firm foundation. ¹¹All power to him forever! Amen.

¹²I have written and sent this short letter to you with the help of Silas, whom I commend to you as a faithful brother. My purpose in writing is to encourage you and assure you that what you are experiencing is truly part of God's grace for you. Stand firm in this grace.

~ 1 Peter 5:5-12

The way to grow

Two Peter 1:5-7 deserves more attention in our hearts and minds than we might realize. Peter gives us a powerful spiritual exercise plan in a nutshell. He writes that faith must grow from dedication to self-discipline; then to endurance, love for God and other believers, and finally to all other people.

[3]By his divine power, God has given us everything we need for living a godly life. We have received all of this by coming to know him, the one who called us to himself by means of his marvelous glory and excellence. [4]And because of his glory and excellence, he has given us great and precious promises. These are the promises that enable you to share his divine nature and escape the world's corruption caused by human desires.

[5]In view of all this, make every effort to respond to God's promises. Supplement your faith with a generous provision of moral excellence, and moral excellence with knowledge, [6]and knowledge with self-control, and self-control with patient endurance, and patient endurance with godliness, [7]and godliness with brotherly affection, and brotherly affection with love for everyone.

[8]The more you grow like this, the more productive and useful you will be in your knowledge of our Lord Jesus Christ. [9]But those who fail to develop in this way are shortsighted or blind, forgetting that they have been cleansed from their old sins.

~ 2 Peter 1:3-9

False teachers

Twisting the gospel is nothing new in the church. Here in chapter 2 the apostle opposes a group of invaders in the church who were falsifying the gospel. He tears their masks off and exposes them as wolves in sheep's clothes. Be on the lookout for such falsifications in your own church.

¹But there were also false prophets in Israel, just as there will be false teachers among you. They will cleverly teach destructive heresies and even deny the Master who bought them. In this way, they will bring sudden destruction on themselves. ²Many will follow their evil teaching and shameful immorality. And because of these teachers, the way of truth will be slandered. ³In their greed they will make up clever lies to get hold of your money. But God condemned them long ago, and their destruction will not be delayed.

⁴For God did not spare even the angels who sinned. He threw them into hell, in gloomy pits of darkness, where they are being held until the day of judgment. ⁵And God did not spare the ancient world—except for Noah and the seven others in his family. Noah warned the world of God's righteous judgment. So God protected Noah when he destroyed the world of ungodly people with a vast flood. ⁶Later, God condemned the cities of Sodom and Gomorrah and turned them into heaps of ashes. He made them an example of what will happen to ungodly people.

⁹So you see, the Lord knows how to rescue godly people from their trials, even while keeping the wicked under punishment until the day of final judgment.

~ 2 Peter 2:1-6, 9

Hurrying the Day of God along

Two Peter 3:12 is the one golden verse in the New Testament that is always overlooked when the Second Coming is discussed. It's the verse that says the date of the Second Coming is adaptable. We can hurry it along by the way we live. This is also what Jesus teaches in The Lord's Prayer.

3Most importantly, I want to remind you that in the last days scoffers will come, mocking the truth and following their own desires. 4They will say, "What happened to the promise that Jesus is coming again? From before the times of our ancestors, everything has remained the same since the world was first created."

5They deliberately forget that God made the heavens by the word of his command, and he brought the earth out from the water and surrounded it with water. 6Then he used the water to destroy the ancient world with a mighty flood. 7And by the same word, the present heavens and earth have been stored up for fire. They are being kept for the day of judgment, when ungodly people will be destroyed.

11Since everything around us is going to be destroyed like this, what holy and godly lives you should live, 12looking forward to the day of God and hurrying it along. On that day, he will set the heavens on fire, and the elements will melt away in the flames. 13But we are looking forward to the new heavens and new earth he has promised, a world filled with God's righteousness.

~ 2 Peter 3:3-7, 11-13

Repent and live

Sin is a reality. We all sometimes break our relationship with God through disobedience. John tells us that we must then confess our sin and not do it again. We must lay our transgressions at Christ's feet. He is still the only One who can reconcile us with God.

[1]We proclaim to you the one who existed from the beginning, whom we have heard and seen. We saw him with our own eyes and touched him with our own hands. He is the Word of life. [2]This one who is life itself was revealed to us, and we have seen him. And now we testify and proclaim to you that he is the one who is eternal life. He was with the Father, and then he was revealed to us. [3]We proclaim to you what we ourselves have actually seen and heard so that you may have fellowship with us. And our fellowship is with the Father and with his Son, Jesus Christ. [4]We are writing these things so that you may fully share our joy.

[5]This is the message we heard from Jesus and now declare to you: God is light, and there is no darkness in him at all. [6]So we are lying if we say we have fellowship with God but go on living in spiritual darkness; we are not practicing the truth. [7]But if we are living in the light, as God is in the light, then we have fellowship with each other, and the blood of Jesus, his Son, cleanses us from all sin.

[8]If we claim we have no sin, we are only fooling ourselves and not living in the truth. [9]But if we confess our sins to him, he is faithful and just to forgive us our sins and to cleanse us from all wickedness.

~ 1 John 1:1-9

Love is an action

John is the apostle of love. Again and again he tells us to love; the *agape* kind of love. This kind of love is sacrificial, serving. *Agape* means loyalty to God and others. It changes you into someone who can put yourself second in favor of others.

⁷Dear friends, I am not writing a new commandment for you; rather it is an old one you have had from the very beginning. This old commandment—to love one another—is the same message you heard before. ⁸Yet it is also new. Jesus lived the truth of this commandment, and you also are living it. For the darkness is disappearing, and the true light is already shining. ⁹If anyone claims, "I am living in the light," but hates a Christian brother or sister, that person is still living in darkness. ¹⁰Anyone who loves another brother or sister is living in the light and does not cause others to stumble. ¹¹But anyone who hates another brother or sister is still living and walking in darkness. Such a person does not know the way to go, having been blinded by the darkness.

¹²I am writing to you who are God's children because your sins have been forgiven through Jesus.

¹³I am writing to you who are mature in the faith because you know Christ, who existed from the beginning.

I am writing to you who are young in the faith because you have won your battle with the evil one.

¹⁴I have written to you who are God's children because you know the Father.

I have written to you who are mature in the faith because you know Christ, who existed from the beginning. I have written to you who are young in the faith because you are strong.

God's word lives in your hearts, and you have won your battle with the evil one.

~ 1 John 2:7-14

God's love is the cross

"Where is the God of love?" many people ask. John's answer is simple: You will meet Him at the cross of Christ. That's where God revealed His heart. That is where God made His heart and love known to us.

[1]See how very much our Father loves us, for he calls us his children, and that is what we are! But the people who belong to this world don't recognize that we are God's children because they don't know him. [2]Dear friends, we are already God's children, but he has not yet shown us what we will be like when Christ appears. But we do know that we will be like him, for we will see him as he really is. [3]And all who have this eager expectation will keep themselves pure, just as he is pure.

[4]Everyone who sins is breaking God's law, for all sin is contrary to the law of God. [5]And you know that Jesus came to take away our sins, and there is no sin in him. [6]Anyone who continues to live in him will not sin. But anyone who keeps on sinning does not know him or understand who he is.

[7]Dear children, don't let anyone deceive you about this: When people do what is right, it shows that they are righteous, even as Christ is righteous. [8]But when people keep on sinning, it shows that they belong to the devil, who has been sinning since the beginning. But the Son of God came to destroy the works of the devil.

[9]Those who have been born into God's family do not make a practice of sinning, because God's life is in them. So they can't keep on sinning, because they are children of God. [10]So now we can tell who are children of God and who are children of the devil. Anyone who does not live righteously and does not love other believers does not belong to God.

~ 1 John 3:1-10

Love is the other way around

Real love is not our love for God, but His love for us. Love is to see that God gave the first big step towards us when He gave His Child to die in our place. Through Him we receive true life.

2This is how we know if they have the Spirit of God: If a person claiming to be a prophet acknowledges that Jesus Christ came in a real body, that person has the Spirit of God. 3But if someone claims to be a prophet and does not acknowledge the truth about Jesus, that person is not from God. Such a person has the spirit of the Antichrist, which you heard is coming into the world and indeed is already here.

4But you belong to God, my dear children. You have already won a victory over those people, because the Spirit who lives in you is greater than the spirit who lives in the world. 5Those people belong to this world, so they speak from the world's viewpoint, and the world listens to them. 6But we belong to God, and those who know God listen to us. If they do not belong to God, they do not listen to us. That is how we know if someone has the Spirit of truth or the spirit of deception.

7Dear friends, let us continue to love one another, for love comes from God. Anyone who loves is a child of God and knows God. 8But anyone who does not love does not know God, for God is love.

9God showed how much he loved us by sending his one and only Son into the world so that we might have eternal life through him. 10This is real love—not that we loved God, but that he loved us and sent his Son as a sacrifice to take away our sins.

~ 1 John 4:2-10

Love is visible

God is invisible, yet His fingerprints and footprints can be seen everywhere. This is because He is visible wherever His children live out His sacrificial and serving love. God's love triumphs when we care for each other and serve Him with our lives.

¹²No one has ever seen God. But if we love each other, God lives in us, and his love is brought to full expression in us.

¹³And God has given us his Spirit as proof that we live in him and he in us. ¹⁴Furthermore, we have seen with our own eyes and now testify that the Father sent his Son to be the Savior of the world. ¹⁵All who confess that Jesus is the Son of God have God living in them, and they live in God. ¹⁶We know how much God loves us, and we have put our trust in his love.

God is love, and all who live in love live in God, and God lives in them. ¹⁷And as we live in God, our love grows more perfect. So we will not be afraid on the day of judgment, but we can face him with confidence because we live like Jesus here in this world.

¹⁸Such love has no fear, because perfect love expels all fear. If we are afraid, it is for fear of punishment, and this shows that we have not fully experienced his perfect love. ¹⁹We love each other because he loved us first.

²⁰If someone says, "I love God," but hates a Christian brother or sister, that person is a liar; for if we don't love people we can see, how can we love God, whom we cannot see?

~ 1 John 4:12-20

Jesus = life

God testifies about Himself and at the heart of this testimony is the fact that He gives us true life. This life is exclusively found in Jesus. Whoever believes in Him has life. Whoever does not know Him does not have everlasting life.

[1]Everyone who believes that Jesus is the Christ has become a child of God. And everyone who loves the Father loves his children, too. [2]We know we love God's children if we love God and obey his commandments. [3]Loving God means keeping his commandments, and his commandments are not burdensome. [4]For every child of God defeats this evil world, and we achieve this victory through our faith. [5]And who can win this battle against the world? Only those who believe that Jesus is the Son of God.

[6]And Jesus Christ was revealed as God's Son by his baptism in water and by shedding his blood on the cross—not by water only, but by water and blood. And the Spirit, who is truth, confirms it with his testimony. [7]So we have these three witnesses—[8]the Spirit, the water, and the blood—and all three agree.

[9]Since we believe human testimony, surely we can believe the greater testimony that comes from God. And God has testified about his Son. [10]All who believe in the Son of God know in their hearts that this testimony is true. Those who don't believe this are actually calling God a liar because they don't believe what God has testified about his Son.

~ 1 John 5:1-10

All about love

Love is still in the foreground as John writes his second letter. As we have heard before, we are again told to love one another. Love means continually keeping God's commandments. God's commandments are in turn all about love!

⁴How happy I was to meet some of your children and find them living according to the truth, just as the Father commanded.

⁵I am writing to remind you, dear friends, that we should love one another. This is not a new commandment, but one we have had from the beginning. ⁶Love means doing what God has commanded us, and he has commanded us to love one another, just as you heard from the beginning.

⁷I say this because many deceivers have gone out into the world. They deny that Jesus Christ came in a real body. Such a person is a deceiver and an antichrist. ⁸Watch out that you do not lose what we have worked so hard to achieve. Be diligent so that you receive your full reward. ⁹Anyone who wanders away from this teaching has no relationship with God. But anyone who remains in the teaching of Christ has a relationship with both the Father and the Son.

¹⁰If anyone comes to your meeting and does not teach the truth about Christ, don't invite that person into your home or give any kind of encouragement. ¹¹Anyone who encourages such people becomes a partner in their evil work.

~ 2 John v. 4-11

Welcome strangers as brothers

Hospitality was one of the basic Christian virtues in the early church. It meant that you even had to open your home to strangers. Gaius, to whom the third letter of John was written, did precisely that. He opened his heart and home to fellow believers. We can learn from him.

¹I am writing to Gaius, my dear friend, whom I love in the truth.

²Dear friend, I hope all is well with you and that you are as healthy in body as you are strong in spirit.

³Some of the traveling teachers recently returned and made me very happy by telling me about your faithfulness and that you are living according to the truth. ⁴I could have no greater joy than to hear that my children are following the truth.

⁵Dear friend, you are being faithful to God when you care for the traveling teachers who pass through, even though they are strangers to you. ⁶They have told the church here of your loving friendship. Please continue providing for such teachers in a manner that pleases God. ⁷For they are traveling for the Lord, and they accept nothing from people who are not believers. ⁸So we ourselves should support them so that we can be their partners as they teach the truth.

~ 3 John v. 1-8

Learn from the past

Jude, Jesus' earthly brother, wrote to believers to remind them of how God dealt with sinners in the past who deliberately disobeyed Him. From this they had to learn that the God of history is also the Lord of the present and the future. He hasn't changed.

¹ This letter is from Jude, a slave of Jesus Christ and a brother of James.

I am writing to all who have been called by God the Father, who loves you and keeps you safe in the care of Jesus Christ.

²May God give you more and more mercy, peace, and love.

³Dear friends, I had been eagerly planning to write to you about the salvation we all share. But now I find that I must write about something else, urging you to defend the faith that God has entrusted once for all time to his holy people. ⁴I say this because some ungodly people have wormed their way into your churches, saying that God's marvelous grace allows us to live immoral lives. The condemnation of such people was recorded long ago, for they have denied our only Master and Lord, Jesus Christ.

⁵So I want to remind you, though you already know these things, that Jesus first rescued the nation of Israel from Egypt, but later he destroyed those who did not remain faithful. ⁶And I remind you of the angels who did not stay within the limits of authority God gave them but left the place where they belonged. God has kept them securely chained in prisons of darkness, waiting for the great day of judgment. ⁷And don't forget Sodom and Gomorrah and their neighboring towns, which were filled with immorality and every kind of sexual perversion. Those cities were destroyed by fire and serve as a warning of the eternal fire of God's judgment.

~ Jude v. 1-7

Snatch them from the fire

You can't turn a blind eye to people sinking in the quicksand of sin. You have to help. Snatch them from the flames like you would a piece of wood. Have mercy on those whose lives are broken. Help the fallen. This is what the gospel of Christ requires you to do.

[17]But you, my dear friends, must remember what the apostles of our Lord Jesus Christ said. [18]They told you that in the last times there would be scoffers whose purpose in life is to satisfy their ungodly desires. [19]These people are the ones who are creating divisions among you. They follow their natural instincts because they do not have God's Spirit in them.

[20]But you, dear friends, must build each other up in your most holy faith, pray in the power of the Holy Spirit, [21]and await the mercy of our Lord Jesus Christ, who will bring you eternal life. In this way, you will keep yourselves safe in God's love.

[22]And you must show mercy to those whose faith is wavering. [23]Rescue others by snatching them from the flames of judgment. Show mercy to still others, but do so with great caution, hating the sins that contaminate their lives.

[24]Now all glory to God, who is able to keep you from falling away and will bring you with great joy into his glorious presence without a single fault.

~ Jude v. 17-24

The Lord is never shackled

The apostle John's imprisonment on the island of Patmos did not incarcerate the gospel. The Lord is never shackled when His children are suffering. For this reason the resurrected Christ appeared to John and told him to encourage the church.

¹²When I turned to see who was speaking to me, I saw seven gold lampstands. ¹³And standing in the middle of the lampstands was someone like the Son of Man. He was wearing a long robe with a gold sash across his chest. ¹⁴His head and his hair were white like wool, as white as snow. And his eyes were like flames of fire. ¹⁵His feet were like polished bronze refined in a furnace, and his voice thundered like mighty ocean waves. ¹⁶He held seven stars in his right hand, and a sharp two-edged sword came from his mouth. And his face was like the sun in all its brilliance.

¹⁷When I saw him, I fell at his feet as if I were dead. But he laid his right hand on me and said, "Don't be afraid! I am the First and the Last. ¹⁸I am the living one. I died, but look—I am alive forever and ever! And I hold the keys of death and the grave.

¹⁹"Write down what you have seen—both the things that are now happening and the things that will happen. ²⁰This is the meaning of the mystery of the seven stars you saw in my right hand and the seven gold lampstands: The seven stars are the angels of the seven churches, and the seven lampstands are the seven churches.

~ Revelation 1:12-20

Wake up

Wake up! This is a well-known exclamation in many homes every morning. But when the congregation in Sardis heard these words, they came from the living Christ. Their spiritual commitment is no more than pretense. Therefore they are called to obey God once again.

[1]"Write this letter to the angel of the church in Sardis. This is the message from the one who has the sevenfold Spirit of God and the seven stars:

"I know all the things you do, and that you have a reputation for being alive—but you are dead.

[2]"Wake up! Strengthen what little remains, for even what is left is almost dead. I find that your actions do not meet the requirements of my God. [3]Go back to what you heard and believed at first; hold to it firmly. Repent and turn to me again. If you don't wake up, I will come to you suddenly, as unexpected as a thief.

[4]"Yet there are some in the church in Sardis who have not soiled their clothes with evil. They will walk with me in white, for they are worthy.

[5]"All who are victorious will be clothed in white. I will never erase their names from the Book of Life, but I will announce before my Father and his angels that they are mine.

[6]"Anyone with ears to hear must listen to the Spirit and understand what he is saying to the churches."

~ Revelation 3:1-6

In the throne room

In Revelation 4 John is invited on the journey of a lifetime. His tour guide is the Holy Spirit. His destination is the throne room of the Almighty. There John saw God on His throne. Using rich imagery John describes how God is in complete control of the universe and how He is still worshiped.

²And instantly I was in the Spirit, and I saw a throne in heaven and someone sitting on it. ³The one sitting on the throne was as brilliant as gemstones—like jasper and carnelian. And the glow of an emerald circled his throne like a rainbow. ⁴Twenty-four thrones surrounded him, and twenty-four elders sat on them. They were all clothed in white and had gold crowns on their heads. ⁵From the throne came flashes of lightning and the rumble of thunder. And in front of the throne were seven torches with burning flames. This is the sevenfold Spirit of God. ⁶In front of the throne was a shiny sea of glass, sparkling like crystal.

In the center and around the throne were four living beings, each covered with eyes, front and back. ⁷The first of these living beings was like a lion; the second was like an ox; the third had a human face; and the fourth was like an eagle in flight. ⁸Each of these living beings had six wings, and their wings were covered all over with eyes, inside and out. Day after day and night after night they keep on saying,

"Holy, holy, holy is the Lord God, the Almighty—the one who always was, who is, and who is still to come."

⁹Whenever the living beings give glory and honor and thanks to the one sitting on the throne (the one who lives forever and ever), ¹⁰the twenty-four elders fall down and worship the one sitting on the throne (the one who lives forever and ever). And they lay their crowns before the throne.

~ Revelation 4:2-10

The Lamb has won

Revelation 5 shares the joy of Christmas as it invites us to share in the safe arrival of Christ after His ascension. Christ is the Lamb that sacrificed His own life to make us kings and prophets in God's service.

¹Then I saw a scroll in the right hand of the one who was sitting on the throne. There was writing on the inside and the outside of the scroll, and it was sealed with seven seals. ²And I saw a strong angel, who shouted with a loud voice: "Who is worthy to break the seals on this scroll and open it?" ³But no one in heaven or on earth or under the earth was able to open the scroll and read it.

⁴Then I began to weep bitterly because no one was found worthy to open the scroll and read it. ⁵But one of the twenty-four elders said to me, "Stop weeping! Look, the Lion of the tribe of Judah, the heir to David's throne, has won the victory. He is worthy to open the scroll and its seven seals."

⁶Then I saw a Lamb that looked as if it had been slaughtered, but it was now standing between the throne and the four living beings and among the twenty-four elders. He had seven horns and seven eyes, which represent the sevenfold Spirit of God that is sent out into every part of the earth. ⁷He stepped forward and took the scroll from the right hand of the one sitting on the throne.

⁸And when he took the scroll, the four living beings and the twenty-four elders fell down before the Lamb. Each one had a harp, and they held gold bowls filled with incense, which are the prayers of God's people. ⁹And they sang a new song with these words: "You are worthy to take the scroll and break its seals and open it. For you were slaughtered, and your blood has ransomed people for God from every tribe and language and people and nation.

~ Revelation 5:1-9

Washed in the blood of the Lamb

One of the most beautiful images in the Bible is found in Revelation 7:14. Here we read that believers who stand before Christ on the last day have clothes that are pure white, having been washed in the blood of the Lamb. Christ's blood-red blood has always been pure white.

⁹After this I saw a vast crowd, too great to count, from every nation and tribe and people and language, standing in front of the throne and before the Lamb. They were clothed in white robes and held palm branches in their hands. ¹⁰And they were shouting with a great roar, "Salvation comes from our God who sits on the throne and from the Lamb!"

¹¹And all the angels were standing around the throne and around the elders and the four living beings. And they fell before the throne with their faces to the ground and worshiped God. ¹²They sang, "Amen! Blessing and glory and wisdom and thanksgiving and honor and power and strength belong to our God forever and ever! Amen."

¹³Then one of the twenty-four elders asked me, "Who are these who are clothed in white? Where did they come from?"

¹⁴And I said to him, "Sir, you are the one who knows."

Then he said to me, "These are the ones who died in the great tribulation. They have washed their robes in the blood of the Lamb and made them white. ¹⁵"That is why they stand in front of God's throne and serve him day and night in his Temple. And he who sits on the throne will give them shelter. ¹⁶They will never again be hungry or thirsty; they will never be scorched by the heat of the sun. ¹⁷For the Lamb on the throne will be their Shepherd. He will lead them to springs of life-giving water. And God will wipe every tear from their eyes."

~ Revelation 7:9-17

Angels can't preach

John saw an angel in front of him and was told to take and eat the scroll in his right hand. This was the Word of God. Then he was told to go and make this Word known all over the world. After all, angels can't preach. That's why John, and you and I, must do it.

[5]Then the angel I saw standing on the sea and on the land raised his right hand toward heaven. [6]He swore an oath in the name of the one who lives forever and ever, who created the heavens and everything in them, the earth and everything in it, and the sea and everything in it. He said, "There will be no more delay. [7]When the seventh angel blows his trumpet, God's mysterious plan will be fulfilled. It will happen just as he announced it to his servants the prophets."

[8]Then the voice from heaven spoke to me again: "Go and take the open scroll from the hand of the angel who is standing on the sea and on the land."

[9]So I went to the angel and told him to give me the small scroll. "Yes, take it and eat it," he said. "It will be sweet as honey in your mouth, but it will turn sour in your stomach!" [10]So I took the small scroll from the hand of the angel, and I ate it! It was sweet in my mouth, but when I swallowed it, it turned sour in my stomach.

[11]Then I was told, "You must prophesy again about many peoples, nations, languages, and kings."

~ Revelation 10:5-11

Believers are marked

There is always great interest in Revelation's 666 mark that the Evil One will place on all his followers. But few seem excited about the fact that Christ has written His and His Father's name on all believers. Everyone on earth is marked. Make sure that you carry Christ's mark.

⁹Then a third angel followed them, shouting, "Anyone who worships the beast and his statue or who accepts his mark on the forehead or on the hand ¹⁰must drink the wine of God's anger. It has been poured full strength into God's cup of wrath. And they will be tormented with fire and burning sulfur in the presence of the holy angels and the Lamb. ¹¹The smoke of their torment will rise forever and ever, and they will have no relief day or night, for they have worshiped the beast and his statue and have accepted the mark of his name."

¹²This means that God's holy people must endure persecution patiently, obeying his commands and maintaining their faith in Jesus.

¹³And I heard a voice from heaven saying, "Write this down: Blessed are those who die in the Lord from now on. Yes, says the Spirit, they are blessed indeed, for they will rest from their hard work; for their good deeds follow them!"

~ Revelation 14:9-13

The Rider will ride again

Revelation 19 tells about the glorious return of the Rider on the white horse. Christ will return triumphantly in the end times to destroy all His enemies. His church share in His victory, now and for all time.

[11]Then I saw heaven opened, and a white horse was standing there. Its rider was named Faithful and True, for he judges fairly and wages a righteous war. [12]His eyes were like flames of fire, and on his head were many crowns. A name was written on him that no one understood except himself. [13]He wore a robe dipped in blood, and his title was the Word of God.

[14]The armies of heaven, dressed in the finest of pure white linen, followed him on white horses. [15]From his mouth came a sharp sword to strike down the nations. He will rule them with an iron rod. He will release the fierce wrath of God, the Almighty, like juice flowing from a winepress. [16]On his robe at his thigh was written this title: King of all kings and Lord of all lords.

[17]Then I saw an angel standing in the sun, shouting to the vultures flying high in the sky: "Come! Gather together for the great banquet God has prepared. [18]Come and eat the flesh of kings, generals, and strong warriors; of horses and their riders; and of all humanity, both free and slave, small and great."

~ Revelation 19:11-18

The Book of Life

John tells us that everyone's deeds are written in the heavenly books. The good news is that there is also a Book of Life. Only the names of Christ's redeemed ones are in this book. God therefore knows us by name or by deeds. Make sure He knows your name.

⁷When the thousand years come to an end, Satan will be let out of his prison. ⁸He will go out to deceive the nations—called Gog and Magog—in every corner of the earth. He will gather them together for battle—a mighty army, as numberless as sand along the seashore. ⁹And I saw them as they went up on the broad plain of the earth and surrounded God's people and the beloved city. But fire from heaven came down on the attacking armies and consumed them.

¹⁰Then the devil, who had deceived them, was thrown into the fiery lake of burning sulfur, joining the beast and the false prophet. There they will be tormented day and night forever and ever.

¹¹And I saw a great white throne and the one sitting on it. The earth and sky fled from his presence, but they found no place to hide. ¹²I saw the dead, both great and small, standing before God's throne. And the books were opened, including the Book of Life. And the dead were judged according to what they had done, as recorded in the books. ¹³The sea gave up its dead, and death and the grave gave up their dead. And all were judged according to their deeds.

¹⁵And anyone whose name was not found recorded in the Book of Life was thrown into the lake of fire.

~ Revelation 20:7-13, 15

I am coming soon!

Jesus' last words in the Bible are, "I am coming soon!" What is our response to this? Well, only to say *maranatha*, which in Aramaic means "Come, Lord Jesus!" Let us continually invite Him to hasten His return to us.

¹⁴Blessed are those who wash their robes. They will be permitted to enter through the gates of the city and eat the fruit from the tree of life.

¹⁵Outside the city are the dogs—the sorcerers, the sexually immoral, the murderers, the idol worshipers, and all who love to live a lie.

¹⁶"I, Jesus, have sent my angel to give you this message for the churches. I am both the source of David and the heir to his throne. I am the bright morning star."

¹⁷The Spirit and the bride say, "Come." Let anyone who hears this say, "Come." Let anyone who is thirsty come. Let anyone who desires drink freely from the water of life.

¹⁸And I solemnly declare to everyone who hears the words of prophecy written in this book: If anyone adds anything to what is written here, God will add to that person the plagues described in this book. ¹⁹And if anyone removes any of the words from this book of prophecy, God will remove that person's share in the tree of life and in the holy city that are described in this book.

²⁰He who is the faithful witness to all these things says, "Yes, I am coming soon!"

Amen! Come, Lord Jesus!

²¹May the grace of the Lord Jesus be with God's holy people.

~ Revelation 22:14-21

Scripture Index

John

Acts

Romans

1 Corinthians